LITERARY CONTEXTS

Postcolonial Literatures

Literary Contexts recognises that literature is always rooted in its social milieu and that we need to study literary cultures in all their complexity and connections. It offers the thrill of locating a text within its context and seeing a context reflected in a literary/cultural text.

Each of the books in the series offers students of English and other literatures concise, informative insights into the history of ideas embodied in literary texts, authors and movements. Organised around themes and ideas with extensive examples from literary and cultural texts, the books enable students to understand how the "literary" takes shape in an intellectual milieu and discover manifestations of abstract ideas in literary texts. Written by scholar-teachers who have taught and researched literature for several years, each volume in the series is a stand-alone reference book for students and teachers alike.

Series editor

Pramod K. Nayar, FEA, FRHistS, teaches at the Department of English, University of Hyderabad, where he also holds the UNESCO Chair in Vulnerability Studies. His most recent books include *Life/Writing* (Orient BlackSwan, 2023), *Nuclear Cultures* (2023), *Alzheimer's Disease Memoirs* (2022), *The Human Rights Graphic Novel* (2021), *Indian Travel Writing in the Age of Empire, 1830–1940* (2020) and *Ecoprecarity* (2019), besides the edited six-volume collection, *The Imperial Archives* (2022).

Also in the series

Shakespeare
American Literature
Modern English Literature, 1890–1960
Victorian Literature
Postmodern Literatures
English Romantic Literature

Literary Contexts

Postcolonial Literatures

Parama Sarkar

Series Editor
Pramod K. Nayar

Orient BlackSwan

POSTCOLONIAL LITERATURES

ORIENT BLACKSWAN PRIVATE LIMITED

Registered Office
3-6-752 Himayatnagar, Hyderabad 500 029, Telangana, India
e-mail: centraloffice@orientblackswan.com

Other Offices
Bengaluru, Chennai, Guwahati, Hyderabad,
Kolkata, Mumbai, New Delhi, Noida, Patna

First published 2016
Reprinted 2020, 2025

040343

ISBN 978 81 250 6283 7

Typeset in Adobe Caslon Pro 11.5/14.3 *by*
Orient BlackSwan

Printed and bound at
B.B. Press, Tronica City, Ghaziabad, UP 201 103

Published by
Orient Blackswan Private Limited
3-6-752 Himayatnagar, Hyderabad 500 029
e-mail: info@orientblackswan.com

CONTENTS

Series Editor's Preface

The idea that the literature of every age is rooted in its social milieu is a truism. Mapping the contours of this milieu often requires, for the student, to read through several specialised texts. Titles in *Literary Contexts*, by bringing together the key contexts – both general and specialised – into one volume, offer the student of English and other literatures short, prescient and informative studies that provide the history of ideas embodied in literary texts, authors and movements.

Intellectual history or the history of ideas has always been intertwined with the cultural practices and shifts within them in every age. Therefore titles in the series track the intellectual history of every age through social and historical contexts, whether these were contexts of imperial voyages, "Westward expansion", the Reformation of the Church, great scientific discoveries or nationalist movements. Considerable attention is paid to the contexts of class, literacy, gender relations, the state and its functions in every age.

The series' titles demonstrate how certain dominant ideas in any age operated. To this end, every title in the series draws upon and cites numerous examples from literary texts. This enables the student to get a sense of the literary themes' origins in the intellectual milieu, and discover manifestations of abstract ideas, such as "exceptionalism", "hybrid and displaced identity" or "division of powers of Church and State", in literary texts.

The authors do not seek to establish a direct correspondence between the literary text and the dominant idea of the age, but they offer the student a sense of the dense exchanges between the idea and the literary text. Each title maps ideas across cultural texts – popular forms, high culture, and scientific and philosophical texts – so that it demonstrates how ideas are mobile and cut across genres and domains. The titles in the series also document the conflicts and tensions in every age so that the student is made aware of the complicated nature of both, the history of ideas and the literary expressions of the same, and is alerted to the messy nature of cultural history of any age, in any nation.

Written by scholar-teachers who have taught and researched literature for several years, *Literary Contexts* is student-friendly, being both jargon-free and incisive.

Pramod K. Nayar

Acknowledgements

I am deeply grateful to everyone whose kindness, generosity and support made this book possible: Pramod K. Nayar for trusting me with this project and for his guidance and patience every step of the way; my editors and copy-editors at Orient BlackSwan for their help with polishing the manuscript into its present form; my colleagues and fellow academics in the English Department at the University of Toledo, especially Sara Lundquist, Jane Bradley, Christina Fitzgerald, Melissa Gregory, Andrew Mattison and Ben Stroud for their invaluable advice and support during the book's writing and tenure process; Sheshalatha Reddy for her insightful comments on my drafts and for the many pep talks that always lifted my spirits; Aryn Bartley, for not only her help with this manuscript, but also for her intellectual and emotional support that has sustained me for many, many years; Lynn Bartley and Tom Bartley, and Adrienne Fricker-Elhai and Jon Elhai for giving me a home away from home; Samantha Davids, Richa Goyal, Cyndee Gruden, Arunima Kashyap, Jason Levine, Rohan Taneja and Jami Taylor for their constant encouragement through the writing process that never failed to invigorate me; and, William Acosta, Anupama Arora, Meghan Bacino, Archana Basu, Emron Esplin, Marlene Hansen Esplin, Rebekah Benson-Flannery, Theng-Theng Fong, Brian Olszewski, Shikha Singh, Deepa Thandaveswara, Kanchana Warnapala for their friendship and for always being there for me through the ups and downs of graduate school and academic life.

Finally, this project would not have been possible without the unwavering love and support of my family: Dada, who taught me to write and instilled his deep love of literature in me; Mummum, for believing in me when others were hesitant; and, Ma, Baba and Runa for their unconditional love, support and encouragement through all these years. My debt to them is immense.

This book is dedicated to Ma and Baba. Thank you for letting me follow my dreams.

Introduction

En route from Bombay to L.A., I happened to stop off for three days in London. There I found West Indian sitcoms crowding the airwaves and *samosas* filling the sandwich bars. Culturally, the talk of the town was a new movie written by a twenty-nine-year-old Pakistani, *My Beautiful Laundrette* . . . . Thus the colonials were effectively staging their own take-over, erecting tandoori palaces in their former rulers' home, introducing their own pungent terms into the mainstream, even seizing control of much of the nation's culture (during the '80s, the highest literary trophy in Britain, the Booker Prize, had been won by an Indian, an Australian, a New Zealander and a South African).

The empire had struck back.

—*Video Night in Kathmandu*
Pico Iyer

What seems to me to be happening is that those peoples who were once colonized by the language are now rapidly remaking it, domesticating it, becoming more and more relaxed about the way they use it – assisted by the English language's enormous flexibility and size, they are carving out large territories for themselves within its frontiers.

—*'Commonwealth Literature' Does Not Exist*
Salman Rushdie

If Pico Iyer and Salman Rushdie's emphatic statements are anything to go by, there seems to have been a seismic shift in the relationship between the erstwhile First and Third Worlds – between the coloniser and the colonised. In order to understand the shifting global power structures, it is imperative to understand the history of colonialism and its traumatic legacies that has left an indelible mark on the global psyche. *Postcolonial Literatures* seeks to provide an introduction to this contested area by uncovering the historical, political, cultural and linguistic contexts that have produced some of the most significant literary texts in the past three hundred years. But before I provide a roadmap for this project, a few words about the field of postcolonial literary studies is in order.

Postcolonial studies as a field of academic specialisation did not emerge till the late 1970s, and today, is a dynamic field that is routinely examined and re-evaluated at international conferences and in scholarly journals throughout the world. Inspired by the pioneering work of Edward Said, Homi Bhabha, Benedict Anderson, Gayatri Chakravorty Spivak, Paul Gilroy and others, postcolonial critics, by combining colonial discourse analysis and poststructuralist theory, have produced an impressive body of theoretical work about European colonialism and anti-colonial struggles. Elleke Boehmer's *Colonial and Postcolonial Literature* (1995), Ania Loomba's *Colonialism/Postcolonialism* (1998), Leela Gandhi's *Postcolonial Theory* (1998), and Robert Young's *Postcolonialism: A Historical Introduction* (2001), are stellar examples of this kind of work. *Postcolonial Literatures*, while relying heavily on these models, particularly that of Boehmer and Loomba, significantly expands the frame of analysis as it seeks to synthesise an overview of intellectual backgrounds ("a history of ideas") of colonialism and its legacies from the seventeenth century onwards with a careful textual analysis of key literary texts from this period. In other words, the book explores in depth the social, historical and political contexts of colonialism, decolonisation, migration, neo-colonialism and globalisation that help us understand the vast array of literature produced in South Asia, Africa and the Caribbean in the past three centuries. Moreover, the book is designed as a useful resource for both specialists and non-specialists; as such, it attempts to go beyond a simple historical and cultural commentary by employing a critical methodology centred on concepts of colonial and postcolonial identity.

Postcolonial and diaspora studies often focus on a predictable discourse about topics like "nationalism", "anti-colonial resistance", "mimicry", "hybridity", "authenticity", etc. While adequately addressing these issues in the analysis of key postcolonial texts, this book engages with a different set of foci: exoticism, commodification, culture making, and strategies of identification in both colonial and postcolonial literature that help anchor both the historical and materialist leanings of the project. Quite understandably, a project of this scope is fraught with complexities, one of the most significant being the problem of exclusion and inclusion. As a field of academic specialisation, postcolonial literary studies is often criticised for being too broad and unwieldy; at other times, it is decried for being too metropolitan, elitist and exclusionary. Moreover, just because postcolonial studies was institutionalised in the late 1970s doesn't mean that there was no writing on colonial and postcolonial societies and cultures before then. Most critics now agree that the history of colonialism dates back to the sixteenth century, when Columbus discovered the New World, and the consequent European mercantile expansion all across the globe. Some criticism even suggests that colonialism began with the Roman conquest of Britain and I draw from Ania Loomba's path-breaking work to elaborate on this issue. As Loomba points out, according to the Oxford English Dictionary (OED), "colonialism" comes from the Roman "*colonia*" and referred to Romans who settled in other lands but still retained their citizenship (7). The word "colonialism" according to the OED means "a settlement in a new country . . . a body of people who settle in a new locality, forming a community subject to or connected with their parent state; the community so formed, consisting of the original settlers and their descendants and successors, as long as the connection with the parent state is kept up" (Loomba 7). This indicates that along with the Roman conquest in second century AD, the Mongol conquest of the Middle East and China in the thirteenth century, the establishment of the Aztec Empire from the fourteenth to the sixteenth century, as well as the growth of the Ottoman Empire would all technically be considered colonial empires. But as Loomba very perceptively points out, the OED definition avoids any reference to the original inhabitants of the colonised lands, thus eclipsing any traces of traumatic encounters, conquests and domination which we know were hallmarks of the European colonising process. So, as she suggests, "the Crusades, or the Moorish invasion of Spain, the legendary exploits of Mongol rulers or the fabled wealth of the Incas or the Mughals were real or imagined fuel for the European journeys to different parts of the world" (8), and, as such, cannot be wholly excluded from the history of colonialism. But unlike the earlier form of pre-capitalist colonialism, modern European colonialism was established along with the rise of capitalism in the western world, and was primarily a mercantile enterprise before it morphed into a venture involving territorial seizures and brutal conquest and domination. As Loomba explains, "Modern colonialism did more than extract tribute, goods and wealth from the countries that it conquered – it restructured the economies of the latter, drawing them into a complex relationship with their own, so that there was a flow of human and natural resources between colonized and colonial countries" (9). In fact, along with the various rationale and strategies that were used to justify occupation of foreign lands, modern European colonialism always remained invested in maintaining the transnational networks that enabled commodities and profits to flow into the "mother country" (Loomba 9). Thus empire was responsible, in no small way, for reshaping the metropolitan centre, both materially and culturally.[1]

Before I explore how the exclusion/inclusion conundrum is often aggravated by issues related to the accessibility and translation of colonial and postcolonial texts, it is important to first understand the various nuances of the term "colonial", "imperial", "colonialist" and "postcolonial". I find Elleke Boehmer's definitions very useful for my purpose. She defines "imperialism" as "the authority assumed by a state over another territory – authority expressed in pageantry and symbolism, as well as in military power" (Boehmer 2), referring particularly to the expansion of European nation-states in the nineteenth and twentieth century. "Colonialism", on the other hand, "involves the consolidation of imperial power, and is manifested in the settlement of territory, the exploitation or development of resources, and the attempt to govern the indigenous inhabitants of occupied lands" (2). In other words, "imperialism" is often the idea or footprint that is used by European countries to legitimise, conquer and occupy foreign territories through the characteristically violent process of colonisation, and "colonialism" is the actual occupation, consolidation and settlement of colonies in foreign lands. In my reading then, the act of colonisation is inherently associated with violence, both metaphorical and actual. It is in this sense I use the words imperialism and colonialism.

Boehmer's distinction between colonial and colonialist literature is also particularly useful. She takes colonial literature to mean "writing concerned with colonial perceptions and experience, written mainly by metropolitans, but also by creoles and indigenes, during colonial times" (2), while colonialist literature, on the other hand, refers to literature that "was specifically concerned with colonial expansion" (3). It is important to emphasise the fact that colonialist literature is predicated on theories of European racial and cultural supremacy and is often invested in explaining or translating native experience to the metropolitan centre. That is how I use the term in this book as well.[2] It is worth noting African writer Chinua Achebe's acerbic comments in his essay "Colonialist Criticism" in response to Albert Schweitzer's proclamation that the African is, in fact, his "junior brother". In this context, Achebe points out,

> The latter-day colonialist critic, equally given to big-brother arrogance, sees the African writer as a somewhat unfinished European who with patient guidance will grow up one day and write like every other European, but meanwhile must be humble, must learn all he can and while at it give due credit to his teachers in the form of either direct praise or, even better since praise sometimes goes bad and becomes embarrassing, manifest self-contempt. (3)

This condescending attitude towards colonised subjects and any form of writing produced by them was not only based on the unquestioned superiority of European languages and cultures, but was also a calculated strategy to keep the native cultures firmly in their place. The desire to write back to the Empire, to reclaim their own voice in the master's language, thus became one of the hallmarks of anti-colonial resistance movements and characterises much of the literature that was produced in the colonies during this time. As Achebe points out, "Let no one be fooled by the fact that we may write in English for we intend to do unheard of things with it" (7), something that other writers like Rushdie have championed in subsequent decades. This is not meant to suggest that all literature produced in Europe between the sixteenth and the nineteenth century was necessarily colonialist. As Ngũgĩ wa Thiong'o emphasises, writers like William Blake, Walt Whitman, Brecht and Sartre showed remarkable sensitivity in cataloguing social ills, even those perpetrated against other people. But "taken as a whole this literature could not avoid being affected by the Eurocentric basis of its world view or global vision, and most of it, even when sympathetic, could not altogether escape from the racism inherent in Western enterprise in the rest of the world" (14).

The term "postcolonial" is also one that has been hotly debated. Critics like Ania Loomba are conflicted about the use of the prefix "post" as it could indicate, chronologically, an era after decolonisation, but also, ideologically, an era that replaced colonial occupation. Both uses are problematic in some ways. Decolonisation was a remarkably uneven process that, in some ways, dates back to the liberation of America, Australia and New Zealand in the eighteenth and nineteenth century, even as European colonisation continued, and often intensified, in Asia and Africa. The decolonisation of Asia, Africa and the Caribbean began in the 1940s and continued well into the 1990s (as in the case of South Africa), leading critics like Ella Shohat to acerbically ask "When exactly, then, does the 'postcolonial' begin?" (103). Also, since a lot of the former colonies in Asia and Africa have continued to deal with economic disparities fostered by colonial rule even after decolonisation, it is difficult to assert that these countries are free of their colonial legacy and hence can be called "postcolonial".[3] Also, as Elleke Boehmer points out, concerns in postcolonial writing are often assumed to be radically opposite to the issues raised in colonial literature, but such a rigid binary is often untenable, and, in fact, may be misleading. It is important, given this context, to underscore that, in this book, I distinguish the term "post-colonial" from the term "postcolonial". "Post-colonial", with a hyphen, is used in a chronological sense to indicate the period after 1945 when decolonisation began in earnest in Asia and Africa. And, again drawing on Boehmer, I define "postcolonial" literature as literature which critically interrogates the coloniser-colonised relationship from all aspects and is invested in reclaiming the voice and agency historically denied to the natives in the many years of colonial occupation and rule. Robert Young defines the function of postcolonial criticism when he remarks: "Postcolonial cultural critique involves the reconsideration of this [colonial] history, particularly from the perspectives of those who suffered its effect, together with the defining of its contemporary social and cultural impact" (1193). His definition is also useful for my methodology. According to Boehmer, "To give expression to colonized experience, postcolonial writers sought to undercut thematically and formally the discourses which supported colonization – the myths of power, the race classifications, the imagery of subordination. Postcolonial literature, therefore, is deeply marked by experiences of cultural exclusion and division under empire" (3).[4] Postcolonial literature then, by definition, is embedded in discourses of cultural exclusion and any study of that literature should necessarily be able to withstand criticism about exclusivity and elitism. But that is hardly the case. Many of the famous postcolonial critics are housed in Western universities and metropolitan centres and often, their critical works, rich in poststructuralist and deconstructionist theory, are considered esoteric and inaccessible to students across the world. Moreover, much of postcolonial criticism and theory is produced in English, and is about literature written in English. This becomes a hotly debated issue with writers and critics writing in vernacular languages who feel that their voices are being forcibly excluded from critical conversation by these Western academic luminaries.

Non-accessibility of literary texts is often a practical problem. A lot of the great works of literature written in the various languages of Africa and Asia are simply not accessible to a wider audience because of a lack of translation. And often, the translated versions available cannot match the nuances and cadences of the original text. In spite of that, veteran critics like Makarand Paranjape rightly question the privileging of English language texts in postcolonial studies and ardently plea for the balancing of the scale: "Who owns the fictional India? Who rules it? Who represents it? To whom does it belong? I am arguing that the end of the empire, likewise, signals a transfer in fiction power. The fictional territory that is India must be repossessed by those who live here and belong here" (Paranjape 41–42). And when a celebrated writer like Salman Rushdie goes on to assert, in his introduction to *The Vintage Book Of Indian Writing, 1947–1997*, that Indian writing in English produced in the last fifty years is not only "a stronger and more important body of work than most of what has been produced in the 16 'official languages' of India but represents the most valuable contribution India has made to the world of books" (x), it is not surprising that he is indignantly accused of being a sell-out to the Western media and the publishing industry.

Questions of cultural authenticity become potent here as writers and critics alike try to decide what should or should not be included within the overarching rubric of postcolonial and diasporic literary studies.[5] But at the same time most postcolonial writers and critics are extremely sceptical of labels forced upon their work. Postcolonial literature is sometimes referred to as Commonwealth literature, Third World literature, New literature in English, etc., and all of these labels have given rise to significant controversy. Just as Rushdie dismisses the moniker of "Commonwealth literature" as a literary ghetto whose purpose is to "confine, to restrain" (68) in his essay "'Commonwealth Literature' Does Not Exist", Chinua Achebe refuses to be fenced in as he struggles to define "African literature". In his essay "The African Writer and the English Language", Achebe ponders if "African literature" is "produced *in* Africa or *about* Africa? Could African literature be on any subject, or must it have an African theme? Should it embrace the whole continent or South of the Sahara, or just *Black* Africa? And then the question of language. Should it be in indigenous

African languages or should it include Arabic, English, French, Portuguese, Afrikaans, etc?" (55). Scalded by years of colonial rule, most of these writers resist speaking about their experience in established binaries and instead make an impassioned plea for pluralism, both socio-cultural and linguistic.[6]

In spite of the fissures and unresolved debates inherent in the field and highlighted here, it is necessary to begin this book by drawing limits, both chronological and spatial. This book is mainly concerned with literature written in English, even though I have occasionally used vernacular texts that have readily available English translations. As such, the book seeks to read the literature of the British Empire, that is, literature related to British imperialism and in opposition to it, produced both at the metropolitan centre and in the colonies. Unlike other critical works that have produced similar socio-cultural narratives about British colonialism, the historical framework in my book dates back to the sixteenth century. It tracks the growth of British mercantile expansion and consolidation through the era of high imperialism and rapid colonisation to the mid-twentieth century collapse of the empire to the nascent neo-colonialism and globalising forces of the twenty-first century. The British Empire persisted for around four hundred years, and in the nineteenth century boasted of occupied areas of land on all five continents.[7] But despite the broad chronological sweep, this is by no means an exhaustive study of the literary negotiations of British colonialism and its legacies. Instead, by focusing on the key terms and themes of identity, commodity and culture, I will use select literary texts to illuminate how specific historical, social and political contexts produced particular literary texts, and how these texts, in turn, shaped the historical and social contexts in which they were produced. Among other things, the book raises some of the following questions through the study of literature – Why did England embark upon its imperial project? What led to the growth and consolidation of the British Empire all across the world? How did this metaphorically and materially affect the societies and cultures that it conquered? Or, conversely, in what significant ways were the British themselves irrevocably changed by empire? What led to the anti-colonial resistance movements that were critical in ushering in decolonisation in the twentieth century? And how are newly formed postcolonial societies dealing with the traumatic legacies of colonialism, plagued as they are with the spectre of neo-colonialism and globalisation?[8]

Given the vast body of colonial and postcolonial literature available for a project of this scope, and despite my concerns about exclusivity, I had to limit the project spatially to a discussion of selected texts produced at the imperial centre and those primarily produced in or concerned with South Asia, Africa and the Caribbean. And even though the first chapter addresses the differing histories of colonialism in America, the settler colonies of Australia and New Zealand and the struggles of Ireland, I have largely excluded them from my larger analysis because of the radically different nature of Britain's relationship with them as distinct from the systematic colonial domination and subjugation of the rest of its colonies. It is also important to underscore here that this is not a book about postcolonial theory, mainly because there are several insightful theoretical commentaries already available influenced by pioneering texts like Edward Said's *Orientalism* (1978), Benedict Anderson's *Imagined Communities: Reflections on the Origins and Spread of Nationalism* (1983), Bill Ashcroft, Gareth Griffiths and Helen Tiffin's *The Empire Writes Back* (1989), and Homi Bhabha's *The Location of Culture* (1994). Instead, I have used postcolonial theoretical discourse to tease out symptomatic patterns and thematic tendencies in colonial and postcolonial literature and the historical, political and socio-cultural contexts in which such writing was produced.

I have tried to generally follow the chronological and historical framework that is mentioned earlier by starting with the narrative of the nascent English colonial expeditions in the sixteenth century and ending with a reading of the rise of neo-colonialism and globalisation in the late-twentieth and twenty-first centuries. Based on this overarching scheme, the book is divided into six chapters. The first chapter of the book introduces postcolonial literature by covering a comprehensive array of historical and political topics, beginning with the fledging European imperial enterprise of the sixteenth century, the rise of the East India Company, the history of settler colonies like Australia and New Zealand, the tumultuous relationship of Britain with Ireland, and ending with the late nineteenth-century imperial consolidation. This chapter briefly outlines issues related to colonial history and illustrates how theories of racial and cultural supremacy reflected in the works of writers such as Daniel Defoe, Sir Rider Haggard, Charles Dickens, Rudyard Kipling, Walter Raleigh, Mungo Park, Fanny Parkes and many others played a major role in validating imperial expansion and rule. As this chapter emphasises, British Empire, from the sixteenth to the nineteenth century, was partly created and sustained by an elaborate imaginative framework mobilised by colonial writings about the New World.

The second chapter continues examining this historical framework with focus on the period of high imperialism in the late nineteenth century and the counter-narratives that emerged as a result of it. The nineteenth century witnessed some major historical changes – unprecedented industrial growth and production following the industrial revolution and Britain's growing mercantile prowess instilled a new sense of hubris in the British imaginary. This led to a period of "high imperialism" characterised by the civilising mission that Britain used as a mantra to justify some of its brutal economic exploitation of the colonies. Interestingly, the late nineteenth century also saw the start of the demise of European colonialism, and by the beginning of the twentieth century and in the aftermath of the First World War, Britain's imperial authority started to develop significant fissures. While English writers like Virginia Woolf, T. S. Eliot and E. M. Forster started voicing their uneasiness and pessimism about the new world order, writers in colonised countries, like Rabindranath Tagore, Mulk Raj Anand, Raja Rao, Frantz Fanon, Claude McKay, C. L. R. James and Aimé Césaire became the intellectual driving force behind anti-colonial resistance movements. This chapter traces the rhetoric of self-representation and national identity that would ultimately lead to organised political movements against European colonial rule by studying some key texts ranging from Joseph Conrad's *Heart of Darkness* (1899), and Rabindranath Tagore's *The Home and the World* (1916), to Aimé Césaire's *A Tempest* (1969) and Jean Rhys's *Wide Sargasso Sea* (1966).

In the third chapter, I discuss Asian and African literature that traces the process of decolonisation and explores the identity crisis of postcolonial countries grappling with a traumatic colonial legacy while simultaneously reinventing themselves as modern nation-states. It can hardly be ignored that decolonisation was one of the most important global phenomenon in the second half of the twentieth century. Even though the liberation struggles and process of decolonisation was far from uniform across the world, one thing seemed fairly constant in all the newly minted sovereign states: a newfound sense of optimism and naïve belief in potential economic and social development. But the initial euphoria reflected in Indian Prime Minister Jawaharlal Nehru's "Tryst with Destiny" speech, for instance, quickly dissipated as the new nation found itself struggling with the carnage that followed the partition of the Indian sub-continent. Most nations in Africa too continued to wrestle with problems of colonial dependency and effective governance amidst inter-ethnic conflicts. Nonetheless, the new nation states remained heavily invested in figuring out a new postcolonial identity amidst a lingering colonial legacy, often centred around controversies about the use of the coloniser's language. This chapter will thus investigate the construction of postcolonial identities through the prism of postcolonial nation-formation by studying the works of Saadat Hasan Manto, Chinua Achebe, Ngũgĩ wa Thiong'o, Wole Soyinka, Salman Rushdie and Khushwant Singh, among others. I specifically look at Achebe's *Things Fall Apart* (1958), Salman Rushdie's *Midnight's Children* (1981), Ama Ata Aidoo's *Changes: A Love Story* (1991), and Chimamanda Adichie's *Purple Hibiscus* (2003) in greater detail in this chapter.

Chapters four and five study colonial and postcolonial migration and the growth of migrant communities primarily in Britain, focusing on the changing notions of Englishness and the re-evaluation of British national identity. There was a significant migrant presence, primarily African and Asian, in England throughout the eighteenth and nineteenth century that has often been overlooked in British national history. Additionally, it is worth noting that alongside the hundreds of black immigrants and travellers who were promptly relegated to the margins on their arrival or when their utility diminished, there were plenty others who were actively engaged in defying all odds and finding a foothold for themselves in an inhospitable society, even at the cost of somewhat compromising their ethnic roots. Critics like Rozina Visram, C. L. Innes and Peter Fryer have done some exemplary work in this field, and drawing on their material, the fourth chapter focuses on literature from pre-1850 Britain and explores the early black presence in the imperial metropolis.[9] First, it investigates the role that Olaudah Equiano's narrative played in the abolitionist movement of the eighteenth century. Later, it reads the British fascination with exotic objects as a facade that masks the undercurrent of xenophobia already palpable in metropolitan attitudes towards an increasing foreign presence in the eighteenth century and the first half of the nineteenth century. While simultaneously reading well-known texts such as that by Equiano, this chapter also sheds light on lesser known works like the travel narratives of Mirza Abu Taleb Khan and Sake Dean Mahomed's fascinating *Shampooing, or Benefits Resulting from the Use of the Indian Medicated Vapour Bath* (1826).

The fifth chapter explores post-1948 colonial migration to Britain. With the Nationality Act of 1948 and the arrival of the *S. S. Empire Windrush* at Britain's shores in the same year, Britain's demographics were fundamentally altered. The optimism and hope felt by the initial group of West Indian immigrants, captured by Calypso singer Lord Kitchener's song "London is the Place For Me", soon turned into disillusionment and despair as they got a taste of British racism over the course of the next five decades. Interestingly, in an apparent acknowledgement of the changing British demographic landscape in the twentieth century, in 2001, British foreign secretary Robin Cook tried to embrace Britain's racial and cultural diversity by declaring chicken tikka masala as "a true British national dish", not only because it was immensely popular in contemporary Britain but "because it is a perfect illustration of the way Britain absorbs and adapts external influences" (Cook).[10] Strikingly different from the vitriolic Powellian rhetoric of the 1960s, this comment, on the surface, seems to herald an acceptance of a new, non-essentialist, hybrid notion of British-ness. Yet, as the 2005 London subway bombings and the recent rise of Islamic fundamentalism – often attributed to second-generation immigrants – point out, all is not perfect in Britain's dreams of multiculturalism and inclusivity. Keeping this trajectory in mind and starting with the demystification of the imperial metropolis in the works of postcolonial writers and focusing on works of writers like Sam Selvon, Caryl Phillips, Hanif Kureishi, Zadie Smith, Monica Ali and critics like Stuart Hall, Paul Gilroy and

Simon Gikandi, this chapter explores how widespread exoticism and xenophobia frustrate attempts by immigrants to assimilate in London and other urban spaces, and consequently, in the larger postcolonial British society. I also examine the recent, much celebrated discourse of multiculturalism and hybridity as explored in the works of these contemporary writers. More specifically, I look at Sam Selvon's *The Lonely Londoners* (1956), Hanif Kureishi's *The Buddha of Suburbia* (1990), Meera Syal's *Anita and Me* (1996), Zadie Smith's *White Teeth* (2000), and Monica Ali's *Brick Lane* (2003), in some amount of detail.

The sixth chapter serves as a conclusion with an exploration of new and emerging concerns in the field of postcolonial studies, primarily the increasing emphasis on globalisation, multiculturalism and neo-colonial politics in contemporary postcolonial and diasporic novels. The events of 11 September 2001 irrevocably altered the global landscape. European colonialism was on its way out following the consistent decolonisation in Asia and Africa in the second half of the twentieth century, and the years following the Cold War witnessed the decline of the former Soviet Union and the unprecedented rise of the United States as a global superpower. On one hand, there is a continued mistrust of what is termed the "McDonaldisation" of the world and its impact on local communities; on the other, there is increased concern about the emerging culture of surveillance in modern Western nation-states that are obsessed with securing its borders against external threats and policing its boundaries through a proliferation of documentation (passports, visas, identity cards, birth certificates, etc.). Thus questions of power dynamics, domination and resistance have acquired a new sense of urgency in the work of contemporary postcolonial writers, albeit in a slightly different context than that of European colonialism. This final chapter attempts to explore some of these issues through a reading of selected texts by Amitav Ghosh, Arundhati Roy, Pico Iyer and others, and tries to highlight some of the newer concerns in the field of postcolonial literary studies. I also include a section on the tenuous position that postcolonial women writers are often forced to occupy in the Western literary marketplace.

In his book *Moving the Centre: The Struggle for Cultural Freedoms*, Ngũgĩ wa Thiong'o proclaims, "Slavery, colonialism, and the whole web of neo-colonial relationships so well analysed by Frantz Fanon, were as much part of the emergence of the modern West as they were of modern Africa. The cultures of Africa, Asia and South America, as much as those of Europe, are an integral part of the modern world" (10). Thus, given the enormous breadth of the field, I want to reiterate that this book is by no means an exhaustive study of colonial and postcolonial literature; rather, it simply offers a brief overview of the contexts and enduring motifs, tendencies and themes that have been an integral part of this field of literature through a selection of literary texts that I find exemplary. The works cited should provide a starting point for anyone interested in a more in-depth reading of these particular ideas.

Works Cited

Achebe, Chinua. *Morning Yet on Creation Day: Essays*. London: Heinemann, 1975. Print.

Bhabha, Homi. *The Location of Culture*. London and New York: Routledge, 1994. Print.

Boehmer, Elleke. *Colonial and Postcolonial Literature*. Oxford: Oxford UP, 1995. Print.

Cook, Robin. "Chicken Tikka Masala Speech." *The Guardian*. 19 April 2001. Web. 16 December 2015. <http://www.guardian.co.uk/world/2001/apr/19/race.britishidentity>

Iyer. Pico. *Video Night in Kathmandu: And Other Reports from the Not-So-Far East.* New York: Vintage, 1988. Print.

Loomba, Ania. *Colonialism/Postcolonialism.* New York: Routledge, 1998. Print.

Paranjape, Makarand. "What About Those Who Stayed Back Home? Interrogating the Privileging of Diasporic Writing." *Shifting Continents/Colliding Cultures: Diaspora Writing of the Indian Subcontinent.* Eds. Ralph J. Crane and Radhika Mohanram. Atlanta: Rodopi, 2000. 225–45. Print.

Rushdie, Salman and Elizabeth West, eds. *The Vintage Book of Indian Writing, 1947–1997.* London: Vintage, 1997. Print.

Rushdie, Salman, "'Commonwealth Literature' Does Not Exist." *Imaginary Homelands: Essays and Criticism 1981–1991.* London: Granta Books, 1991. 61–70. Print.

Thiong'o, Ngũgĩ wa. *Moving the Centre: The Struggle for Cultural Freedoms.* London: James Currey, 1993. Print.

Young, Robert. *Postcolonialism: An Historical Introduction.* Malden, Massachusetts: Blackwell, 2001. Print.

Notes

1. For more on this, see Ania Loomba's insightful analysis on pages 10 and 11 of *Colonialism/Postcolonialism.*
2. I define "native" to mean the people originally inhabiting lands that were colonised. Boehmer points out that for a while the word was often used in a derogatory way, but postcolonial critics have recently reclaimed the word to merely mean "belong to a particular place by birth" (8).
3. For more on this, see pages 12 and 13 of Loomba's book.
4. I also want to draw attention to Homi Bhabha's description of the postcolonial since he was so instrumental in shaping the trajectory of postcolonial theory. In *The Location of Culture*, Bhabha talks about postcolonial criticism at length:

   Postcolonial criticism bears witness to the unequal and uneven forces of cultural representation involved in the contest for political and social authority within the modern world order. Postcolonial perspectives emerge from the colonial testimony of Third World countries and the discourses of 'minorities' within the geopolitical divisions of East and West, North and South. They intervene in those ideological discourses of modernity that attempt to give a 'hegemonic' normality to the uneven development and the differential, often disadvantaged, histories of nations, races, communities, peoples. . . . As a mode of analysis, it attempts to revise those nationalist or 'nativist' pedagogies that set up this relation of Third World and First World in a binary structure of opposition. The postcolonial perspective resists the attempt at holistic forms of social explanation. It forces a recognition of the more complex cultural and political boundaries that exist on the cusp of these often opposed political spheres. (171, 173)

5. Rushdie, in his essay "'Commonwealth Literature' Does Not Exist", indignantly dismisses the demands for cultural authenticity by suggesting that authenticity is the "respectable child of old fashioned exoticism" (67). He adds:

> It demands that sources, forms, style, language and symbol all derive from a supposedly homogenous and unbroken tradition. . . . One of the most absurd aspects of this quest for national authenticity is that – as far as India is concerned, anyway – it is completely fallacious to suppose that there is such a thing as a pure, unalloyed tradition from which to draw. The only people who seriously believe this are religious extremists. The rest of us understand that the very essence of Indian culture is that we possess a mixed tradition, a mélange of elements as disparate as ancient Mughal and contemporary Coca-Cola American. . . . The reality of the mixed tradition is replaced by the fantasy of purity. (67)

6. In his essay "Colonialist Criticism", Achebe talks at length about the problems with colonialist literature and criticism.

> The colonialist critic, unwilling to accept the validity of sensibilities other than his own, has made particular point of dismissing the African novel. He has written lengthy articles to prove its non-existence largely on the grounds that it is a peculiarly Western genre, a fact which would interest us if our ambition was to write

'Western' novels. But in any case, did not the black people in America, deprived of their own musical instruments, take the trumpet and the trombone and blow them as they had never been blown before, as indeed they were not designed to be blown? And as a result, was it not jazz? Is anyone going to say that this was a loss to the world or that those first Negro slaves who began to play around with the discarded instruments of their masters should have played waltzes and foxtrots and more Salvation Army hymn tunes? No! Let every people bring their gifts to the great festival of the world's cultural harvest and mankind will be all the richer for the variety and distinctiveness of the offerings. (17)

7. Even though there is some critical debate about the difference between "Englishness" and "Britishness," I am using the term English and British interchangeably in this book to denote the inhabitants of Great Britain (comprising of England, Scotland and Wales).
8. Again, drawing on Boehmer, "neo-colonialism signifies the continuing economic control by the West of the once-colonized world, under the guise of political independence" (9), something that I deal with in significant detail in the final chapter.
9. I am using the word "black" here in the inclusive sense to talk about all non-white ethnicities present in England at that moment. This has a critical trajectory that is discussed more in the relevant chapter.
10. For more on this speech, see Robin Cook's *Guardian* article.

ONE

Writing Empire

The rise of European imperialism and images of empire from the sixteenth to the nineteenth century

> The writer is the ultimate colonizer, conquering the space of consciousness with the exclusionary and divisive structures of representation. This metaphorical notion of the writer as colonizer ought to be considered as more than a mere figure of speech, given the practical role which writing plays in the actual processes of colonial expansion and administration. In fact the structures of writing and those of political power can never be wholly distinguished from one another.
>
> —*The Rhetoric of Empire*, David Spurr

As David Spurr and other postcolonial critics have convincingly argued, the European colonial project from the sixteenth to the nineteenth century did not simply involve the actual conquest of far-flung lands, but was also (in large measure), a literary and imaginative project, based on fantastical accounts of strange countries and their mysterious inhabitants. Europe's mercantile ambitions, which triggered its imperial ambitions, ensured that colonial and metropolitan sites were connected most obviously through "material flows of capital, commodities and labour" (Lester 6). As part of these developing circuits of global commerce, "Indian calicoes moved to Africa to purchase slaves, Tahitian breadfruit was taken to the Caribbean to feed those slaves, Caribbean molasses were transported to New England where it was made into rum for trade with Native Americans, and tea, coffee, chocolate, tobacco, sugar, rice and potatoes converged, from sites dispersed across the globe, on the British metropole" (6). In fact, as early as 1708, Daniel Defoe in *The Review* commented on the insidious influence of Eastern textiles, among other imports, on the British mindset.[1] In the statement quoted below, he talks specifically of Indian cottons that were becoming so indispensable in British homes that the British Parliament eventually had to prohibit their import into Britain.

> The general fansie of the people runs upon East India goods to that degree that the chints and painted calicoes . . . become now the dress of our ladies. . . . Nor was this all, but it *crept* into our houses, our closets, and bedchambers; curtains, cushions, chairs, and at last, beds themselves, were nothing but calicoes or Indian stuffs; and in short, almost everything that used to be made of wool or silk . . . was supplied by the Indian trade. (Thomas 48; emphasis added)

If Defoe's statement is any indication, the growing dependence on Eastern commodities, fostered by the activities of the East India Company (hereafter referred to as EIC), created considerable anxiety about the corrupting influence of Eastern trade among British intelligentsia as early as the beginning of the eighteenth century.[2] At the same time, the ubiquitous presence of Indian commodities in European households enabled the British to "see India as the English imagined it, or India not necessarily as it was, but as it was understood to be" (Daly 10). In fact, this imaginative appropriation of India and other colonised countries aided the imperialist spirit and Britain's civilising mission. In his *Travels in the Interior of Africa* (1799), Mungo Park perceptively points out that European mercantile ambitions were irrevocably tied up with the supposedly "benign" discourse of enlightenment, that "Nothing is wanting to this end but example, to enlighten the minds of the natives, and instruction, to enable them to direct their industry to proper objects" (238–9). Closer attention to this twin trajectory of imperial ambition and greed masked by the rhetoric of the civilising mission in this chapter will help us understand how Europe, specifically Britain, created and maintained a vast imperial network from the sixteenth to the nineteenth century that helped them establish control over vast sections of the world ranging from India, Africa and the West Indies to the settler colonies of Canada, Australia and New Zealand.

Britain's initial forays into the Americas, Africa and the Far East

While Britain undoubtedly emerged as one of the main driving forces behind Europe's imperial expansion from the eighteenth century onwards, it was by no means the first European power to venture into unknown lands. In 1498, when Portuguese explorer Vasco da Gama opened up the sea route to the East and landed in Malabar on the western coast of India, Portugal gained access to the famed riches of the East. English sailors often joined the Portuguese in their voyages to West Africa, the Far East and South America. By the sixteenth century, Spain had not only annexed Portugal between 1580 and 1640 but had also made significant inroads into both central and South America as a powerful Catholic imperial power. At the same time, the Dutch were making their presence felt in Southeast Asia by dominating the East Indies spice trade and slowly edging out the Portuguese from some of their established West African trading posts. Till then, Britain had only managed minor expeditions into the New World – "a brief exploration of the north-east North American seaboard by John Cabot in 1497; summer settlements in Newfoundland for the north

Atlantic fishery; and exploration/privateering voyages against the Spanish by men like Francis Drake and Walter Raleigh" (Samson 8). Bill Nasson remarks, "At first, the English seemed to be preoccupied more with cod than colonisation" (25). But emboldened by Britain's defeat of the Spanish Armada in 1588, and egged on by reports of the fabulous and endless acquisitions the Spanish were making in the New World, Britain began to covet West African outposts where the Portuguese had been formerly trading for gold, ivory, spices and slaves. Still, Britain's interest in the African commodity and slave trade remained erratic compared to the other European powers and did not suggest any sustained imperial commitment. It was the first successful plantation in Virginia in North America in 1607 that gave Britain its first colonial possession. The Virginia settlement, modelled on earlier colonial plantations by the British and Scots in Ireland, was based largely on British royal patronage where colonists obtained permission from the Crown to acquire land grants and begin farming (Samson 9). Gradually, Britain made inroads into Central America and the West Indies by acquiring former Spanish colonies like Barbados in the West Indies (1620–30) and Jamaica in 1655. The victory over France and Spain in the Seven Years War (1756–63) consolidated Britain's position in the area (Fhlathúin 23). By the end of the seventeenth century, British plantations across the Americas were growing a wide variety of crops including cotton, tobacco and sugar. In exchange for the land grants, British plantations were required to trade exclusively with Britain, thus pumping significant amounts of money into the British economy. But the back-breaking work on the plantations required a steady supply of labour, and by the end of the seventeenth century, "England was routinely shipping many thousands of African slaves . . . and well on its way to becoming the leading slave-trading nation of the Western world" (Nasson 38).

Britain's growing maritime supremacy did not go unnoticed among the English intelligentsia. William Shakespeare wrote a speech for the character of John of Gaunt, in *Richard II* (1597), that celebrated Britain's burgeoning identity as Europe's leading empire builder.

> This royal throne of kings, this sceptered isle,
> This earth of majesty, this seat of Mars,
> This other Eden, demi-paradise,
> This fortress built by nature for herself
> Against infection and the hand of war,
> This happy breed of men, this little world,
> This precious stone set in the silver sea,
> Which serves it in the office of a wall,
> Or as a moat defensive to a house,
> Against the envy of less happier lands . . .
>
> This blessed plot, this earth, this realm, this England,
> This nurse, this teeming womb of royal kings,
> Feared by their breed, and famous by their birth,
> Renowned for their deeds as far from home,
> For Christian service and true chivalry,
> As is the sepulcher in stubborn Jewry
> Of the world's ransom, blessed Mary's Son:
> This land of such dear souls, this dear, dear land
> Dear for her reputation through the world . . .
> (Shakespeare 59–60)

However, when slavery was made illegal in all British territories in 1833, the ensuing confusion led to a rapid decline of the West Indian plantation culture. Although indentured labourers were then shipped in from far-flung countries like China and India, this did little to alleviate the fortunes of English plantations. Furthermore, the American Revolution began in 1775 and when the Declaration of Independence was signed in 1776, it was clear that Britain's empire across the Atlantic was on its way out. Even as economists like Adam

Smith, in his influential *The Wealth of Nations* (1776), decried Britain's management of the colonies by insisting that "Great Britain derives nothing but loss from the dominion which she assumes over her colonies" (151), and argued for free trade and a move away from Britain's protectionist policies in the colonies, it became clear that Britain had to look for other markets to expand its mercantile empire.[3] A movement eastward into countries like Turkey, India and consequently the Far East became almost imperative.

Britain's love affair with Eastern imports had started as far back as 1662 when Catherine of Braganza's bridal dowry introduced various objects like cane, tea, porcelain, lacquer and textiles to Britain. Before this first material contact with its objects, the European mainland had, at best, fantastical images of the East; lands where cotton "grew six yards tall; of a city in China where all people dressed in silk, yet still had plenty to spare for foreign merchants; and of fortunes to be had in Java in 'pepper, nutmegs, spikenard, cubebs, cloves and all the other valuable spices and drugs'" (Thomas 9). Even though travellers like Marco Polo, who Gertrude Thomas quotes here, were publicly derided for embellishing their travel narratives, it was the lure of these eastern luxuries that prompted constant expeditions from Europe to the East. This particular event, as Thomas's book demonstrates, had a lasting impact on Renaissance England, and more generally on British commodity culture. In many ways, as Thomas insists, "it was the demanding desire for such exotic extravagances that in great measure shaped geography and wrote the history of the world" (vi). As the consumer demand for spices, cotton and silk textiles, coffee and tea grew exponentially, a group of merchants keen on exploiting the spice and silk routes previously dominated by the Portuguese and the Dutch set up the EIC as "a joint-stock enterprise to bid for a monopoly charter for English trade in Asia, a warrant granted in 1600" (Nasson 43). This singular event spearheaded Britain's mercantile and consequent imperial expansion for the next three hundred years.

British traders had long been fascinated with the opulence of imperial China, gleaned through multiple travel accounts, and had long hoped for a trade relation with that country that would necessitate a conquest of the vast China seas. So China's dogged refusal to open its economy and trading routes to British merchants, who were viewed as "inferior foreign barbarians and devils" (Nasson 110), was extremely frustrating not only for the merchants themselves, but also to the British government. Quite predictably, Britain was looking for some kind of a dispute between British merchants and their Chinese counterparts that would require a military intervention. That opportunity came in the form of the Opium Wars of 1839–1842 and 1856–1860. It was provoked by the Chinese imprisonment of British merchants who had not handed over their imported shipments of opium, a commodity that had been specifically banned by the Chinese because of the negative effects they believed it had on its citizens. The British claimed that such persecution was in violation of laws that governed international free trade, but in reality, they were thrilled by the opportunity to challenge and subdue the Chinese with their military prowess. The Opium Wars ended in a series of treaties in which Chinese sovereignty was severely compromised as Britain gained access to ports, concessions and privileges that would make it easy for Western merchants to conduct free trade. These initial gains were consolidated with the later seizures of Hong Kong and Kowloon. As Nasson mentions, by the second half of the nineteenth century, "control of China's foreign trade was in British hands, without the territorial costs and risks of accompanying colonial responsibilities" (111).

The Rise of the East India Company and the colonisation of India

By the time Britain's conflict with the Chinese over trade routes and policies was being played out in the seas of China in the first half of the nineteenth century, Britain was already beginning to consolidate its claim on India, the "jewel" in the British crown. British traders, along with the French and Portuguese, had long maintained small trading outposts along the coast of India during the rule of the Mughal dynasty. But with the demise of the Mughal Empire in the eighteenth century, both the British and the French moved with alacrity to form alliances with local rulers in an attempt to further consolidate their presence. A series of British victories over the French-allied Indian forces between 1746 and 1761, particularly the Battle of Plassey of 1757 under the leadership of Robert Clive (commander of the EIC's army), cemented the dominion of the EIC in the subcontinent. When the Mughal emperor gave Clive the *diwani*, or contract, which entitled him to an annual fee in exchange for the right to form a civil government and complete control over the revenues of the rich territory of Bengal, the EIC made its foray into a new set of political responsibilities. The transformation of the EIC from a trading company to wielding legislative powers over several provinces was quite rapid. From the metropolitan centres of Calcutta, Bombay and Madras, they quickly brought areas as far as Burma, Ceylon and even modern day Malaysia under their administrative control, sometimes through strategic alliances with local rulers, but often through military coercion. Even though it lost its monopoly on trade in 1813 and functioned as a branch of the British government, the EIC persisted in its drive to impose direct rule over most territories and quickly became extremely unpopular through its annexation policies such as the Doctrine of Lapse. Widespread backlash against their unpopular policies as well as the struggling economy in once prosperous regions like Bengal culminated in the Indian Mutiny of 1857. Even though the Mutiny shook the British administration in unprecedented ways, it failed to permanently banish the British and the country was quickly brought under direct British rule. The Royal Proclamation of 1858 established Queen Victoria as the Empress of India. In the Royal Proclamation, the Queen assured her imperial subjects:

> We declare it to be Our Royal Will and Pleasure that none be in any wise favoured, none molested or disquieted by reason of their Religious Faith or Observances; but that all shall alike enjoy the equal and impartial protection of the Law . . . . And it is Our further Will that, so far as may be, Our Subjects, of whatever Race or Creed, be freely an impartially admitted to Offices in Our Service, the Duties of which they may be qualified, by their education, ability, and integrity, duly to discharge. (Samson 173)

Lofty words. But ironically, it was the Victorian era that witnessed a calculated consolidation of Britain's empire. Spain and France, Britain's main imperial rivals had recently witnessed a decline in their fortunes, and with France's defeat in the Napoleonic Wars, Britain's position as the leading European superpower was further consolidated. Moreover, as Fhlathúin points out:

> The Treaty of Nanking provided for British commercial ventures to be granted access to China in the wake of the First Opium War (1839–42); it also gave Britain possession of Hong Kong. As mentioned earlier, although China was never colonized or directly subject to British rule, it remained part of the 'informal empire' of British influence until the rise of Japan altered the balance of power in the region at the end of the nineteenth century. (27)

THE CURIOUS CASE OF IRELAND AND BRITAIN'S SETTLER COLONIES

The issue of whether Ireland can be imagined as a postcolonial state has been an ongoing debate in academia starting in the 1980s and going on well into the 2000s. According to some critics, the Field Day Theatre Company's staging of Brian Friel's *Translations* in 1980 inaugurated the study of Irish literature through the postcolonial lens. Joe Cleary claimed, "the play raised a cluster of issues about British state expansion in nineteenth-century Ireland, about the politics of cultural collision and language change, and about the role of knowledge in the imaginative appropriation of territory" (14), all key issues investigated in postcolonial theory. But the Field Day Theatre Company did not simply stage the play. As Cleary points out, they also published a series of pamphlets that contained critical analyses of Irish culture within a framework of English imperialism and Irish anti-colonial nationalism by noted postcolonial theorists like Frederic Jameson, Edward Said and Terry Eagleton. These pamphlets, along with a growing body of Irish postcolonial criticism like David Cairns and Shaun Richards's *Writing Ireland: Colonialism, Nationalism and Culture* (1988), Lynn Innes's *The Devil's Own Mirror: The Irishman and the African in Modern Literature* (1990), and David Lloyd's *Anomalous States: Irish Writing and the Post-Colonial Moment* (1993), have at least ensured a vigorous critical discussion of Ireland's relationship with England. Moreover, Bill Nasson argues that even though British economic investments in Ireland remained minimal, Irish tax contribution to the maintenance of the British army and its imperial missions around the world was heavily overstretched and almost bordered on the point of exploitation, making the Irish situation distinctly colonial (123). British politicians, frustrated with the continuous internal dissensions in Ireland, often employed racist language to characterise the Irish, and comparisons to the barbarous, uncivilised natives of Asia and Africa were plentiful: "In the 1890s, the Conservative Prime Minister, Lord Salisbury, and the Fabian Socialists, Sydney and Beatrice Webb, were not at all unusual in sharing the view that in their evolutionary imperfections, the incapable Irish resembled the 'Hottentots' of South Africa" (Nasson 124). But other critics like Stephen Howe in his *Ireland and Empire: Colonial Legacies in Irish History and Culture* (2000) and Norman Vance in *Irish Literature since 1800* (2002) furiously refuted this perspective by insisting that:

> . . . the language of colony, colonialism and imperial domination increasingly misrepresents and oversimplifies, the complicated and idiosyncratic relationship between Ireland and mainland Britain . . . by the standards of normal colonial and postcolonial economic performance, Ireland never was a really poor country, let alone a unique exemplar of misery and oppression among European peoples. (Vance 3)

Critics like Glenn Hooper and Edna Longley warn that even though the word "colonial" might be applicable to some aspects of the Irish experience and its relationship with Britain, caution must be used with the methodological approach being used before abruptly forcing Ireland into a postcolonial framework. Clearly, the jury is still out on whether Irish literature can be included in postcolonial studies. One curious fact worth noting here is that while Irish nationalists in the nineteenth century often railed against the perceived injustices of British administrators, well-educated Protestant loyalists often found employment in colonial service and were often deployed in the settler colonies of Australia and Canada. At the same time, mass-Irish emigration to these countries increased by leaps and bounds as thousands left the mainland to escape religious persecution and poverty.

Australia and New Zealand had long been regarded as vast unexplored regions of imperial opportunity. But while New

Zealand, after some initial skirmishes with the Maoris, was shaping up to be a "classic complementary imperial economy, virtually a rainy extension of Lincolnshire or Wiltshire" (Nasson 128), centred around wool farming, meat and dairy produce, Australia created some amount of apprehension in the British public imagination in the early nineteenth century. The British people were initially unsure of what to make of a country that supposedly housed thousands of convicted felons and poor Irish immigrants amidst a verdant, but wild natural landscape. But the massive opportunity for wool farming and the discovery of minerals like coal, copper, lead, silver, zinc and the Gold Rushes, especially in the province of Victoria between 1851 and 1870, saw an enormous surge in the British expatriate population in Australia. Moreover, "profitable export production linked the new Australian economy to the international trading system, providing the earnings that could be used to fund essential infrastructure – the development of railways, roads, urban services and so on" (129). But towards the end of the nineteenth century, Australian writers started growing tired of paying obeisance to Britain and, following the Eureka stockade of 1854, ushered in a new era characterised by "a rejection of British [cultural, social and political] supremacy and a new Australian self-confidence which – along with strong feelings of Unionism – led up to the literary nationalism of the 1890s" (Bader 137).[4] This crystallising of Australian identity continued into the first two decades of the twentieth century and is epitomised in A. D. Hope's 1939 poem "Australia".[5] By the beginning of the twentieth century, even though Australia, like other settler colonies, was somewhat indebted to London for its economy, it had also asserted its own unique identity in the form of a responsible government and a certain degree of constitutional liberty.

Britain's "civilising mission" in the second half of the nineteenth century

The nineteenth century saw a radical revision of the way British people thought about their colonised subjects, resulting in a discourse that was increasingly shaped by notions of racial and cultural superiority. Much of the imperial expansion and consolidation during the Victorian era was thus legitimised by the narrative of uncivilised people in strange, exotic lands, created and nurtured in popular imagination by European colonisers. When Robert Clive was granted the *diwani* of Bengal, Bihar and Orissa by the Mughal Emperor Shah Alam II in 1765, there was actually some thought about the EIC's identity and purpose in India and the proper way of governance. "Should it confine itself to commercial matters, or should it wield political influence in the subcontinent? If the latter, should it rule according to Indian custom or should it bring Christianity, western government, and British law to India?" (Samson 93). But the thoughts of good governance based on the colonised subjects' needs and aspirations quickly faded away as the discourse about the civilising mission began to gain ground in Victorian England. As early as 1839, Charles Darwin's *Voyage of the Beagle* reveals not only pride in the British conquest of the South Sea, but also a condescending satisfaction that the benefits of Christianity were being brought to these remote parts of the world. "It is impossible for an Englishman to behold these distant colonies, without a high pride and satisfaction. To hoist the British flag, seems to draw with it as a certain consequence, wealth, prosperity, and civilization" (Darwin 376). Books like Sir Charles Dilke's *Greater Britain* (1868), and J. R. Seeley's *The Expansion of England* (1883), cemented Darwin's early impulses about bringing Western civilisation to the poor, spiritually bereft and morally abject natives. Such books "identified empire with Britishness, or more specifically with Englishness, and argued for the value to Britain of its overseas possessions as well as the special fitness of the English to rule over other people" (Fhlathúin 27). As Samson suggests, Indians who were "once defined as commercial and political allies (or rivals) with an ancient civilization, . . . were now identified as cultural inferiors requiring guidance and reform" (94). Especially after the Sepoy Mutiny of 1857 and Queen Victoria's formal coronation as the Empress of India, missionary work in India was justified by defining the natives as being "immersed in the most appalling depths of bestial superstition and social corruption" (Lester 30). Quite understandably thereafter, John Ruskin, in his inaugural lecture at Oxford University in 1870, declared that England "must found colonies as fast and as far as she is able, formed of her most energetic and worthiest men; – seizing every piece of fruitful waste ground she can set her foot on, and therefore teaching these her colonists that their chief virtue is to be fidelity to their country, and that their first aim is to be to advance the power of England by land and sea" (Fhlathúin 27). Much of this fervent desire to establish colonies and save the world was directed at the dark continent of Africa. In their influential books about Britain's imperial conquests, Patrick Brantlinger and Alan Lester have convincingly demonstrated that this humanitarian discourse was paradoxically constructed out of the discourse of abolitionism. In the early nineteenth century, an emergent Evangelical morality was gaining ground in England where "the eighteenth-century concept of individual 'virtue' was being superseded by a notion of collective responsibility for the plight of others" (Lester 25). The brutal oppression and exploitation characteristic of the trans-Atlantic slave trade became the focal point around which such debates started being played out and ideas of what constitutes a "civilised" nation started to be re-evaluated. As Lester points out, by the early nineteenth century, not only had anti-slavery become a "defining quality of being British" (25) and proof of the empathy and divine aura of the

British, but the abolition of the slave trade in 1807 also "served both to secure national atonement for the wrongs which Britons had inflicted on the world through their participation in the trade, and to reinforce patriotic discourse by distinguishing freedom-loving Britons from tyrannical Continental Catholics" (25). But as Patrick Brantlinger points out, with reference to Eric Williams's thesis in *Capitalism and Slavery*, Britain's attempts at reinforcing a new found sense of patriotism with the altruistic discourse of abolitionism paradoxically led to more significant colonial inroads into Africa. Brantlinger suggests that although Williams acknowledges the idealism fuelled by the nascent evangelicalism that led to the abolition of slavery, he demonstrates that at this point Britain had much less to lose than the other European powers because it had already lost much of its slave-owning territory after the American Revolution. So, in other words, "as the leading industrial power in the world Britain found in abolition a way to work against the interests of rivals who were still heavily involved in colonial slavery and a plantation economy" (Brantlinger 174). Nonetheless, the public campaign against slavery reached a crescendo in the 1830s, and in 1833, slavery was completely outlawed in all British-owned territory when the British Parliament passed the Emancipation Act. Once the Emancipation Act went into effect, deliberations began on how to integrate emancipated slaves into the social fabric of the colonies. In the West Indies, for instance, between 1834 and 1838, newly emancipated slaves were forced to work under an apprenticeship system, after which former slave owners were compensated monetarily for each slave. Ironically, the slaves, who were still considered property, received no compensation of any kind, leading to unstable, and often, bitter relations between former plantation owners and their slaves in the Caribbean. In Africa, the question of the rehabilitation of slaves was tied up with shifting representations of the Africans. In much of the abolitionist literature from the 1790s to the

1830s, the African native was the noble savage – innocent, child-like victims of European brutality – in contrast to the images of indolent, animalistic Africans of early travel narratives and accounts by plantation owners. In "Africa Delivered; or The Slave Trade Abolished" (1809), for instance, James Grahame writes, "In that fair land of hill, and dale, and stream/the Simple tribes from age to age had heard/No hostile voice" (Graham 58).[6] Such characterisations of Africans were patronising, if not downright offensive, but also gave the British public, re-imbued with a spirit of benevolence, the desire to support the work of Christian missionaries who were tenaciously arguing for the redemption of the poor natives.

After abolishing slavery in British-owned colonies, the British now set out to quell savage customs in Africa and save the Africans from themselves. This humanitarian enterprise started with the virtuous Niger Expedition in 1841 that aimed to establish outposts throughout the continent that would enable Christian missionaries and anti-slavery reformers to bring "light" and western civilisation into the darkest recesses of the continent. This culminated in the infamous land grab that became the "Scramble for Africa". As Brantlinger points out, "By the time of the Berlin Conference of 1884–85, which is often identified as the start of the Scramble for Africa, the British tended to see Africa as a center of evil, a part of the world possessed by demonic darkness or barbarism, represented above all by slavery, human sacrifice, and cannibalism, which it was their duty to exorcise" (179). Although Rudyard Kipling wouldn't come up with his infamous phrase "The White Man's Burden" till he published his poem of the same name in 1899, it was clear that was the driving force and rationale behind the increasing involvement of both missionaries and explorers in the African continent.

Interestingly, as British explorers went on their moral crusades in India, Africa and even in the far flung colonies of Australia and New Zealand, and Britain's imperial empire was becoming inextricably linked to British identity, the rather dubious discourse of exoticism, centred around foreign bodies and commodities, was gaining ground in Victorian England.

Exoticism, as a descriptive category, emerged out of the genre of travel writing. Various travelogues and writing about the Orient by writers like Richard Burton, Benjamin Disraeli, W. M. Thackeray, as well as *The Arabian Nights,* with their plentiful, picturesque descriptions of minarets, bazaars, harems and dervishes, managed to conjure up an image of the exotic East in the British public's imagination. Malek Alloula corroborates this in his brilliant book, *The Colonial Harem*: "Arrayed in the brilliant colors of exoticism and exuding a full-blown yet uncertain sensuality, the Orient, where unfathomable mysteries dwell and cruel and barbaric scenes are staged, has fascinated and disturbed Europe for a long time. It has been its glittering imaginary but also its mirage" (3). Alloula goes on to show how this search for the exotic, in many cases, the mythical harem, brought an army of missionaries, anthropologists, photographers and writers into places like Algeria. There they set up camp to dream "of the Orient, its delights and its beauties"(3) and capture the phantasm of the Orient into a very specific commodity – a postcard. Alloula goes on to demonstrate how the postcard then became a harbinger of stereotypes, a tool of imperialist rhetoric and "the fertilizer for colonial vision" (4). Brantlinger also emphasises that the exotic Orient was a source of endless fascination: "Fixated on the harems and veiled women of various Muslim societies, the Victorians found the Orient's alleged sensuality both abhorrent and endlessly fascinating" (136). But this fascination with the exotic turned into palpable fear when some of these exotic bodies began to appear on the European mainland. For instance, as early as 1845, Parisian critic Theophile Gautier wrote anxiously about the Algerian influence on France.

> It is strange, we believe we have conquered Algeria, but Algeria has conquered us. Our women already wear scarves interwoven with threads of gold, streaked with a thousand colours, which have served the harem slaves . . . hashish is taking the place of champagne; our Spahi officers look so Arab one would think they have captured themselves in a *smala*; they have adopted all the Oriental habits, so superior is primitive life to our so-called civilization. If this goes on, France will soon be Mahometan and we shall see the white domes of mosques rounding themselves on our horizons . . . we should indeed like to live to see the day. (Root 19)

Gautier's anxiety about national identity being threatened by Oriental influence is also applicable to the British context. Daniel Defoe, whom I quoted in the beginning of this chapter, was no less concerned about the debilitating effect the influx of Eastern bodies and commodities had on British national identity. In fact, critics have suggested that, in Victorian England, the impulse to exoticise and codify cultural difference stemmed primarily from the fear of British identity being tainted by the influx of Oriental culture, and the discourse of exoticism became a mode of control by which Oriental bodies and commodities were frozen into a state of stasis, and as such, kept in check and at a distance from the British public.

We see the discourse of exoticism put in practice during the celebrated Great and Colonial Exhibitions in Victorian England. It was the Great Exhibition of 1851, organised at the initiative of Queen Victoria's consort, Prince Albert, at the newly constructed Crystal Palace in London's Hyde Park, that marked an official acknowledgement of Britain's fascination with material objects, especially those imported from other countries and particularly from Britain's ever-expanding colonies. The exhibition was an exaggerated show of mercantile prowess and was intended to demonstrate the burgeoning supremacy of British trade among its European counterparts. Prince

Albert, on the opening day of the exhibition, declared that "the products of all quarters of the globe are placed at our disposal, and we have only to choose which is the best and cheapest for our purposes" (Richards 28). The display of objects from India, the jewel in Britain's imperial crown, was particularly necessary to create this myth. It is also worth emphasising that Indians in their ethnic costumes were an integral part of the display along with all other material objects imported from the colony, lending credence to the discourse of exoticism. As Deborah Root suggests in her book *Cannibal Culture*, exoticism "works through a process of dismemberment and fragmentation in which objects stand for images that stand for a culture or a sensibility as a whole" (42). So, by displaying Indian bodies in all their ethnic glory but framing them within a tableau of picturesque Oriental life, their potency is minimised and effectively controlled. Root also points out that eroticism is one of the most persistent tropes of exoticism. "The notion that sex is somehow more interesting in a colonial setting, particularly if accompanied by accoutrements the Westerner finds unusual, such as colorful clothing or oddly shaped furniture, is extremely persistent. Exotic accoutrements of sex have always titillated the colonist, which fits in with Malek Alloula's study of erotic postcards in French colonial Algeria in which he observes that French colonists wanted to see Moorish women behind bars" (39–40).[7] Spectacular events like the Great Exhibition of 1851 and the Colonial and Indian Exhibition of 1886 had a very specific purpose. As Aviva Briefel points out, the Colonial and Indian Exhibition that opened in South Kensington on 4 May 1886 attracted a record number of visitors:

> Featuring extravagant displays from British colonial holdings, the exhibit was organized by the Prince of Wales as an "imperial object lesson" in England's power and grandeur. In the words of an article from the *Saturday Review*, "Now if any man can look at this and not come away with a new and a lively sense of

> the greatness of the country he belongs to, he must be a fellow of a very dull imagination and a very stupid temperament" ("Imperial Object" 633). The exhibition was intended to provide ocular proof of the "commercial wealth and power of England beyond the seas" (Peripatetic 511), the "solidarity of a world-wide Empire, its unity of interest, and its manifold resources" ("Colonial and Indian," *Saturday Review*). The fact that it was located in South Kensington, an "exhibitionary complex" that, since its establishment in 1857, had become a monument to "Victorian high imperialism" (Kriegel 6), confirmed its dedication to perpetuating the colonial project. (Briefel 2)[8]

But some other messages also become clear. As Samson suggests, "Britain's zeal for exploration was not only about commercial or national prestige. The empire was also becoming an empire of knowledge where everything from coastlines and wind patterns to animals and plants was being observed, catalogued, and analyzed" (54). Peter Hoffenberg also points out that "The use of South Asians as ethnographic exhibits was part of a more general Victorian-era project to construct an ethnographic survey of the subcontinent . . . . Human subjects were labeled, displayed, and studied much as were complementary commercial and artistic exhibits" (219). This process of mapping and cataloguing was hardly a benign process, as Edward Said so lucidly explained in his seminal work, *Orientalism* (1978). This was a deeply political and calculated enterprise to construct an Orient according to the needs of the West and the discourse of exoticism was effectively marshalled to that effect in Victorian England. Literary texts both helped sustain and provide a rationale for the insular and problematic imperial vision from the sixteenth to the nineteenth century.

THE IMPERIAL MISSION IN BRITISH LITERATURE

Many years after decolonisation, modern readers can learn about the European empire through multiple nineteenth- and twentieth-century novels, travel narratives and administrative documents preserved in library collections in Britain. But, as Elleke Boehmer rightly suggests, the empire, in itself, was a textual project. "The Empire in its heyday was conceived and maintained in an array of writings – political treatises, diaries, acts and edicts, administrative records and gazetteers, missionaries' reports, notebooks, memoirs, popular verse, government briefs, letters 'home' and letters back to settlers" (13). This is corroborated by Mary Louise Pratt who, in her book *Imperial Eyes: Travel Writing and Transculturation* (1992), famously writes:

> Borders and all, the entity called Europe was constructed from the outside in as much as from the inside out. While the imperial metropolis tends to understand itself as determining the periphery . . . it habitually blinds itself to the ways in which the periphery determines the metropolis – beginning, perhaps, with the latter's obsessive need to present and re-present its peripheries and its others continually to itself. Travel writing, among other institutions, is heavily organized in the service of that imperative. (6)

The multitude of travel narratives that emerged at this time, ranging from those by Richard Hakluyt, Richard Burton, Mungo Park, H. M. Stanley and David Livingstone, to those by female travellers like Fanny Parkes, Mary Kingsley, Maud Diver and Flora Annie Steele, contributed to Britain's imperial project, as did writings by popular writers like Charles Dickens, Wilkie Collins, Rudyard Kipling, Rider Haggard, W. M. Thackeray, Joseph Conrad and others. Earlier, critics like C. A. Bodelson and Karl de Schweinitz had claimed Britain's burgeoning empire was often outside the peripheral vision of writers on the mainland. Schweinitz stated, "At the most the colonies in that [Victorian] literature were far off-stage, a distant world to which the dramatis personae could be banished if it were convenient for the development of the novel. No one in Dickens, Thackeray,

Eliot, or Trollope brooded about the imperial relationship" (34). But with the advent of postcolonial studies in the late 1970s and inspired by Edward Said's famous analysis of Jane Austen's awareness of colonisation in *Mansfield Park* (1814) in *Culture and Imperialism* (1993), postcolonial critics have looked as far back as early modern travel narratives to understand how the imperial project was undoubtedly shaped by British literature. While books like Mary Louise Pratt's *Imperial Eyes: Travel Writing and Transculturation* (1992) and Barbara Korte's *English Travel Writing from Pilgrimages to Postcolonial Explorations* (2000), have looked at travel narratives to understand Britain's imperial ambitions, books like Patrick Brantlinger's *Rule of Darkness: British Literature and Imperialism, 1830–1914* (1988), Suvendrini Perera's *Reaches of Empire: The English Novel from Edgeworth to Dickens* (1991), Jenny Sharpe's *Allegories of Empire* (1993), and Deirdre David's *Rule Britannia: Women, Empire and Victorian Writing* (1995), have exhaustively studied Victorian novels to demonstrate how colonial politics influenced every aspect of life in Victorian England. While Brantlinger states that "Imperialism, understood as an evolving but pervasive set of attitudes and ideas toward the rest of the world, influenced all aspects of Victorian and Edwardian culture" (8), Deirdre David points out that in Victorian England:

> The wealth derived from empire served to create a curious and mainly middle-class reading public: the audience for Victorian writing about Britain's geopolitical power, whether in the form of political essays, travel narratives, missionary tales, or novellas that question the imperial project. In turn, this writing imaginatively collaborates, consciously or not, with structures of civil and military power to constitute and secure the red spaces that prove so comforting to Marlow, and to Conrad's British readers.[9] (*Rule Britannia* 3)

The rest of this chapter, then, will briefly outline these issues related to colonial history and illustrate how theories of racial and cultural supremacy, reflected in select travel narratives and Victorian novels, played a major role in validating imperial expansion and rule.

The nascent imperialist rhetoric in early modern travel writing

As mentioned earlier in the chapter, it was not until the second half of the sixteenth century that British explorers were able to catch up with their European counterparts, primarily the Spanish and the Portuguese, in their quest for adventure and discovery of new lands. In 1577, Francis Drake set out on a voyage that would make him the first Englishman to circumnavigate the globe, and in 1585, Sir Richard Grenville was the first Englishman to attempt to set up a colony in North America. Since then, the sheer volume of travel narratives written by British merchants and explorers has been staggering, prompting William Sherman to claim that "early modern travel writing was so varied that it may not even be appropriate to describe it as a single genre" (30). Critical writing on early modern travel writing has also been wide ranging. Sherman's essay "Stirrings and Searchings" (1500–1720) in *The Cambridge Companion* situates early modern travel writing within its political and social context. To emphasise the immense diversity of narrative voices, he divides travellers into ten different categories – editors, pilgrims, errant knights, merchants, explorers, colonisers, captives and castaways, ambassadors, pirates, and scientists. Others like Joan Pau Rubies highlight the anthropological function of travel narratives. In an essay titled, "Travel Writing and Ethnography", he mentions that Richard Willes, one of the earliest compilers of travel accounts, had proclaimed in 1577 that the sixteenth century was the age of the flourishing of ethnography. For instance, Francis Drake's account is entirely focused on the English attacks on Spanish colonies, and a lot of the merchants of the EIC were specifically asked to maintain detailed descriptions of the places they visited and the people they encountered in a methodical fashion (244). Others maintain that early modern travel writers engaged in nascent but sustained imperialist rhetoric in order to stake claims to new lands and economic markets in the sixteenth century amidst stiff European competition. Richard Helgerson analyses the conflict of aspiration and insecurity in Elizabethan England in his book *Forms of Nationhood* and encapsulates the crisis succinctly – "Were England to rival the greatness of Greece and Rome, something decisive needed to be done" (3). Simple ethnographic documentation of the native experience in travelled lands thus often become secondary to the construction of an imperialist ideology under the overarching slogan of "Hail Britannia".

One of the earliest pioneers of this imperialist ideology in the sixteenth century was Richard Hakluyt (1553–1616). Hakluyt's compendium of travel documents entitled *The Principal Navigations, Voyages, Traffiques and Discoveries of the English Nation* was first published in 1589 and the 1600 edition of the compendium ran into three volumes. Hakluyt's aim in this massive collective effort wasn't simply to whet the appetite of future British travellers to explore mythic lands. Instead, it was a deliberate political gesture to arouse British national pride and to encourage policymakers in Queen Elizabeth's service to seriously consider expansion of British authority to distant lands, an activity which had already been embarked upon by Britain's continental rivals – Spain, France, Portugal, and Denmark. As Barbara Korte points out, "Hakluyt was convinced that England was destined to take on a leading role in the expansion of the world, and he thus collated the knowledge gathered by his countrymen with particular care, demonstrating the extent to which England had already adopted this new role" (31). His feverish catalogue of travel accounts to distant places – ranging from Syria, Aleppo, Babylon and Basra to Chile, Peru and Java and China – clearly reveals an attempt to trigger British national pride and to instil a sense of superiority that would motivate Britain to work on more expansionary strategies and emerge as a forerunner of empire building overseas. In the preface to the compendium, Hakluyt immediately attempts to make up for Britain's late start by re-instating belief in Britain's prowess at expeditions at sea. Even though he is uncomfortably aware that Britain had not yet produced a great adventurer of the likes of Vasco da Gama and Christopher Columbus, he makes a valiant attempt to salvage some pride by mentioning explorers like Richard Chancellor, Sir Hugh Willoughby, Stephen Burrough, Arthur Pet and Charles Jackman (2). He claims that the British were not lacking in the spirit of adventure; in fact, the paths traversed by these explorers were far more difficult and challenging than their continental counterparts, as they had to constantly combat inclement weather in the northern seas and the dangerous waters of the Caspian Sea. Moreover, British expeditions were not a recent phenomenon and, if not in terms of conquests, the British were at least pioneers of "foreign trade and merchandise" (36), dating back to the reign of the Danish King Canute. In fact, a lot of the voices that we hear in the three volumes are of the merchants themselves, making it clear how much value Hakluyt placed on mercantile expansion. As Richard Helgerson explains, "Seen through the eyes of merchants, the world emerged as a vast network of markets offering unlimited commodities and vent, and England itself emerged as the aggressive commercial entity required from the first by Hakluyt's strategic thinking" (171). The rhetoric of imperial domination slowly acquires more urgency as Hakluyt ties it in with the notion of difference – particularly notions of religious difference between Europeans and the inhabitants of the New World, in his dedicatory epistle in the second edition of 1599 to Sir Robert Cecil, Principal Secretary to Queen Elizabeth. He emphasises that the second edition contains a lot of narratives chronicling the perilous expeditions of brave British adventurers to expel "the Saracens and Mahometans", filled "with a zealous devotion and ardent desire to protect and dilate the Christian faith" (37). The lofty goals of the Europeans to save the world by converting the heathens to Christianity can thus effectively be traced back to the beginning of the seventeenth century.

Hakluyt's desire for bringing civilisation to the natives is also tied to his territorial ambitions. Throughout his collection, North America is portrayed as a country teeming with wealth and natural resources, and he repeatedly mentions the enticing economic prospects that the country has to offer. He declares that if the Queen is willing to dispatch her adventurers to this hitherto untrammelled land, "she shall by God's assistance, in short space, work many great and unlooked for effects, increase her dominions, enrich her coffers, and reduce many pagans to the faith of Christ" (37). But his desires of colonising the New World does not in any way dampen his mercantile ambitions. The more he travels, the more he is enamoured by new trade routes that British merchants can forge far beyond the European mainland, and he emphasises that such trailblazing merchants and explorers are "worthy inhabitants of this city of London" (38). Hakluyt is thus one of the first Englishmen to conjure up an imperial network centred around the metropolis of London as he repeatedly talks about the necessity of establishing trade routes all across the world that would enable British commodities like wool cloth to be exported easily to countries as distant as China and Japan.

In the first edition, Hakluyt was invested in urging the Queen to expand Britain's borders. In the second edition, he provides specific details about the execution of such a project. He also mentions his gratitude at being consulted on the subject of British expansion on the island of Guiana. It is quite clear from this that Hakluyt perceives his role as being more significant than that of an ethnographer. His selection of materials is designed with a specific political purpose in mind and he increasingly sees himself as an indirect partaker or a catalyst in the growing imperial ambitions of Britain. As the above analysis shows, Hakluyt's narrative was thus ideologically motivated to reignite British nationalist pride, and by showing the British to be a dynamic civilisation capable of engaging in both territorial and mercantile expansion, he was reinventing "both England and the world to make them fit one another" (Hakluyt 153).

This analysis of Hakluyt's objectives begs the question whether the genre of travel writing was always aligned with political and ideological objectives in the sixteenth century. Helgerson affirms this when he claims that Hakluyt and the communities he represented "mapped the physical world and strove to impress on it the designs of collective desire" (153). Sir Walter Raleigh's account, *The Discovery of the Large, Rich, and Beautiful Empire of Guiana* (1595), as well as those of Samuel Purchas including *Purchas his Pilgrimage* (1613) and *Hakluytus Posthumus or Purchas his Pilgrimes* (1625), also reveal not only an ethnographic bent but a desire to expand Britain's influence overseas. As Mary Fuller explains, "Sir Walter Raleigh's early projects . . . were heralded in a vocabulary which cast discovery as apocalypse: flinging open the doors to the east, unveiling the earth's hidden secrets, bringing light to benighted people" (13). Like Hakluyt before him, Raleigh too can be said to be one of the early supporters of Britain's imperial project. Their portrayal of the travelled land is largely refracted through their lens as explorers and colonisers and "the travelers/writers, as far as they present themselves in their texts, largely identify with the official purpose of their voyages" (Korte 35).

The Colonial Project in the long eighteenth century

The nineteenth century has been traditionally regarded as a period of high imperialism when Britain enjoyed an unimaginable material prosperity, in no small measure due to its control of a significant part of the world's landmass. But before we discuss that, it is important to note that Britain was able to reach this level of prosperity only because its expansionary tactics had continued unabated through the seventeenth and long eighteenth century, often through ethnographic expeditions. As Boehmer pointed out, "From the European point of view . . . colonialism was a metaphoric and cartographic – as well as a legalistic – undertaking" (17), and the process of identifying the blank spaces on the map and imagining, classifying, populating these spaces continued unabated through the seventeenth and eighteenth century, aided by travel narratives, merchant's tales and explorer's documents. Travelogues like Peter Kolb's *The Present State of the Cape of Good Hope* (1719), Anders Sparrman's *Voyage to the Cape of Good Hope* (1775), William Paterson's *Narrative of Four Voyages in the Land of the Hottentots and the Kaffirs* (1789), Mungo Park's *Travels in the Interior Districts of Africa* (1799), and John Barrow's *Travels into the Interior of Southern Africa* (1801), aided Europe's ethnographic project by providing insight into the mysterious African continent. As Korte points out, after Europeans had staked claims to Australia, and no more new lands were to be found, European explorers turned their attention to existing continents about which their knowledge was relatively limited, like the Arctic regions, South America and, most importantly, Africa (87). As part of this concerted effort, European countries continued to send explorers and researchers into previously unexplored regions, particularly into the heart of the "Dark Continent". First published in German, Peter Kolb's book was translated into English in 1731 and remains a veritable compendium of information on southern Africa in the first half of the eighteenth century. Even though Kolb was initially sent by his Prussian patron to Africa to carry out astronomical and meteorological research, Kolb's book is hardly just a scientific treatise. In fact, it contains detailed ethnographic accounts of the Khoikhoi society and contains chapters on "forms of government, religion, ceremonies, domestic economy, cattle management, medicine, and so on" (Pratt 43). What distinguishes Kolb's narrative from other travel narratives of his time is his latent humanism and his recognition of the Hottentots as "cultural beings" (43). As Pratt explains, "Without denying the repugnance to Europeans of many Khoikhoi practices, he rejects paradigms of essential difference that make it 'natural' for Europeans to deal with the Africans differently from the ways they deal with each other" (44).

Like Kolb, Sparrman and Paterson – both sent to Southern Africa as naturalists to document the geography, the flora and fauna – were quick to distinguish themselves from European colonisers and merchants. Paterson claims:

> If ambition never instilled in the conquerors of the world the desire to extend their empire to the deserts of Africa, if commerce had not tempted men to examine a country whose outer appearance could never seduce anyone whose sole object is to increase his wealth . . . nevertheless there exist men who, despite all the terrors of these countries find them objects capable of adding to their satisfaction. (Pratt 50)

Both these narratives thus differed significantly from the dominant narrative about Africa as a place of monstrosities and savagery and can be said to have inaugurated a new sub-genre of scientific travel.

In contrast to Kolb, Sparrman and Paterson, John Barrow's narrative is unmistakably written from a colonial perspective, precisely because he was sent to the Cape colony as part of a British imperial project. After Britain annexed the Cape from the Dutch in 1795, Barrow was sent there as a personal secretary to the new governor, Lord George McCartney. As such, even though much of his narrative is ethnographic, documenting the geography of the land, a pride in the British imperial project is unmistakable in his tone. In fact, Pratt mentions that Barrow was so distraught when Britain returned the Cape Colony to the Dutch in 1803, he wrote a second volume of his *Travels* to convince the British of the strategic importance of the Cape to Britain's imperial mission (Pratt 67). Maybe because of his impassioned arguments, Britain forcibly re-annexed the Cape in 1806, although it was not before 1815 that they definitively established their control in that region.

In fact, in the last decades of the eighteenth century, as Pratt points out, most of the countries in Europe were having a difficult time holding on to their imperial dominance as they were plagued by a series of indigenous resistance movement (72). The American Revolution and the murder of James Cook seriously destabilised the British and they were struggling to hold on to their colonies while the slave revolt in Santo Domingo in 1790 had overthrown French colonial rule and an uprising of the Andean population in 1781 had undermined the Spanish authorities. Meanwhile, even as the intra-European rivalries sapped the adventurous spirit and created tensions on the mainland, this competition with each other was what "bound European powers together in finding new forms of Euroimperial interventions, and new legitimating ideologies: the civilizing mission, scientific racism, and technology-based paradigms of progress and development" (Pratt 74). All of these new ideologies started crystallising into the imperialist rhetoric of the nineteenth century and can also be observed in turn-of-the-century travelogues like that of Scottish explorer, Mungo Park.

Even though detailed ethnographic accounts about the African continent routinely appeared throughout the eighteenth century, the deepest recesses of Africa, for some reason, had eluded the grasp of European colonisers.[10] The explorers had been unable to locate the famed Niger which was reportedly the hub of commercial activity in the African interior, or explore the mythical city of Timbuktu which, since the publication of Leo Africanus's *History and Description of Africa* in 1550, had existed "in European mental maps as a city of gold at the center of a wealthy and cultured kingdom" (Pratt 70). So in 1788, just a few months before the establishment of the Society for the Abolition of the Slave Trade, the Association for Promoting the Discovery of the Interior Parts of Africa (or the African Association) was founded under the leadership of Joseph Banks. The association's manifesto clearly states that they were determined to get rid of "this stigma, and desirous of rescuing the age from a charge of ignorance . . . strongly impressed with a conviction of the practicability and utility of thus enlarging the fund of human knowledge, have formed the plan of an Association for Promoting the discovery of the interior parts of Africa" (Pratt 69). Aside from the lofty goal of knowledge gathering, the association was primarily interested in commercial ventures as the heavily populated interiors of Africa, with its cities and established commercial networks, was imagined as a rich market for British goods. So, even as the anti-slavery movement was gaining urgency within the British intelligentsia at the end of the eighteenth century, interest in the discovery of Africa continued unabated, except, there was a significant change in the perception of Africa at the turn of the century. Pratt explains, "the reimagining of the African interior in the late eighteenth century coincided with the extraordinary acceleration of the anti-slavery movement after 1770 and the reconception of Africans as a market rather than a commodity" (71).

As part of the newly found African Association's knowledge-gathering project in 1795, Mungo Park, a Scottish surgeon, started on a mission to discover the Niger and gather relevant information that might be used to establish trade routes into the interior of Africa. Since earlier expeditions by the association's many volunteers had failed spectacularly, Mungo Park's successful completion of his mission and discovery of the Niger bolstered the British imperialist spirit. 1500 copies of the first edition of Park's *Travels in the Interior Districts of Africa* (1799) were sold out within a month, and the book was translated into French and German by 1800. Even though Park states in his preface that his narrative is "a plain unvarnished tale, without pretensions of any kind, except that it claims to enlarge, in some degree, the circle of African geography" (xv), he is clearly invested in widening British commercial interests in the region. He writes:

> It appears that slaves, gold, and ivory, together with the few articles enumerated in the beginning of my work, viz., bees-wax and honey, hides, gums, and dye-woods, constitute the whole catalogue of exportable commodities . . . It cannot, however, admit of a doubt, that all the rich and valuable productions, both of the East and West Indies, might easily be naturalized and brought to the utmost perfection in the tropical parts of this immense continent. (238–239)

At the same time, Park's account is remarkable for its dramatic quality; the lone adventurer against the elements of nature – a narrative that acted as a catalyst to the British adventurous spirit and consequently led to a series of African expeditions by explorers like David Livingstone and H. M. Stanley in the second half of the nineteenth century.

NINETEENTH-CENTURY TRAVEL WRITING AND THE IMAGES OF EMPIRE

The industrial and technological advancements made following the industrial revolution, and unprecedented revenues generated by trade with Asia and Africa, produced in the early nineteenth century British mind-set a sense of economic and cultural superiority that was reflected in every aspect of the literature produced during that period. In the Victorian era, travelogues achieved bestseller status due to their being a combination of ethnographic document and imperialist rhetoric, and largely aided Britain's imperial project. For instance, when David Livingstone's *Missionary Travels* was published in 1857, it sold over seventy thousand copies and made him such a celebrity that he would often be mobbed in public. H. M. Stanley's *In Darkest Africa* (1890), sold over one hundred and fifty thousand copies and was frequently translated into several languages. Narratives like that of Livingstone's, Stanley's and Richard Burton's were heavily invested in documentation and knowledge gathering, which critics like Thomas Richards, Barbara Korte and Elleke Boehmer believe was "a seminal instrument of control over the Empire" (Korte 90). In fact, Richard Burton, the author of almost two dozen travelogues, is often credited as "one of the founders of the new science of anthropology" (Brantlinger 159). At the same time, as Korte points out, "The Victorian explorers became *national* heroes if their expeditions could be claimed for the imperial cause" (90), and we see marvellous examples of Britain's philanthropic civilising mission in the works of most of these writers.

Richard Burton, in his *Personal Narrative of a Pilgrimage to Al-Madinah and Meccah* (1855), travels disguised as a Dervish, a false identity he adopts as he journeys through Mecca and Medina and painstakingly documents the social mores and customs of the Arabs. Barbara Korte draws on Pratt's argument to point out: "The apparently strictly object-orientated description of 'manners-and-customs', that is the anthropological content of these accounts, is a strategy which allows the writers to avoid the portrayal of culture *contact*: the text constructs an 'other' with whom the European traveller does not establish a genuine interpersonal relationship" (92). Burton's disguise is possible because of his ingenuity and understanding of foreign races, but as he emphasises at every step, the potential of unmasking is very real and fraught with dangers. Yet, disguises like this, or his disguise of a half-Arab, half-Persian merchant on his travels through India, was a necessity because, as Burton writes, "the European official in India seldom, if ever, sees anything in real light, so dense is the veil which the fearfulness, the duplicity, the prejudice and the superstitions of the natives hang before his eyes" (*Falconry* 65). Though severely critical at times of the British imperialist process, Burton never ceases to be racist and imperialist in his narratives. His journey to Medina was prompted by the classic imperialist desire to fill in the blank spaces on the map. "I volunteered in the autumn of 1852 to explore the Great Waste of Eastern and Central Arabia. That huge white blot which still disgraces our best maps" (Hayman 17). Elsewhere he claims that "Like the fox in the fable, fulsomely flattering at first . . . the Indian will befriend the Englishman, but in the latter's absence he will . . . look forward to the hour when enlightened Young India will arise and drive the 'foul invader' from the land" (Brantlinger 163), thus reinforcing all the racist stereotypes already in play in the Victorian mindset.[11]

Unlike earlier travelogues discussed here, Victorian travel narratives are also dominated by an overwhelming urge to keep the realms of the coloniser and the colonised separate. This was a time when the threat of miscegenation and the contamination of the imperial metropolis by colonial agencies was gathering force in British public discourse, and "the strict separation of description of a country's population from geographical and topographical descriptions, so that the country, which is, after all, the real object of the imperial gaze, comes across as 'unpopulated'" (Korte 92) becomes a dominant writing strategy. In Victorian travelogues, the controlling and delimiting of colonial life was organised around the discourse about the "picturesque". The term, borrowed from landscape painting, is particularly useful to encapsulate some of the imperialist ideas at work in these travelogues. Indira Ghose suggests, "The organizing trope of the picturesque was evoked in colonial travelogues in the service of an imaginative appropriation of the other world" (*Women Travelers* 41). Referring to a particular scene as "picturesque" belies its willingness to be framed, and this metaphor of containment, a move towards freezing the reality and vibrancy of native life into an aesthetic vignette, can be read symbolically as a desire to seal the boundaries of native experience. The particular moment is framed in time and the observer/traveller remains very much detached from the actual experience and hence free from the threat of contaminating the readers back home.

In his *The Lake Regions of Central Africa* (1860), Richard Burton describes the Tanganyika Lake as "picturesque", but as Korte points out, the people and densely populated villages of the region are reduced to just components of a landscape – "Villages, cultivated lands, the frequent canoes of the fishermen on the waters, and on a nearer approach the murmurs of the waves breaking upon the shore, give a something of variety, of movement, of life to the landscape" (Burton 307–308). In fact, Fanny Parkes's travel account is entitled *Wanderings of a Pilgrim in Search of the Picturesque* and this motif is constantly reiterated throughout her writing. Labelling India as a "picturesque" place enables these women to experience the beauties of the natural, verdant land, but maintains a necessary distance between the observer and the observed, thus ensuring the well-being of British domestic life, free from threats of intermingling.

This leads us to the vast array of travelogues written by women in the Victorian period and forces us to examine whether accounts by women present a different ideology or employ different rhetorical strategies than their male counterparts. Critics like Deirdre David argue that in Victorian women's writing, there is a shift in tone from the expansionist discourses of male travel accounts and the spirit of adventure is often replaced by musings about questions of home and belonging. David affirms that "Almost always, the travel narratives, memoirs, and letters produced by Victorian women disclose a more domestic and therefore different picture of empire than that to be found in conventionally male genres such as the essay, the government report, and the public speech" (*Rule Britannia* 27). But as the following analysis will reveal, notwithstanding the inward gaze and the occasional moments of anti-imperialist critique by travellers like Mary Kingsley, most Victorian women's travel writing very much remains embedded within the larger imperial project.

In the second half of the nineteenth century, British colonial rule was well underway in India and in some parts of Africa, and many of these women had travelled to the colonies with their husbands or male relatives. Instead of focusing on the public sphere and larger issues of administration, they turned their gaze inward into the private sphere and started meticulously documenting the details of their transplanted lives. The focus of these women was very much on their subjective experiences and many of them were preoccupied with mapping India in contrast to the beloved land that they had left behind. More often than not, their catalogue of ethnographic details of life in India became a catalogue of what seems to be encapsulated in the words "absence" and "recognition". They evaluated and valorised a lot of their experiences in comparison to what they recognised as familiar to their prior lives in England. Any observation of colonial Indian life is characterised either by a sense of loss, because it reminds them of what they had left behind in Britain, or has nostalgic power because it evokes thoughts of some beloved object back home. Thus the travelogues of these women writers become an imaginative space where their subjective experiences in India are constantly evaluated against a thoroughly internalised standard of British domesticity. Korte points out that "The foreignness of a traveled country is always the result of an act of construction on the part of the perceiver, who defines the country's otherness against his or her own sense of identity, his or her own familiar contexts" (20), and nowhere is this more apparent than in some of these female authored travelogues. Ghose quotes Emma Roberts, who finds the principal street, or Chandery Choke, in Delhi, fascinating because "the houses are of various styles of architecture, partaking occasionally of the prevailing fashions of the west; Grecian piazza, porticos, and pediments" (*Memsahibs Abroad*, 25), and she sees the city of Benares as the "Indian Venice" (*Memsahibs Abroad*, 33). Flora Annie Steel even writes a practical guide titled *The Complete Indian Housekeeper and Cook* dedicated to those "English Girls to whom Fate may assign the task of being Housemothers in our Eastern Empire" (Barr 152). Pat Barr points out that Lady Dufferin, the wife of the eighth Viceroy of India, Lord Dufferin, provides minute details of the sage-green moiré coat embroidered in silver and worn by the native rajah in one official gathering, but asserts that the natives "remain picturesque oriental oddities with whom she seems to have had little verbal communication" (174). In fact, as Indira Ghose perceptively points out, "With the increasing stultification of Anglo-Indian society in India and the stricter patrolling of racial boundaries, travelers focused their attention more and more on the social life within the British community in India and less on interrelations between Indians and English" (*Memsahibs* 9–10). The travelogues, like Fanny Parkes's *Wanderings,* become more of a catalogue of the "picturesque" sights of India than accounts of cultural encounters in what Pratt calls "contact zones" (4), and thus in some ways can be said to be as reflective of an imperialist ideology as seen in male travelogues.[12]

This is not to say that "contact zones" don't exist at all in women's travel narratives. Interestingly, these "contact zones" were liminal spaces populated by women in the *zenana* or native servants employed in the colonial household. As Susan Bassnett suggests, in the accounts by women, "There is a clear assertion of femininity, either through attention to details of clothing, accounts of domestic life, or the inclusion of romantic episodes" (239). Their femininity gives them privileged access to Indian aristocratic women in the *zenana*, something which is outside the purview of male travellers unless, like Richard Burton, they travelled in disguise. A lot of the travel accounts by women contain detailed and colourful descriptions of these encounters. But like in the sixteenth-century travelogues, where limited understanding of native customs would often create fictive versions of native experience, the process of "cultural interpretation" here is often hampered by the lack of access to native languages, and descriptions of these meetings often become stereotypical portrayals of beautiful but indolent Oriental women. Fanny Parkes, for instance, has a fascinating description of the attire of Mulka Begum. She is clearly enthralled by the beauty, gracefulness and splendour of Oriental women, but even such descriptions acquire value only when pitted against descriptions, albeit negative ones, of European women:

> [Mulka Begum] walks very gracefully and is as straight as an arrow. In Europe how rarely – how very rarely does a woman walk gracefully! Bound up in stays, the body is as stiff as a lobster in its shell; that snake-like undulating movement – the poetry of motion – is lost, destroyed by the stiffness of the waist and hip, which impedes the free movement of the limbs. A lady in European attire gives me the idea of a German manikin; an

Asiatic, in her flowing drapery, recalls the statues of antiquity. (Dalrymple 194)

Though the Eden sisters and Fanny Parkes reveal a careful fascination with aristocratic women, they are clearly dismissive, even contemptuous of the servants, especially the ayahs and the ambiguous figure of the wet-nurse. Parkes clearly states that the servants are "great plagues; much more troublesome than English servants" (Dalrymple 19), labels her ayah as being "excessively idle", and is even more caustic in an indirect reference to a wet-nurse – "The children of Europeans in India have a pale sickly hue, even when they are in the best of health; very different from the chubby brats of England" (23). In this case, these British women felt compelled to uphold their superior class positions and maintain a marked distance by insisting on racial differences. As Laurence Kitzan explains, "The emphasis constantly was on difference and not on similarities, because difference was inherently more interesting, but also because too much emphasis on similarities carried with it the danger that wrong conclusions might be reached about the relationship of native peoples to the British" (8). With their insistence on the "picturesque" as a writing strategy and their obvious attempts to keep the coloniser-native realm of experience markedly distinct, thus upholding the dominant British discourses to which they would return at the end of their travels, Victorian female travellers were as complicit in the imperial process as the men of their ilk. As Indira Ghose rightly points out, female travel accounts are often not about a real India but one that is "created in the colonial Imagination" (*Memsahibs* 11). Ghose starts her introduction by quoting Adela Quested's words in E. M. Forster's novel, *A Passage to India,* where Adela claims "I want to *see* the *real* India" (1). The question remains how much of the "real" India these women travellers actually cared to see.

RACE AND IMPERIALISM IN THE VICTORIAN NOVEL

As I have noted earlier in the chapter, critics like Edward Said, Patrick Brantlinger, Jenny Sharpe, Deirdre David and others have vigorously refuted early criticism like that of C. A. Bodelson who, in a book published in 1925, claimed that "the part played by the colonies in mid-Victorian fiction is surprisingly small. A person dependent on [that] fiction . . . might be excused if he failed to discover that the Empire consisted of more than the islands of Great Britain and Ireland" (41). In fact, the nineteenth century not only saw an unprecedented rise in the power and prestige of Britain, both because of its military and mercantile triumphs, but the reign of Queen Victoria from 1837–1901 came to be characterised as the age of "high imperialism", distinguished by "geographic magnitude; the mass organization and institutionalization of colonial power, often expressed in forms of aggressive nationalism; and, as the century matured, the formalization of imperialist ideologies, especially those pertaining to race, encouraged in part by the spread of Social Darwinist thought" (Boehmer 31). As we have seen previously, Victorian travel narratives advanced the imperial project in various ways, and even if Victorian novels often did not actively engage with the question of empire, most novelists, at the very least, reflected an awareness of the empire-building process. As Edward Said emphasises in *Culture and Imperialism*, nineteenth-century realist novels could be *of* imperial domination, even if they were not *about* it, and "when we come to Kipling, Conrad, Arthur Conan Doyle, Rider Haggard, R. L. Stevenson, George Orwell, Joyce Cary, E. M. Forster, and T. E. Lawrence, the empire is everywhere a crucial setting" (63). Contradicting the popular critical view that Jane Austen wasn't aware of contemporary events, Said has pointed out that in *Mansfield Park* (1814), Sir Thomas Bertram's Mansfield Park estate was clearly sustained by sugar plantations he owned and periodically visited in Antigua. Others, like Boehmer, point out that in the nineteenth-century novel, empire was often synonymous with commodities or objects that were circulated among the wealthy (26). She mentions the cashmere scarves, turquoise bracelets, ivory chess-men and other objects liberally sprinkled through Elizabeth Gaskell's *North and South* (1855) and W. M. Thackeray's *Vanity Fair* (1847–1848) to indicate that the ubiquitous presence of these foreign objects in British society had to have created an awareness of the world outside.

In fact, awareness of British colonising impulses can be traced as far back as Shakespeare's *The Tempest,* where Prospero colonises the island belonging to Caliban and enslaves him. Daniel Defoe's *Robinson Crusoe* (1719), is also regarded as an early text referencing the European colonial experience. Defoe was keenly aware that British identity was increasingly being tied up with the spirit of adventure and conquest. In *The Compleat English Gentleman* (1730), he claims:

> [He may] make a tour of the world in books, he may make himself master of the geography of the universe in the maps, atlases and measurements of our mathematicians. He may travel by land with the historians, by sea with the navigators. He may go round the globe with Dampier and Rogers, and kno' a thousand times more doing it than all those illiterate sailors. (Pratt 15)

In *Robinson Crusoe,* Defoe shows this adventurous, indefatigable spirit in action as his protagonist Crusoe sets out to build a small estate for himself along the lines of his Protestant ideals after he is shipwrecked on a remote island. But as it was for colonial explorers, the lure of the unknown is both fascinating and terrifying, as embodied in his fear of cannibalism. As Boehmer points out, "This explains Crusoe's concern to make of the cannibal survivor Friday, an image of himself, an opposite who will confirm the reality of his own being.

He is 'my man Friday,' dressed like Crusoe, named for the day Crusoe saves him" (18). In true colonial fashion, Crusoe writes a journal that helps him record his experiences for posterity and is not hesitant to deploy all the characteristic colonialist tropes of savagery and cannibalism. As many postcolonial critics point out, *Robinson Crusoe*, with its colonial settlement, subjugation of the native, remaking him in the image of his own self and the coalescing of the writer/coloniser trope, clearly becomes an allegory for empire.

Early nineteenth-century novels like Austen's *Mansfield Park* (1814), and Fanny Burney's *The Wanderer* (1814), reveal an awareness of the empire, albeit tangentially. But it was the 1850s, the decade of transformations in the history of the British Empire, that significantly altered relations between Britain and its "crown jewel" colony of India. A couple of specific events aided this transformation. As seen before, at the beginning of this decade, British imperialism was beginning to gather steam following the exaggerated celebration of Britain's mercantile prowess in the Great Exhibition of 1851. Although the English Ethnological Society was founded earlier in 1843, discourses around racial hierarchy became more pronounced with the 1859 publication of Charles Darwin's *Origin of the Species*. Suddenly, colonial subjects were being perceived and categorised in much more racialised terms than before. Specifically, it was the "recent events" in this comment, alluded to by Dr Cumming in his 1859 text, *The Great Tribulation*, which fundamentally changed Anglo-Indian relations:

> It used to be said of the Hindoos that they were such a mild, amiable, and gentle race . . . But what is the disclosure? That greater liars do not exist in the world than the Hindoos; that you cannot always trust them out of sight; that they are deceptive; and we have seen by *recent events* such outbursts of fanaticism, cruelty, bloodshed, and crime, that we wonder how

> any that knew them thirty years ago could give them such and so splendid a character. (Bolt 182–183; emphasis added)

Prior to the Indian Mutiny, or Sepoy Rebellion of 1857, Indians were mostly regarded as "docile, harmless, and industrious" people who make "capital servants"; and potential masters were advised that "the great secret in the management of them is kindness and fair dealing, with a tolerance of their harmless prejudices" (Bolt 178–179).[13] Even in the middle of the decade, before 1857, the stereotype of the mild-mannered Indian servile to British authority was dominant in Victorian imagination. In other words, the "tractable, mild Hindu" (Bolt 178) belonged to a gentle race who could be objectified at will and who welcomed the benevolent rule of the British Raj as long as their "harmless" religious practices and prejudices were indulged. The events of 1857 thus came as a huge shock and created complete outrage in Victorian Britain, primarily because "it seemed to indicate a gross ingratitude on the part of the Indian people" (Bolt 157). Eyewitness accounts of the rebellion were grossly embellished and feverishly circulated in Britain. Suddenly Indians were no longer fetishised objects but wild, savage brutes capable of unspeakable cruelties and in desperate need of strong governance. Even the normally reticent *Spectator* reflected this xenophobia and spoke of that "strange pit full of jewels, rags, and filth, of gleaming thoughts, and morbid fears, and horrid instincts – the Hindoo mind" (Bolt 166). The immediate effect of the revolt and the public outrage that followed was a set of radical administrative reforms whereby the rule of the EIC was terminated and power assumed by the Crown with Queen Victoria promising to rule her native subjects with "Paternal care" (Samson 82). But the most significant effect of 1857 was the post-mutiny re-evaluation of the Indian character in "contact zones". Racial and commodity fetishism of the first half of the nineteenth century was transmuted into a palpable anxiety about foreign bodies and commodities both in the colonial space and in the imperial metropolis. Victorian literature both recorded and stoked this heightened awareness and apprehension of the "other". In her book, Mary Poovey has pointed out that in post-1857 English imagination, India was often constructed as a place of savagery, poverty and ailments in need of healing "by an efficient head nurse cum Bourgeois mother (England, middle-class woman)" (196). But even as the need for this compassionate undertaking was emphasised, there was considerable trepidation about the safety of the virtuous English rose. We see this reflected in the literature of the time when, in Charlotte Bronte's *Jane Eyre* (1847), Diana Rivers tries to discourage Jane from going to India with St John by insisting that Jane is "much too pretty, as well as too good, to be grilled alive in Calcutta" (462). Deirdre David rightly explains that what Diana meant is that the "Englishwomen who go out to India are sacrificed to the climate and to native threats of molestation precisely in response to Victoria's imperative, articulated through the ideology and practices of her subjects, to civilize barbaric societies" (*Rule Britannia* 7).

One school of critical thought believes that many nineteenth-century novelists, including Charles Dickens and Wilkie Collins, were apologists for the empire. Cannon Schmitt elaborates in his discussion of Dickens's famous passage from *Dombey and Son*:

> Their fictions reflected imperialist assumptions and aspirations, including most crucially an Anglocentric world view and a sense of obvious, perhaps divinely sanctioned British superiority. With that superiority came, in turn, the implication of a right or obligation to seize other lands, subdue other peoples, replace outmoded customs and pernicious superstitions with British laws, mores, and religion – in short, to rule the globe. (5)

After all, the description of the East India House in *Dombey and Son* as a place "teeming with suggestions of precious stuffs and stones, tigers, elephants, howdahs, hookahs, umbrellas, palm trees, palanquins, and gorgeous princes of a brown complexion sitting on carpets, with their slippers very much turned up at their toes" (32) does evoke an exotic India which was very much a part of the popular imagination. Dickens's engagement with the empire is also evident in other novels. In *Bleak House*, Mrs Jellyby declares her philanthropic intentions when she claims that "one hundred and seventy families . . . averaging five persons in each, either gone or going to the left bank of the Niger" (381) as part of the Borrioboolan project to cultivate coffee and educate the natives. Deirdre David points out that Dickens here is critical of overseas philanthropy at the cost of domestic neglect and misery (*Rule Britannia* 45). Patrick Brantlinger confirms this when he points out that Dickens, in an 1848 essay on the Niger Expedition, scathingly attacks Britain's philanthropic efforts by suggesting that Africa was not fit for civilisation. "Between the civilized European and the barbarous African there is a great gulf set . . . To change the customs even of civilized . . . men . . . is . . . a most difficult and slow proceeding; but to do this by ignorant and savage races, is a work which, like the progressive changes of the globe itself, requires a stretch of years that dazzles in the looking at" (178).[14] It was not simply the "savage races" incapable of upliftment who were the objects of his ire; it was also the missionaries whom he felt were "perfect nuisances who leave every place worse than they find it" (178). Thomas Carlyle, another of Dickens's contemporaries, voiced the same concerns in "The Nigger Question" (1849) and in his response to the Jamaica Rebellion of 1865. According to Brantlinger, both Carlyle and Dickens felt that "abolitionist and missionary activities were distractions from more appropriate concerns about poverty and misgovernment at home" (178).

Wilkie Collins, a contemporary of Dickens, was less virulent in his criticism of the Indian mutineers and more ambivalent in his response to the mass hysteria surrounding the events of

1857. Although Joy Connolly maintains that Wilkie Collins is "probably best seen not as an apologist for the British empire but as a tentative judge of its ills" (xxxi), Collins's celebrated novel *The Moonstone* is a novel deeply embroiled in the post-mutiny discourse of fear and mistrust that dominated the Victorian public imagination. The events of the novel are set in 1848–1849, but Collins's novel, published in 1868, actively participates in the new culture of fear-mongering being formulated by mutiny literature, and records the anxiety and trepidation surrounding foreign objects and bodies produced out of post-1857 xenophobic discourses in England. Collins seems to be critical of British conduct in India at certain points in the narrative, especially in the description of the plunder of the royal armoury at Seringapatam, where Colonel Herncastle seized a diamond after very possibly murdering a Hindu priest responsible for the safekeeping of the jewel. This leads some critics to read the novel as an anti-imperialist text. Yet, Collins's narrative seems to employ all the stereotypes prevalent in the post-mutiny Victorian imagination in his representation of Indian characters. In a striking departure from early nineteenth-century popular discourse, which rampantly fetishised Indian objects and bodies and displayed them as permanent fixtures in both private and public spaces, Collins's narrative raises concerns about "security and infiltration" (Perera 13) and presents the Indian diamond and the Indian priests who accompany it to England as invasive threats who would create fissures in the Victorian social fabric.

Collins imagines the colonial space and its people as a metaphorical quicksand that threatens to engulf all that comes into contact with it. Much has been written about the exchange between Gabriel Betteredge and Rosanna Spearman in connection with the patch of deadly quicksand called the "Shivering Sands," a place where Rosanna ultimately finds her resting place:

> The horrid sand began to shiver. The broad brown face of it heaved slowly and then dimpled and quivered all over. "Do you know what it looks like to me?" says Rosanna, catching me by the shoulder again. "It looks as if it had hundreds of suffocating people under it – all struggling to get to the surface, and all sinking lower and lower in the deeps! Throw a stone in, Mr. Betteredge! Throw a stone in, and let's see the sand suck it down! (Collins 40)

Critics have debated whether the people trapped in the brown sands are the British caught up in the counter-effects of colonialism, or the colonial subjects trying to fight their way out of domination by the British (Connolly xxxi). This sinister image of quicksand seems to be the central leitmotif in Collins's narrative and seems to indicate the insidious effect the colonial space has on the coloniser. The passage acknowledges the struggles of colonial subjects against imperial domination, but the image of the stone being engulfed by the sands suggests the deadly effect of colonialism on anybody who comes in contact with it, maybe even British colonisers. Rosanna urging Betteredge to throw the stone into the heaving sands and see the sand suck it down brings to mind Betteredge's immediate impulse to throw the cursed moonstone into the quicksand (or back into the colonial quagmire) so as to preserve the domestic harmony of the Verinder household. This metaphor, early on in the narrative, paves the way for the manner in which India and its influence are imagined in the text. The magnificent Indian diamond, the Moonstone, the three Indian priests in pursuit of the diamond and the opium (under whose influence the crime is induced) form the triumvirate around which Collins's narrative re-evaluates the empire-colony relation following the 1857 rebellion.

In her fascinating study of *The Moonstone*, Deirdre David identifies the trope of invasion and counter-invasion as framing the narrative. "In *The Moonstone*, the trope of counter-invasion gathers together in Britain the Indians, the diamond and the opium, all produced through the British appropriation of large parts of the Indian subcontinent and all wrested, as it were, from their own ahistorical 'natural' places" (*Rule Britannia* 20). Within the narrative, this moment of counter-invasion is captured most succinctly by the colonialist butler, Gabriel Betteredge:

> Here was our quiet English house suddenly invaded by a devilish Indian Diamond – bringing after it a conspiracy of living rogues, set loose on us by the vengeance of a dead man. . . . Who ever heard the like of it – in the nineteenth century, mind; in an age of progress, and in a country which rejoices in the blessings of the British constitution? (Collins 48)

Betteredge's comment not only fuses the object with the accompanying bodies by reiterating the "devilish" presence of both, he at once establishes the contrast between the rational British identity "in an age of progress" and the backward Indians who are apparently thought to be strolling conjurors but are actually revealed to be three Indian priests in disguise, pursuing the moonstone.

In his insightful study that traces the emergence of criminality in the English novel vis-à-vis Britain's relation to its colonies, Upamanyu Mukherjee rightly identifies the figure of the "criminal" Indian in Collins's novel as a legacy of mutiny fiction that dominated the Victorian imagination in the 1860s (Mukherjee 166). The three Indians come under suspicion right at the beginning simply because of their race and without any possible proof of their having committed a crime. Even though the imperial-at-heart, *Robinson Crusoe*–toting butler refuses to acknowledge his racist sensibilities, claiming that he would be "the last person in the world to distrust another person because he happens to be a few shades darker" (Collins 30) than him, his first instinct, when the Indians appear, is to protect the family silver and warn the Indians off the estate. As soon as he discovers the diamond is missing and there is a small vial of ink in the estate grounds, he is convinced that he has disturbed the activities of the three Indians "lurking about the house, and bent, in their heathenish way, on discovering the whereabouts of the diamond" (63). Even the well–travelled Franklin Blake believes that "The idea of certain chosen servants of an old Hindoo superstition devoting themselves, through all difficulties and dangers, to watching the opportunity of recovering their sacred gem, appears to me to be perfectly consistent with everything that we know of the patience of Oriental races, and the influence of Oriental religions" (54). Herncastle's purported crime of wresting the diamond in blatant disregard of Hindu religious beliefs is side-lined while the imagined "conspiracy" of the Hindu priests to reclaim the jewel, which was originally theirs, becomes the central concern of the narrative. If Betteredge had his way it would just be easy "to shy the Diamond into the quicksand, and settle the question in *that* way" (55). In other words, Betteredge emerges as the cautionary voice bent on preserving Victorian social order by casting off the spell of the East and by disposing it in its own colonial quagmire.

The creation of the mixed-race Ezra Jennings, who proposes the experiment of re-enacting the scene of crime to exonerate Franklin Blake, have made critics like Deirdre David argue that Jennings's work reveals him to be "a colonized figure so trusted by his masters, so purged of the native savagery that flourished at the time of the thuggee gangs, that he can be assigned the labor of cleansing the centre of empire itself of its own corruption" (*Rule Britannia* 143). Such an observation is only partly true. In his role as an amanuensis for the demented Dr Candy that helps him discover the mysterious effects of opium on Franklin Blake, thus leading to the unravelling of the mystery of the moonstone, Jennings is mistakenly assumed to have considerable narrative agency. In reality, Jennings is repeatedly tortured and persecuted because of his extraordinary appearance and his role is limited almost to that of being the "native informant" who alerts his white masters of the ill effects of opium because he himself has been subject to its deleterious effects. Jennings, it must be noted, cannot shed light on how the moonstone made its way to the pawnbroker in London. It is the re-entrance of Sergeant Cuff, the archetypal white law-enforcement officer, who is able to uncover the crime of Godfrey Ablewhite. Collins's narrative is clearly sceptical of the presence of mixed-race individuals within Victorian social order and Jennings's story is not a happy one. Ezra Jennings is as disabled by his race as Rosanna Spearman and Limping Lucy, both of whom are clearly indicated as occupying the margins of Victorian society.

In the second half of the nineteenth century then, racial fetishism of the earlier decades made way for a more pronounced xenophobic discourse where the magical East was denigrated into the malevolent East that would corrupt and destabilise Victorian society if the public was not made aware of its insidious influence. This particular moment of crisis in Victorian London provided rich material for the literary intelligentsia, and narratives like *The Moonstone* provide valuable insight into Victorian social life vis-à-vis its relation to the colonies in the late nineteenth century. As Deirdre David so graphically points out, literature produced in the Victorian age was either directly or tangentially, pictorially or literally, very invested in the imperial project based on a hegemonic racial structure:

> Victorian attitudes toward empire are almost always unambiguously racist, occasionally worried about the European erosion of native customs, often uneasy about the domestic prices demanded for the maintenance of distant territories, frequently fearful of the consequences of British invasion and subjugation, sometimes infatuated with the exotic delight of alien cultures, and periodically attentive to what is construed as the moral responsibility of imperial rule. (*Rule Britannia* 8)

It is not until the very end of the nineteenth century that we slowly see some of the shifting paradigms of colonial-subject relations in the metropolitan centre.

As this chapter emphasises, the English empire, from the sixteenth to the nineteenth century, was partly created and sustained by an elaborate imaginative framework mobilised by colonialist writings about the newly discovered lands, even though this imagined world was far from reality. Since the middle of the nineteenth century, the Orient was no longer a dreamland, but had "inched closer. Colonialism makes a grab for it, appropriates it by dint of war, binds it hand and foot with myriad bonds of exploitation, and hands it over to the devouring appetite of the great mother countries, ever hungry for raw materials" (Alloula 3). Towards the very end of the nineteenth century, a different voice began to emerge which recognised the pitfalls of the imperialist rhetoric and its very practical consequences. In the preface to *The Story of an African Farm*, Olive Schreiner, under the pseudonym of Ralph Iron, caustically remarks:

> It has been suggested by a kind of critic that he would better have liked the little book if it had been a history of wild adventure; of cattle driven into inaccessible *kranzes* by Bushmen; 'of encounters with ravening lions, and hair-breath escapes.' This could not be. Such works are best written in Piccadilly or in the Strand; there the gifts of the creative imagination, untrammelled by contact with any fact, may spread their wings. (8)

Schreiner here is clearly criticising the view that representations of Africa consistent with existent stereotypes in the Victorian imagination and completely devoid from reality were the only acceptable ones. Early twentieth-century novels like Conrad's *Heart of Darkness* and E. M. Forster's *A Passage to India* among others appeared increasingly ambivalent about the colonial project even as voices of resistance in the colonies – like that of Rabindranath Tagore, Claude McKay, Aimé Césaire, Frantz Fanon, etc. – were beginning to reach a crescendo. The systematic anti-colonial resistance that was emerging at the turn of the century will be discussed at length in the next chapter.

Works Cited

Alloula, Malek. *The Colonial Harem*. Trans. Myrna Godzich and Wlad Godzich. Minneapolis: U of Minnesota P, 1986. Print.

Bader, Rudolph. "Australian Literature." *Companion to the New Literatures in English*. Ed. Christa Jansohn. Berlin: Erich Schmidt Verlag, 2002. 137–174. Print.

Bassnett, Susan. "Travel Writing and Gender." *The Cambridge Companion to Travel Writing*. Eds. Peter Hulme and Tim Youngs. Cambridge: Cambridge UP, 2002. 225–241. Print.

Barr, Pat. *The Memsahibs: The Women of Victorian India*. New Delhi: Allied Publishers, 1976. Print.

Bodelsen, C. A. *Studies in Mid-Victorian Imperialism*. New York: Knopf, 1925. Print.

Boehmer, Elleke. *Colonial & Postcolonial Literature*. Oxford: Oxford UP, 1995. Print.

Bolt, Christine. *Victorian Attitudes to Race*. London: Routledge, 1971. Print.

Brantlinger, Patrick. *Rule of Darkness: British Literature and Imperialism, 1830–1914*. Ithaca: Cornell UP, 1988. Print.

Briefel, Aviva. "On the 1886 Colonial and Indian Exhibition." *BRANCH: Britain, Representation and Nineteenth-Century History*. Ed. Dino Franco Felluga. Extension of *Romanticism and Victorianism on the Net*. Web. 18 November 2015.

Bronte, Charlotte. *Jane Eyre*. London: Penguin, 1996. Print.

Burton, Richard. *Falconry in the Valley of the Indus*. London: J. Van Voorst, 1852. Print.

———. *The Lake Regions of Central Africa*. New York: Dover, 1995. Print.

Cleary, Joe. *Outrageous Fortune: Capital and Culture in Modern Ireland*. Dublin: Field Day Publications, 2006.

Collins, Wilkie. *The Moonstone*. New York: Barnes & Noble Classics, 2005. Print.

Connolly, Joy. Introduction. *The Moonstone*. By Wilkie Collins. New York: Barnes & Noble Classics, 2005. Print.

Dalrymple, William, ed. *Begums, Thugs and White Mughals: The Journals of Fanny Parkes*. London: Sickle Moon Books, 2002. Print.

Daly, Suzanne. *The Empire Inside: Indian Commodities in Victorian Domestic Novels*. Ann Arbor: U of Michigan P, 2011. Print.

Darwin, Charles. *Voyage of the Beagle*. Harmondsworth: Penguin, 1839. Print.

David, Deirdre. "Empire, Race, and the Victorian Novel." *A Companion to the Victorian Novel*. Eds. Patrick Brantlinger and William B. Thesing. Massachusetts: Blackwell, 2002. 84–100. Print.

———. *Rule Britannia: Women, Empire, and Victorian Writing*. Ithaca: Cornell UP, 1995. Print.

Dickens, Charles. *Bleak House*. New York, Penguin Books, 2006. Print.

———. *Dombey and Son*. London: Oxford UP, 1950. Print.

———. "The Niger Expedition." *The Examiner*, 19 August 1848, reprinted in *National Library Edition: The Works of Charles Dickens – Volume 18: Miscellaneous Papers, Plays and Poems*. New York: Bigelow, Brown, 1903. 18:64. Print.

Fhlathúin, Máire Ní. "The British Empire." *The Routledge Companion to Postcolonial Studies*. Ed. John McLeod. New York: Routledge, 2007. 21–31. Print.

Fuller, Mary C. *Voyages in Print: English Travel to America, 1576–1624*. Cambridge: Cambridge UP, 1995. Print.

Ghose, Indira, ed. *Memsahibs Abroad: Writings by Women Travelers in Nineteenth Century India.* Delhi: Oxford UP, 1998. Print.

———. *Women Travelers in Colonial India.* Delhi: Oxford UP, 1998. Print.

Grahame, James. "Africa Delivered; or, The Slave Trade Abolished." *Poems on the Abolition of the Slave Trade.* Eds. James Montgomery, James Grahame and E. Benger. New York: Books for Libraries P, 1971. Print.

Hakluyt, Richard. *Voyages and Discoveries.* Ed. Jack Beeching. London: Penguin Books, 1972. Print.

Hayman, John, ed. *Sir Richard Burton's Travels in Arabia and Africa: Four Lectures from a Huntington Library Manuscript.* San Marino, California: Huntington Library, 1990. Print.

Helgerson, Richard. *Forms of Nationhood: The Elizabethan Writing of England.* Chicago: Chicago UP, 1992. Print.

Hoffenberg, Peter. *An Empire on Display: English, Indian, and Australian Exhibitions from the Crystal Palace to the Great War.* Berkeley: U of California P, 2001. Print.

Hooper, Glenn. Introduction. *Irish and Postcolonial Writing: History, Theory, Practice.* Ed. Glenn Hooper and Colin Graham. New York: Palgrave, 2002. Print.

Keay, John. *The Honourable Company: A History of the English East India Company.* London: Harper Collins, 1991. Print.

Kingsley, Mary. *Travels in West Africa.* London: Macmillan & Co. Ltd, 1897. Print.

Kitzan, Laurence. *Victorian Writers and the Image of Empire: The Rose-Colored Vision.* Connecticut: Greenwood P, 2001. Print.

Korte, Barbara. *English Travel Writing from Pilgrimages to Postcolonial Explorations.* Trans. Catherine Matthias. London: Macmillan, 2000. Print.

Lester, Alan. *Imperial Networks: Creating Identities in Nineteenth-century South Africa and Britain.* London: Routledge, 2001. Print.

Lloyd, Christopher. *The Search for the Niger*. London: Collins, 1973. Print.

Mukherjee, Upamanyu. *Crime and Empire: The Colony in Nineteenth-Century Fictions of Crime.* Oxford: Oxford UP, 2003. Print.

Nasson, Bill. *Britannia's Empire: Making a British World.* Gloucestershire: Tempus Publishing, 2004. Print.

Park, Mungo. *Travels into the Interior of Africa*. London: Eland, 1983. Print.

Perera, Suvendrini. *Reaches of Empire: The English Novel from Edgeworth to Dickens*. New York: Columbia UP, 1991. Print

Poovey, Mary. *Uneven Developments: The Ideological Work of Gender in Mid-Victorian England.* Chicago: U of Chicago P, 1988. Print.

Pratt, Mary Louise. *Imperial Eyes: Travel Writing and Transculturation*. New York: Routledge, 1992. Print.

Richards, Thomas. *The Commodity Culture of Victorian England.* New York: Verso, 1991. Print.

Richardson, Joanna. *Theophile Gaultier: His Life and Times*. New York: Coward and McCann, 1959. Print.

Root, Deborah. *Cannibal Culture: Art, Appropriation, and the Commodification of Difference.* Colorado: Westview P, 1996. Print.

Rubies, Joan Pau. "Travel Writing and Ethnography." *The Cambridge Companion to Travel Writing.* Eds. Peter Hulme and Tim Youngs. Cambridge: Cambridge UP, 2002. 242–260. Print.

Said, Edward. *Culture and Imperialism.* New York: Vintage, 1993. Print.

———. *Orientalism.* New York: Vintage, 1979. Print.

Samson, Jane, ed. *The British Empire*. Oxford: Oxford UP, 2001. Print.

Schmitt, Cannon. "'The Sun and Moon were made to Give Them Light': Empire in the Victorian Novel." *A Concise Companion to the Victorian Novel*. Ed. Francis O' Gorman. Oxford: Blackwell Publishing, 2005. Print.

Schreiner, Olive. *The Story of an African Farm*. Boston: Roberts Brothers, 1890. Print.

Schweinitz, Karl de. Jr. *The Rise and Fall of British India: Imperialism as Inequality*. London: Methuen, 1983. Print.

Shakespeare, William. *Richard II*. Ed. John M. Lothian. Oxford: Clarendon P, 1938. Print.

Sherman, William. "Stirrings and Searchings (1500–1720)." *The Cambridge Companion to Travel Writing*. Eds. Peter Hulme and Tim Youngs. Cambridge: Cambridge UP, 2002. 1736. Print.

Smith, Adam, *An Inquiry into the Nature and Causes of the Wealth of Nations*. Ed. Edwin Cannan. 1904. Library of Economics and Liberty. Web. 22 November 2015. <http://www.econlib.org/library/Smith/smWN.html>

Spurr, David. *The Rhetoric of Empire: Colonial Discourse in Journalism, Travel Writing, and Imperial Administration*. Durham & London: Duke UP, 1993. Print.

Thackeray, William M. *Vanity Fair*. New York: Barnes & Noble Books, 2003. Print.

Thomas, Gertrude Z. *Richer than Spices: How a Royal Bride's Dowry Introduced Cane, Lacquer, Cottons, Tea, and Porcelain to England, and so Revolutionized Taste, Manners, Craftsmanship, and History in both England and America*. New York: Alfred A. Knopf, 1965. Print.

Vance, Norman. *Irish Literature since 1800*. London: Pearson, 2002. Print.

Notes

1. I use the term "Eastern" interchangeably with the "Orient" in this essay to suggest any of the countries in the Far East, the Indian subcontinent and the Middle East that comprised the Orient in nineteenth-century British imagination. By eastern imports

here, I mean objects that were imported into England from any country in the Near East like Turkey, Far East like China, Japan, Java, Sumatra or from the Indian subcontinent. I use the term imports to designate any item ranging from spices to textiles that were brought into the European mainland through the trade routes with the East.

2. The language of invasion is also seen in John Keay's *The Honourable Company*:

   > Instead of English tweeds revolutionizing Eastern fashions, Indian cottons were about to invade English domestic life. Napkins and table-cloths, bed-sheets and sofa furnishings, not to mention underwear and dress fabrics, quite suddenly became indispensable to every respectable household. A new vocabulary of chintzes and calicoes, taffetas, muslins, ginghams and cashmeres entered everyday use. Having first invaded the larder, Eastern produce was about to take over the linen cupboard. (98–99)

3. For more on this, see page 56 of Jane Samson's *The British Empire.*

4. Bader mentions that the Eureka Stockade was "the clash over the license-fee system which took place between rebellious miners from the Ballarat Diggings and British soldiers [and Victorian police] on Bakery Hill, Ballarat, on December 3rd, 1854. This unique uprising of Australian workers against the arrogance of the [British] authorities is seen as the root and origin of the Australian egalitarianism, republicanism and democratic fervor which characterized the 1890s" (138).

5. For the complete poem, see pages 139 to 140 of Bader's essay.

6. For more examples of this, see pages 175 to 176 of *Rule of Darkness*, Patrick Brantlinger's detailed analysis of abolitionist literature.

7. In *The Colonial Harem*, Malek Alloula describes how photographers would often recruit models from the fringes of society to reconstruct a particular image for postcards: "In her role as substitute, the model presents three distinct and yet closely

related advantages: she is *accessible*, *credible*, and *profitable*. This is the three-legged foundation upon which will come to stand the whole of the enterprise pursued so relentlessly by the colonial postcard" (18).

8. For a fascinating account of the 1866 exhibition, see Aviva Briefel's "On the 1886 Colonial and Indian Exhibition." Briefel refers to the work of Lara Kriegel on Victorian culture. See Lara Kriegel's *Grand Designs: Labor, Empire, and the Museum in Victorian Culture*.
9. In Joseph Conrad's famous novel *Heart of Darkness*, his protagonist Marlow mentions that he was happy to see large chunks of the world coloured red, marked as British imperial possessions. Postcolonial critics often use this passage to demonstrate Marlow's imperialist leanings. For a detailed analysis of Conrad's novel, please see Chapter 2.
10. In fact, as early as 1552, Joao de Barros had lamented that "It seems that for our sins, or for some inscrutable judgement of God, in all the instances of this great Ethiopia [i.e. Africa] that we sail along, he has placed a striking angel with a flaming sword of deadly fevers, who prevents us from penetrating into the interior to the springs of this garden, whence proceed rivers of gold that flow to the sea in so many parts of our conquest" (Lloyd 13–14).
11. For a more detailed analysis of Burton's complex narrative, see pages 162 to 164 of Brantlinger's *Rule of Darkness*.
12. For Pratt, "contact zones" are "social spaces where disparate cultures meet, clash, and grapple with each other, often in highly asymmetrical relations of domination and subordination – like colonialism, slavery, or their aftermaths as they are lived out across the globe today" (4).
13. This is from an 1855 document by H. B. Evans, which Bolt quotes in *Victorian Attitudes to Race*.
14. The original citation can be found in Charles Dickens's "The Niger Expedition".

TWO

THE EMPIRE WRITES BACK

High imperialism, anti-colonial resistance and the rise of nationalism in the late nineteenth and early twentieth centuries

Long before direct colonialism had robbed the African of his geography through military conquest and settler economic occupation, of his history through the usurpation of the means of making it, of his culture through alien religions, he had already been robbed of all of these in the literature that was inspired by the slave system or that took that system as the everlasting norm in human relations. Colonialist literature was built on that tradition. The only difference was that during the colonial era the racism in the academic and imaginative literature could now be passed on as gospel truth into the education system. The geography, history, languages, names and all the gods of Europe became the centre of the academic universe of the African child. Racism as a doctrine had left its hiding place in between the hardcovers and was now being paraded as academic brilliance in the colonial classroom.

—Ngũgĩ Wa Thiong'o, *Moving the Centre*

In the second half of the nineteenth century, Germany and other European countries, as well as the United States, were well industrialised and were beginning to challenge Britain's status as a major imperial power. Germany, France, Belgium and others carved up large chunks of the African continent in what came to be known as the "Scramble for Africa". The United States expanded its influence in Latin America by acquiring Cuba and then went on to occupy the Philippines and other lands after the Spanish-American war in 1898. Further East, Japan was engaging in its own set of "expansionist wars" (Samson 106). Determined not to be outdone by its competitors, Britain cranked up its efforts and the end of the nineteenth century saw a surge in both patriotism and xenophobia summed up in the pithy phrase "Rule Britannia" that started doing the rounds. In an inaugural lecture in 1870, John Ruskin proudly proclaimed:

> There is a destiny now possible to us – the highest ever set before a nation to be accepted or refused. We are still undegenerate in race; a race mingled of the best northern bloods . . . . There is indeed a course of beneficent glory open to us, such as never was yet offered to any poor group of mortal souls. But it must be – it *is* with us, now, 'Reign or Die.' . . . This is what she must do, or perish: she must found colonies as fast and as far as she is able, formed of her most energetic and worthiest men; – seizing every piece of fruitful waste ground she can set her foot on, and there teaching these her colonists that their chief virtue is to be fidelity to their country, and that their first aim is to be to advance the power of England by land and sea. (28–30)

Critics like Elleke Boehmer and Deirdre David have suggested that after 1870, Britain saw the rise of a new, more aggressive form of imperialism that was reflected in the Victorian literature briefly discussed in the previous chapter. This chapter will focus in greater detail on this period of high imperialism and the counter-narratives that emerged as a result of it.

Britain, along with the other European nations, had seen its fair share of technological triumphs throughout the nineteenth century. With the introduction of the steam engine and railways, Britain's access to remote places became even easier. The invention of modern telegraphy improved communication networks significantly, and quite predictably, led to increased collaboration between the mainland and the imperial employees overseas, even in the farthest outposts of the empire. This easier access to both natural and commercial resources all across the world resulted in the conversion of England into a nation of consumers, even more so than before. Not only were Indian textiles much in demand, tea, imported largely from China, developed into an unmistakable British ritual even as sugar consumption during the course of the nineteenth century increased by a whopping 700 percent (Boehmer 41). Books like Suzanne Daly's *The Empire Inside: Indian Commodities in Victorian Domestic Novels* (2011), and Anandi Ramamurthy's *Imperial Persuaders: Images of Africa and Asia in British Advertising* demonstrate the crucial role African and Indian commodities played in the British domestic imagination and reveal how these commodities were slowly reshaping British identity. If anything, this meant that Britain had to maintain an even stronger hold on its colonies while continuing to downplay colonisation as a commercial and profitable venture. This is when language about European racial supremacy assumes a new sense of urgency.

Late nineteenth-century "high imperialism" and the civilising mission in the colonies

As Patrick Brantlinger, Deirdre David, Barbara Korte and others have pointed out, Victorian high imperialism was characterised by "the civilizing mission" that Britain used as a mantra to justify its often brutal economic exploitation of the colonies. Rudyard Kipling's "The White Man's Burden" (1899), sums up the ideas behind this mission that many Victorians had come to consider their manifest destiny.

> Take up the White Man's burden . . .
> Send forth the best ye breed . . .
> Go bind your sons to exile
> To serve your captives' need;
> To wait in heavy harness,

> On fluttered folk and wild . . .
> Your new-caught, sullen peoples,
> Half-devil and half-child. (Damrosch 20–21)

Kipling's call to the imperial officers to selflessly serve and save "the silent, sullen peoples" and lead them to freedom is unmistakably tinged with a sense of white supremacy over non-white peoples, and illustrates the obvious racial prejudices inherent in the late Victorian mind-set. The idea that English officers were often engaged in the thankless task of bringing progress to the natives in the form of industry and infrastructure, that included the installation of railways and roads in India and different countries in Africa, was aligned with a sense of moral responsibility that conveniently edited the native response out of the picture. As Samson asserts, "The British believed that only Europeans were capable of improving and developing African natural and human resources, and were proud of their ability to survey landscapes and create the borders of new countries" (116). She points to a passage from Charles Eliot's *The East Africa Protectorate* (1905), where Eliot gloats over the British accomplishment with the Ugandan Railway:

> It is not an uncommon thing for a line to open up a country, but this line has literally created a country. As a civilized territory and a possible residence of Europeans, East Africa may be said to have come gradually into existence at exactly the same rate as the rails advanced . . . the whole enterprise offers the most extraordinary example of the pluck and luck which characterize the British race. (Eliot 208–209)

This astonishing view of the European supremacy was almost always tied to demeaning images of the colonised subjects. The natives were most often regarded as "half-devil and half-child", an image that was solidified in the public imagination with the publication of Charles Darwin's *The Origin of Species* in 1859. As Boehmer succinctly argues, Social Darwinism reinstated the idea that:

> ...cultural differences, ranged hierarchically, were based in nature and formed an intrinsic part of evolutionary development .... Race classifications, therefore could be used to explain not only biological variety but the superiority or inferiority of different cultural types ranged on a scale of evolutionary progress. A great gap, based in biology, was believed to separate white races from black. (Boehmer 84)

British missionaries also aided and abetted this civilising mission with their message of bringing the glories of Christianity to the uncivilised heathens. Even though their outreach in India and other parts of South Asia were somewhat limited, they managed to garner a large following in a lot of African countries. In fact, some of the dissension that started in the nineteenth century between converts and non-converts have continued into the twentieth century and have resulted in protracted civil wars in countries like Sudan and Nigeria. But simply bringing the light of Christianity to the colonies was not enough. As Samson points out, along with advocating English language education, most of the missionaries were proponents of British trade and labour practices and encouraged the import of British manufactured goods. In fact, John Williams, a missionary working in the South Pacific islands in the nineteenth century, argued that this could be a hallmark of imperial policy.

> I am convinced that the first step towards the promotion of a nation's temporal and social elevation, is to plant amongst them the tree of life, when civilization and commerce will entwine their tendrils around its trunk, and derive support from its strength. Until people are brought under the influence of religion, they have no desire for the arts and usages of civilized life; but that invariably creates it. (Williams 152–3)

All this rhetoric in the colonies ushered in a new sense of urgency about imperial policymaking in London. As early as 1872, the leader of the Opposition Party, Benjamin Disraeli, urged a "greater imperial pride, reinventing his Conservative

Party as the promoter and defender of empire" (Samson 177). Disraeli's aggressive imperialism had some serious consequences. Following nationalist uprisings and the restlessness in Egypt that followed Disraeli's acquiring of some shares in the Suez Canal, the Liberal Prime Minister William Gladstone found himself ordering the invasion of Egypt in 1882 to protect British interests in the Suez Canal (Samson 177). More serious expansionist measures were soon to follow. As European nations squabbled for natural resources and commercial markets in the colonies, large sections of Africa that were still left untapped came to their attention. What followed has come to be infamously referred to as the "Scramble for Africa".

"The Scramble for Africa"

As we have seen in the first chapter, European explorers and merchants had set up several trading outposts along the coast of Africa from as early as the 1500s. But no single European country had been able to wrestle or maintain control over large parts of Sub-Saharan Africa. The rapid industrialisation in the nineteenth century along with the invention of the steam engine, progress in railways, and in the communication system changed all that and enabled several European countries to systematically carve up the African continent into smaller colonies. This process of deliberately occupying the African landmass between 1880 and 1914 by European nations with complete disregard for the African natives came to be known as "The Scramble for Africa". As David Damrosch explains, "Some rules for this scramble were established by a conference held in Berlin in 1884, at which the European powers divided the continent into different spheres of influence and control, agreeing to respect each other's 'rights' to their holdings" (217). One of the most prominent beneficiaries of this enterprise was King Leopold of Belgium, who was granted access to the Congo region. King Leopold named the colony "Congo Free State" and promoted it as a "perfect marriage of the noble work of civilization and the profits of free enterprise" (Damrosch 124), and journalist-explorers like Henry Morton Stanley were quick to laud King Leopold's benevolent enterprise. In books like *In Darkest Africa* and *Through the Dark Continent*, Stanley talks of his journey through the African heartland and the dire need to bring the glories of civilisation to these areas.

> No part of Africa, look where I might, appeared so promising to me as this neglected tenth part of the continent. I have often fancied myself – when I had nothing to do better than dream – gazing from some loft height, and looking down upon this square compact patch of 800,000,000 acres, with its 80,000 native towns, its population of 40,000,000 souls, its 17,000 miles of river waters, and its 30,000 square miles of lakes, all lying torpid, lifeless, inert, soaked in brutishness and bestiality, and I have never yet descended from that airy perch in the empyrean and touched earth but I have felt a purpose glow in me to strive to do something to awaken it into life and movement . . . . (Damrosch 249–250)

But soon enough a much darker picture began to emerge about the oppression and brutalities that Belgian colonial officers had imposed on African natives through the ivory trade.

In his book *King Leopold's Ghost*, Adam Hochschild provides a graphic picture of the shocking abuses that were carried out in the so-called Free State under the directions of King Leopold. Joseph Conrad too encountered the grim reality of the Congo on his journey there that largely informed his novel *Heart of Darkness*, serialised in *Blackwood's Magazine* in 1899 and published in book form in 1902. Conrad wrote several stories and novels that explicitly engaged with the subject of empire including *Lord Jim* (1900) and *Nostromo* (1904), but *Heart of Darkness* has probably been the novel that has given rise to the most amount of heated critical discussion. In the novel, structured as a framed narrative, Conrad's protagonist Marlow (a modern day Robinson Crusoe), driven by a desire for adventure to explore the many blank spaces on the map and especially "the biggest – the most blank, so to speak – that I had a hankering after" (Conrad 11), sets off on an expedition down the Congo River into the heart of Africa. This desire for filling up the blank spaces was not something new in Europe. Henry Morton Stanley already had such designs on Africa as detailed in a letter he wrote to his friend Frank Pocock, dated 26 December 1876:

> I assure you, Frank, this enormous void is about to be filled up. Blank as it is, it has a singular fascination for me. Never has white paper possessed such a charm for me as this has, and I have mentally peopled it, filled it with most wonderful pictures of towns, villages, rivers, countries, and tribes – all in the imagination – and I am burning to see whether I am correct or not. (Damrosch 236)

What follows in Conrad's novel is an account of the horrendous exploitation of the heartland of the Congo by Belgians in the late nineteenth century, and the brutal atrocities and innumerable maimings and murders of native Africans driven by the sheer greed of European merchants and traders. At one point, Marlow describes the European mission in what can be taken as being one of the strongest indictments of colonialism in the novel:

> They grabbed what they could get for the sake of what was to be got. It was just robbery with violence, aggravated murder on a great scale . . . The conquest of the earth, which mostly means the taking it away from those who have a different complexion or slightly flatter noses than ourselves, is not a pretty thing when you look at it too much. (Conrad 10)

But it is Marlow's responses to the world in which he finds himself and his part-fascination, part-revulsion with the mythical Kurtz figure that has garnered the most critical reaction.

English travellers, like Richard Burton in his *The Lake Regions of Central Africa* (1860), had already exalted Arab civilisations as being superior to African ones and had berated Africans for being "lazy, childlike, lost to barbarity" (Boehmer 85). Such images started appearing with startling regularity all through the second half of the nineteenth century, and when Conrad referred to African natives in animalistic terms, many critics alleged that he was as much of a proponent of imperialism as Rudyard Kipling. In a ground-breaking article titled "An Image of Africa: Racism in Conrad's *Heart of Darkness*", published in 1977, the famous Nigerian writer Chinua Achebe unequivocally accused Conrad of being a racist and asserted that "*Heart of Darkness* projects the image of Africa as 'the other world,' the antithesis of Europe and therefore civilization, a place where man's vaunted intelligence and refinement are finally mocked by triumphant bestiality" (*An Image of Africa* 252). Others, like Peter Manthorpe, have taken issue with Achebe's accusation.

> His reading of *Heart of Darkness* makes no allowance for the story's pervading mood of deep disquiet or, more accurately, of unease amid the quietude of complicity. Marlow is profoundly unsettled, not only by what he has seen in Africa, but by the kind of wilful blindness he finds back in Europe. And while *Heart of Darkness* can be read as an indictment of Belgian colonial practice, the fact that Marlow's yarn is addressed to the director, the lawyer and the accountant of a British colonial trading company makes it clear that whatever truth he wants them to see about Belgian colonial practice should be extended to the British colonial experience as well. (Manthorpe 162)

While it might be too reductive to read this complex novel through either of these lenses, Achebe's main arguments that lead him to his conclusion are most definitely worth noting. Achebe rightly points out that the African people do not have a voice in a novel that is ostensibly about Africa, except in a couple of instances, most notably when one of them announces "Mistah Kurtz – he dead" (Conrad 69). Now, it can be argued that the announcement of Kurtz's death coming from a native is indicative of achieving freedom from Kurtz's terrorising regime that had stultified all native African speech. So the brief statement is indicative of a newfound sense of freedom from the brutality the natives in the trading outpost had been subjected to for years. In that case, the novel might be offering an indictment of colonialism. But at the same time, it is also worth noting, along with Achebe, that the African people are almost always portrayed as savage and animalistic – magnificent to look at but hard to interact with as they made "a violent babble of uncouth sounds" (Conrad 22) even among themselves and projected a "complete, deathlike indifference of unhappy savages" (19).

At one point in the novel, as Marlow is journeying up the river, he comes across a boat paddled by some African natives – "You could see from afar the white of their eyeballs glistening. They shouted, sang; their bodies streamed with perspiration; they had faces like grotesque masks – these chaps; but they had bone, muscle, a wild vitality, an intense energy of movement that was as natural and true as the surf along their coast . . . They were a great comfort to look at" (17). The Africans here are very clearly reduced to objects under the intense gaze of the white colonisers; their grotesque faces and bodies and intense animalistic force is simultaneously intimidating and awe-inspiring. So is the description of Kurtz's so-called mistress who appears suddenly along the river in all her native splendour.

> She walked with measured steps, draped in striped and fringed cloths, treading the earth proudly with a slight jingle and flash of barbarous ornaments . . . She was *savage and superb*, wild-eyed and magnificent; there was something *ominous* and stately in her deliberate progress. And in the hush that had fallen suddenly upon

> the whole sorrowful land, the immense wildness, the colossal body of the fecund and mysterious life seemed to look at her, pensive, as though it had been looking at the image of its own tenebrous and passionate soul. (60; emphasis added)

As Achebe rightly points out, this vision of savage splendour is contrasted with the modest femininity of Kurtz's Intended, the epitome of Victorian domesticity and womanhood – "She had a mature capacity for fidelity, for belief, for suffering . . . This fair hair, this pale visage, this pure brow, seemed surrounded by an ashy halo from which the dark eyes looked out at me. Their glance was *guileless,* profound, confident, and *trustful*" (73; emphasis added). These descriptions seem to suggest that it is not only appearance and temperament that differentiate the two women; it is the feeling they inspire in the onlooker. While Kurtz's Intended's innocence prompts Marlow to lie and tell her that Kurtz died with her name on his lips instead of the iconic and mysterious words, "The horror! The horror!" (68), Kurtz's mistress is clearly an object of intense gaze and scrutiny, almost bordering on the ominous, primarily because of her mysteriousness and inscrutability. In fact, this darkness and the accompanying fear based on the inscrutability and impenetrability of the colonised land and people becomes a recurrent trope in colonialist fiction at the turn of the century. Added to that is the idea that to be touched by some of these colonial landscapes is to be possessed by it, but without coming any closer to understanding it, as exemplified by Kurtz's final words.

In E. M. Forster's *A Passage to India* (1924), the Marabar Caves become the symbol of impenetrability, as does India in Alice Perrin's collection of stories, *East of Suez* (1901). Even the celebrated Mary Kingsley talks about feeling unmoored when faced with the immensity of the African forest – "I just lose all sense of human individuality, all memory of human life, with its grief and worry and doubt, and become part of the atmosphere"

(178). Boehmer points out – "What happens, typically, is that description admits defeat, submitting to the horror of the inarticulate. The native or the colonized land is evoked as the quintessence of mystery, as inarticulateness itself" (95). In earlier centuries, like we have seen in the first chapter, the desire to control, born out of the inability to fully comprehend one's surroundings, was carried out through discursive practices. In the nineteenth century and beyond, these controlling mechanisms, coded in the language of racial supremacy, became more material and violent, and it is not surprising that the late nineteenth century saw the rise of anticolonial resistance movements all across the colonised world as a resistance to this discourse.

COLONIAL EDUCATION AND THE BEGINNINGS OF ANTI-COLONIAL RESISTANCE IN INDIA

Dissenting voices like that of Aimé Césaire and Frantz Fanon were beginning to build to a crescendo in the first few decades of the twentieth century. Following the chaos of the First World War, so eloquently captured by T. S. Eliot in *The Waste Land*, England was starting to feel the weight of the imperial burden. Even as writers like Virginia Woolf and D. H. Lawrence described unprecedented scenes of chaos of post-war London, writers all across the colonial world, encouraged by the increasing number of nationalist rebellions and emerging dissident voices, started asserting the validity of their own subjective experiences. Critics like Boehmer mention some of the important historical events that led to the cracks in England's imperial armour and its astonishingly rapid decline within a span of forty years. The humiliations of the Boer War in South Africa from 1899–1902 in particular, was a reminder that all was not well with the Empire. India saw the emergence of the Swadeshi movement in 1905 to 1908, followed by the Civil Disobedience Movement in 1921 to 1922, and the Quit India movement in 1942, all paralleling the decline in moderate politics of the Indian National Congress. There were widespread nationalist uprisings in Africa, especially in Kenya, Nigeria and South Africa, with the South African Native National Congress, later the African National Congress, being formed in 1912 (Boehmer 99). Marcus Garvey and his Back to Africa movement in the 1920s inspired nationalist movements in many other colonised countries. Amidst this tumultuous political backdrop, writers like Rabindranath Tagore, Claude McKay, Aimé Césaire and others were beginning to use both European narratives as well as multiple genres like the short story, novel, drama and poetry, to articulate their own colonial experiences, thus ensuring that the coloniser's voice was no longer the dominant one. As Boehmer suggests, "literary conventions and discourses inherited from the colonizer were appropriated, translated, decentred, and hybridized in ways we now name postcolonial but were in fact at the time anti-colonial, often opportunistic, tactical, and *ad hoc*, and which formed an important means of self-expression" (Boehmer 100). As many critics such as Priyamvada Gopal and Gauri Vishwanathan have pointed out:

> The first phase of British rule in India from the late eighteenth century onwards, was broadly Orientalist in its educational policy, combining 'the initiation of the West to the vast literary treasures of the East [and] the reintroduction of the natives to their own cultural heritage, represented . . . as being buried under the debris of foreign conquests and depredations.' (Gopal 15)

But by the early nineteenth century, when the EIC was plagued by financial trouble, a counter movement called Anglicism emerged. The Anglicists advocated the introduction of European education in the colonies as they believed the earlier movement towards Orientalism was leading EIC officials down a path of degeneration. This movement solidified in 1835 when Thomas Babington Macaulay declared in his "Minute on

Indian Education" that an English education was imperative for the state of affairs in the colonies to be improved, and what was needed was "a class who may be interpreters between us and the millions whom we govern; a class of persons, Indian in blood and colour, but English in taste, in opinions, in morals, and in intellect" (249). Even though highly controversial in his reference to racial hierarchy, Macaulay's words were quickly embraced in the form of Lord Bentinck's English Education Act of 1835 that formalised the necessity of English language teaching and learning in India. However, Gopal points out that the "would be interpreters" were not passive recipients of this undertaking, but that "native subjects engaged with the new power structure in their own self-interest . . . . Colonial policy on education shifted and changed in relation to the response of its subjects who had ideas of their own on how they could benefit from new educational initiatives, including English education" (17). The Hindu College, fashioned as the "Oxford of the East", had already been established in Calcutta in 1817, and according to Jasodhara Bagchi, the Hindu College came to epitomise "the integration of Anglicism and Orientalism, the powerful mixture that enabled the Bengal bhadralok to fashion themselves into modern Hindus, Bengalis, and, over time, into Indians" (Gopal 17).

Calcutta had already been the home of the phenomenon known as the Bengal Renaissance. "For the intelligentsia of Bengal, the 'Renaissance' inaugurated a search for cultural and, eventually, national identity, a place from where they could articulate a sense of individual and collective selfhood" (Gopal 18). Henry Vivian Derozio, a young Hindu College lecturer, was at the centre of the Young Bengal movement, a strand of the Bengal Renaissance, and is credited as being one of the first Anglophone poets who merged Indian themes with English rhythms and cadences in his poetry. Michael Madhusudhan Dutt, a student of Derozio, acquired some degree of notoriety initially with his proclamations of love of the English language – "Yes – I love the language – the glorious language of the Anglo Saxon. My imagination visions forth before me the language of the Anglo-Saxon in all its radiant beauty; and I feel silenced and abashed" (Gopal 18), but his relationship with English literature and language became fraught over time and he is now remembered as one of the greatest poets of the Bengali language after his publication of the epic poem, *Meghanadabadha Kavya*, inspired by Milton's *Paradise Lost* (Gopal 19). Perhaps one of the most influential books on the emergence and rise of nationalism is Benedict Anderson's *Imagined Communities: Reflections on the Origin and Spread of Nationalism*, published in 1991. As the title indicates, Anderson thought of the modern nation-state as an "imagined community" born as feudal societies gave way to capitalist societies. He suggested that the bourgeoisie who came into existence in capitalist societies attempted to create a sense of community based on a sense of shared interests and cultures within a nation. Newspapers, novels and other newly developed means of communication, or in Anderson's words, "print capitalism", aided such an imaginative construction. Anderson thus suggests that "The convergence of capitalism and print technology on the fatal diversity of human language created the possibility of a new form of imagined community, which in its basic morphology set the stage for the modern nation" (46). But as Partha Chatterjee argued in his book *Nationalist Thought and the Colonial World* (1986), print capitalism and a nationalist consciousness developed in a different way. Even though most of the culturally elite intelligentsia were educated in the coloniser's language, some even in Europe, they simultaneously engaged with their mother tongue and attempted to re-invigorate and popularise them – "The bilingual intelligentsia came to think of its own language as belonging to that inner domain of cultural identity, from which the colonial intruder had to be kept out; language therefore became a zone over which the nation first had to declare its sovereignty and then had to transform in order to make it adequate for the modern world" (Chatterjee 7).[1]

Given this literary/historical background, it is not surprising that the Bengal of the 1880s and 1890s was a breeding ground of ideas about a new nationalism, pioneered by writers like Bankim Chandra Chatterjee and Rabindranath Tagore. Both writers primarily wrote in their native Bengali; most of the narratives were aimed at awakening a nationalist consciousness. Written in the fashion of a Gothic novel and set amidst the rapidly changing society of nineteenth century Bengal, Chatterjee's *Rajmohan's Wife* (1864), is credited as being the first known Anglophone Indian novel by an Indian writer (Gopal 29). But it his Bengali novel *Anandamath* (1882) – imagined as a fictional history of a rebellion against a tyrannical rule – that inspired the nationalist Swadeshi movement that developed in 1905 as the main form of resistance to the purported Partition of Bengal. The anthem "Bande Mataram", written by Chatterjee as a rallying cry for his rebels in the novel is "still India's 'national song' and is to this day touted by Hindu nationalists as a more genuinely 'Indian' alternative to the existing national 'anthem,' 'Jana Gana Mana,' written by Rabindranath Tagore in a self-consciously secular spirit incorporating a diversity into a unity" (Gopal 33). Tagore had been prolific as a writer, but it is his novel *Ghare Baire* on the Swadeshi movement (first translated by his nephew Surendranath Tagore as *The Home and the World*) and serially published from 1915 to early 1916, that created a storm of controversy. Tagore was vilified by domestic readers as an apologist for empire, further aggravated by his being awarded the Nobel Prize for Literature and his acceptance of a knighthood in 1916 (though he returned it later as a protest against the Jallianwala Bagh Massacre of 1919). The novel didn't fare much better in Europe either. Anita Desai, in her introduction to Tagore's novel, mentions that Georg Lukacs panned the novel as "a petit bourgeois yarn of the shoddiest kind" (xxi) and E. M. Forster dismissed it as "boarding-house flirtation" with its "Babu sentences" (xxi), but the importance of the novel as a critical study of the nature of nationalism, when anti-colonial feelings were at its peak, can hardly be overemphasised.

ANTI-COLONIAL NATIONALISM IN TAGORE'S *THE HOME AND THE WORLD*

The Swadeshi movement of 1905 was born as a mark of protest against Lord Curzon's arbitrary decision, citing administrative difficulties, to slice the province of Bengal into two parts. But as the intelligentsia immediately recognised, the partition was a euphemism for the notorious British policy of "divide and rule", which had been erratically implemented with disastrous consequences all across India, and had been very useful to the British in quelling any kind of resistance movements. A partition of Bengal would be very useful to snuff out the incipient nationalism that was taking root all across the state. Tagore himself was an early supporter of this nationalist movement that involved the boycott of all kinds of foreign goods in favour of domestic products. Not only did he compose patriotic songs to rally supporters, he was also partly responsible for setting up a weaving centre and a matchstick factory in Bengal. But when he realised that the driving force of the movement was the wealthy land-owning class, who had nothing to lose with the burning of cheap foreign stuff, and the victims were peasants and merchants, particularly Muslims, who had little or no understanding of the abstract concept of Swadeshi but were terrified at the prospect of losing their only means of livelihood, Tagore became completely disenchanted with the Swadeshi ideology. His ideological confusion found expression in *The Home and the World* through the characters of the wealthy landowner Nikhil, his wife Bimala and Nikhil's friend, the revolutionary leader Sandip, who uses their palatial mansion as a seat of the Swadeshi movement. Tagore's novel opens with Nikhil established as the modern Renaissance man with liberal Western ideas about the equality of the sexes who, as Bimala says, "would not give me any opportunity for worship. That was his greatness" (Tagore 19). Instead, he is keen to get her out of purdah and into the real world, to try to get her to think for herself. "I would have you come into the heart of the outer world and meet reality. Merely going on with your household conventions and the drudgery of household tasks – you were not made for that! If we meet, and recognize each other, in the real world, then only will our love be true" (23). Bimala already had a vision of herself as "the *Shakti* of Womanhood, incarnate" (36), and when the charismatic Sandip with his rousing patriotic rhetoric makes an appearance in their house, some gentle coaxing from Nikhil is enough to make Bimala cross the threshold into the public space of the living room, much to the chagrin of the other female members of the household. But Nikhil and Bimala's happy marriage is put under serious strain as Sandip recognises the naïve Bimala's need for a meaningful role in the current political climate. He is quick to give her the importance she desires by telling her "You are far above all modesty and diffidence. You are the Queen Bee of our hive, and we the workers shall rally around you. You shall be our centre, our inspiration" (44). Bimala fails to see that Sandip is a deeply narcissistic individual, so wrapped up in his ideology and his heightened self-importance that he would spare no pains to reach his goal, even if that involves emotionally manipulating his friend's unsuspecting wife. As the narrative progresses, the unsuspecting Bimala gets increasingly drawn into an affair with Sandip. When Sandip asks her for a significant amount of money for the nationalist cause, Bimala, suspecting her husband won't be in favour of it, gives it to him by stealing from the family safe. But soon, along with Amulya, a young protégé of Sandip, Bimala discovers his true colours and the emptiness of his rhetoric – something that Nikhil had known all along but had hesitated to tell Bimala, fearing she might suspect him of some sort of jealousy. Given Bimala's passion for the cause, Nikhil knew it would "be difficult to explain to Bimala today that Sandip's love of country is but a different phase of his covetous self-love" (43). The novel ends with Bimala grappling with her emotions as she learns that Amulya has been killed in a raid and that her husband Nikhil has sustained serious injuries while trying to save his tenants from violence perpetrated by Swadeshi activists led by Sandip.

The novel clearly casts Bimala as the fulcrum between two opposing ideologies, as well as two different forms of masculinity. But what is remarkable about the novel is that Bimala is not a passive character in the dramatic events that engulf her; she clearly represents the motherland to Tagore and is repeatedly referred to as "Mother" by multiple characters, even by her husband towards the end of the book. As Anita Desai points out, "When Tagore writes of how her adoring husband begs Bimala to leave the *zenana* to which custom has kept her confined and come out into 'the world', he seems to be coaxing Bengal out of the orthodoxy and superstition he so hated into the light of the modern age, to make her a fit deity for independent India" (Desai xxv). And even though the three characters have a distinct voice in the novel and distinct views on nationalism, Tagore's sympathies seem to unmistakeably lie with the gentle and wise Nikhil as he proclaims, "I am willing . . . to serve my country; but my worship I reserve for the Right which is far greater than my country. To worship my country as a god is to bring a curse upon it" (29). Tagore is clearly making a distinction here between "service" and "worship" emphasising that blind obeisance to anything can potentially have dangerous consequences. As Gopal points out, "Swadeshi is figured here as essentially destructive and tyrannical and as such, derivative of the violence of colonial power itself" (37). Nikhil and Sandip embody opposing ends of the nationalist spectrum and their ideological difference represent a distinction between restraint and rational reform as opposed to inflammatory rhetoric and passionate jingoism. In fact, it is his vision of nationalism as an amalgamation of rational thinking coupled with the power of imagination rather than a narrow vision of patriotism that made Tagore's poetry so marvellously evocative to the masses and established him as the greatest Bengali poet of all times. His poem "Where the Mind is Without Fear", first published in Bengali in 1910 and then published in English in 1912 as part of the collection *Gitanjali*, is worth quoting here in its entirety.

> Where the mind is without fear and the head is held high
> Where knowledge is free
> Where the world has not been broken up into fragments
> By narrow domestic walls
> Where words come out from the depth of truth
> Where tireless striving stretches its arms towards perfection
> Where the clear stream of reason has not lost its way
> Into the dreary desert sand of dead habit
> Where the mind is led forward by thee
> Into ever-widening thought and action
> Into that heaven of freedom, my Father, let my country awake.
> (27–28)

Here, Tagore makes an impassioned plea to his countrymen to not get embroiled in fear and divisive rhetoric and instead embrace reason on the march towards freedom and justice. Tagore's message inspired countless people then and continues to be relevant a hundred years after it was first published.

Reworking the English language in anti-colonial literature

While there was an upsurge of nationalistic pride and self-expression in India, West Indian writers like Claude McKay and Aimé Césaire, inspired by Black American movements like Marcus Garvey's "Back to Africa" movement, "began to proclaim African cultural dignity. Race pride, they believed was to be recovered in the excavation of 'ancestral origins'" (Boehmer 113). Claude McKay was a Jamaican contemporary of Marcus Garvey and spent his early years in the Caribbean. Those childhood years inevitably shaped his poetry as is evident from the images of black rural life and customs in some of his early works. Later in life, outraged by racial inequality and oppression in the American South, McKay became a major figure in the Harlem Renaissance and wrote some of his major novels including *Home to Harlem* (1928), and *Harlem Shadows* (1922), about that experience. *Home to Harlem* and his famous later novels *Banjo* (1929), and *Banana Bottom* (1933), incorporated "black vernacular traditions, or as he put it 'the necromancy of [black] language'" (Boehmer 113). In fact, the use of language became a key element in the fashioning of the Caribbean identity. Frantz Fanon has talked about the use of the coloniser's language in *Black Skin, White Masks*:

> Every colonized people – in other words, every people in whose soul an inferiority complex has been created by the death and burial of its local originality – finds itself face to face with the language of the civilizing nation; that is, with the culture of the mother country. The colonized is elevated above his jungle status in proportion to his adoption of the mother country's cultural standards. He becomes whiter as he renounces his blackness, his jungle. (Fanon 18)

In the West Indian context, language became complicated in a different way. As Louis James points out, "To advance socially, the 'black' people were required to speak a language which simultaneously devalued them, in which 'Negro' signified the physical and brutish, and 'white' the moral and intellectual. The creation of Creole out of the language of the colonizer therefore offered not so much an alternative language as 'a new way of being'" (120), and it is not surprising then that different forms of Creole started emerging in various parts of West Indies as slaves began to figure out ways to communicate with each other using dialects different from that of their owners. Kamau Braithwaite points out, "it was in language that the slave was perhaps most successfully imprisoned by his master, and it was in his (mis-)use of it that he perhaps most effectively rebelled" (James 120). But along with reinventing the coloniser's language, dismantling colonial stereotypes about their land and taking pride in their own history and culture became important themes in the writing of some of the West Indian and African Negritude writers like Aimé Césaire. As Boehmer elaborates, "Negritude therefore meant celebrating all that had been identified as negative and inferior by the colonizers – the instinctual and the mysterious darkest Africa. The poetry rejoiced in the 'earth-loving' sensuality, visceral rhythms and ancestral mystique of an imaginary pre-conquest Africa" (105). Césaire's retelling of Shakespeare's *The Tempest* is worth noting here. Shakespeare's monster Caliban is not only given a stronger voice; in some ways, he becomes the hero of Césaire's play by calling Prospero's motives into question. Even though Prospero tries to portray himself as a victim of the European lust for greed and power, in the form of his brother who forced him into exile, Caliban repeatedly chastises him for being a coloniser in his own way. One of the many altercations between Prospero and Caliban in Shakespeare's play was on the issue of language. Prospero repeatedly reminds Caliban that he gave him language – "When thou didst not, savage,/Know thine own meaning, but wouldst gabble like/A thing most brutish, I endowed thy purposes/With words that made them known" to which Caliban replies "You taught me language; and my profit on't/ Is, I know how to curse. The red plague rid you/ For learning me your language" (14). As Thiong'o points out, Shakespeare doesn't deny Caliban a voice, but the play "has all the images that are later to be reworked into a racist tradition particularly in popular European literature about the colonised peoples: the savage as a rapist, lazy, a lover of whisky, stupid, cannibalistic" (15). In Césaire's play, Caliban is more energetic in his dismissal of Prospero's attempts at colonising his mind. He balks at the suggestion that Prospero civilised him:

> You didn't teach me a thing! Except to jabber in your own language so that I could understand your orders; chop the wood, wash the dishes, fish for food, plant vegetables, all because you're too lazy to do it yourself. And as for your learning, did you ever impart any of *that* to me? No, you took care not to. All your science you keep for yourself alone, shut up in those big books. (17)

As the play progresses, Caliban becomes increasingly defiant by answering with his native "Uhuru" greeting to Prospero's calls, criticising Ariel for his servility, asking "What good has your obedience done you, your Uncle Tom patience and your sucking up to him. The man's just getting more demanding and despotic everyday" (26) and generally refusing to answer to the name that Prospero had imposed on him. But one of the key moments in the play comes after Ferdinand and Miranda's marriage, where Caliban enunciates the colonial condition of estrangement and loss of identity forced upon him by the coloniser, as he tells Prospero:

> And you lied to me so much,
> about the world, about myself,
> that you ended up by imposing on me
> an image of myself:
> underdeveloped, in your words, undercompetent

that's how you made me see myself!
And I hate that image . . . and it's false!
But now I know you, you old cancer,
And I also know myself!
And I know that one day
My bare fist, just that,
will be enough to crush your world!
The old world is crumbling down! (62)

It was this rhetoric that gave impetus to the multitude of resistance movements and outcries for freedom that we see in different parts of the world. While Caliban doesn't hesitate to indict Prospero in this, he is quick to realise that the negative self-image hoisted on colonised subjects by their rulers has, to some degree, sustained colonial rule. This self-knowledge becomes crucial in the fight for freedom. As Claude McKay sums up in a 1912 poem titled "Passive Resistance":

There'll be no more riotin',
Stonin' p'lice an' burnin' car;
But we mean to gain our rights
By a strong though bloodless war.
We will show an alien trust
Dat Jamaicans too can fight
An' dat while our blood is hot,
They won't crush us wi'deir might. (McKay 13)

Dismantling colonial myths in Jean Rhys's *Wide Sargasso Sea*

Colonialist fiction also seemed to suggest that any kind of meaningful interaction with the natives is naturally doomed to fail, and often a conscious attempt was made to keep social and cultural spheres markedly separate. In *A Passage to India*, one of the British characters, Mr Turton, observes "I have never known anything but disaster result when British people and Indians attempt to be intimate socially. Intercourse, yes. Courtesy, by all means. Intimacy – never, never. The whole weight of my authority is against it" (Forster 182). Mr Turton's remarks obviously refers to the events in the novel when the encounter between Adela Quested and Dr Aziz in the Marabar Caves leads to accusations of rape and breeds racial tension between the natives and the English. W. M. Thackeray wittily observes in *Vanity Fair*, "Those who know the English colonies abroad, know that we carry with us our pride, pills, prejudices, Harvey-sauces, cayenne-peppers, and other Lares, making a little Britain wherever we settle down" (634), deliberately masking the very real fear of sexual and cultural miscegenation that was becoming a source of worry for the British intelligentsia. Boehmer observes:

> Despite efforts at containment, the fear of other cultures, or of the primitive, found its way into texts, cropping up in all manner of images of contamination, infection, and bewitching. Constant anxiety was expressed about the degeneration allegedly caused not only by direct encounters with natives, but by the proximity to savage passions, or simply by the malign influence of the alien environment. (69)

The Jamaican Morant Bay Rebellion of 1865 and the Indian Mutiny of 1857 brought to the forefront some of Darwin's theories, and even leading writers like Anthony Trollope "described West Indian Creoles as a degenerate race belonging neither to Africa nor to Europe, with no language but 'their broken English'" (James 17). Nowhere is this feeling of in-betweenness created and fostered in the West Indian colonial mind-set captured more eloquently than in Jean Rhys's novel *Wide Sargasso Sea*. Published in 1966, *Wide Sargasso Sea* is set in the West Indies in the 1840s and is a retelling of the classic Victorian novel *Jane Eyre* by Charlotte Bronte. Rhys's novel gives a voice to Bertha Mason, Mr Rochester's first wife who is secretively locked away in the attic of Thornfield Manor and must be disposed of before Jane Eyre can achieve a happy union with Mr Rochester in the eyes of prudish Victorian society. After Richard Mason disrupts Mr Rochester and Jane Eyre's marriage proceedings in Bronte's novel, Rochester tells a stunned audience, including Jane, that he is indeed married, but to Bertha Mason, who is "mad; and she came of a mad family; – idiots and maniacs through three generations! Her mother, the Creole, was both a mad woman and a drunkard! – as I found out after I had wed the daughter: for they were silent on family secrets before" (Bronte 326). Rochester seems to indicate that he was tricked into a marriage with an unsuitable girl with a troubled family history, and the reference to the Creole lineage is unmistakable here. Further on in the novel we, along with the other wedding guests, see Bertha in the mysterious attic under the observation of Grace Poole.

> In the deep shade, at the further end of the room, a figure ran backwards and forwards. What it was, whether beast or human being, one could not, at first sight, tell: it grovelled, seemingly, on all fours; it snatched and growled like some strange wild animal: but it was covered with clothing; and a quantity of dark, grizzled hair, wild as a mane, hid *its* head and face. (327-8; emphasis added)

The above lines, about the madwoman in the attic described in animalistic terms, caught Rhys's attention. In a letter to Diana Athill in 1966, Rhys mentions that *Jane Eyre* was one of the first books she read when she came to England: "Of course, Charlotte Bronte makes her own world, of course she convinces you, and that makes the poor Creole lunatic all the more dreadful. I remember being quite shocked, and when I re-read it rather annoyed. 'That's only one side – the English side' sort of thing" (Raiskin 144). She also tells us in the same letter that she started her novel quite light-heartedly much later in life and it was supposed to be a story of one of the many unfortunate marriages of convenience that were quite commonplace during the colonial era between gold-digging

Europeans and daughters of wealthy West Indian planters and merchants. "This was the story of one arranged marriage, with the bridegroom young, *unwilling*, rather suspicious and ready to believe the worst, not liking the semi tropics at all, and the bride poor bride very romantic, with some French or Spanish blood, perhaps with the seeds of madness, at any rate hysteria" (Raiskin 144–5). But Rhys's novel has been much celebrated as a complex postcolonial novel and is worth a lengthy critical discussion.

Wide Sargasso Sea brought Rhys widespread acclaim and recognition and even the honour of Commander of the Order of the British Empire at the age of 88 for her contributions to literature. Set in the 1840s on the Coulibri estate in the West Indies, the novel starts by documenting the precarious social position of the white Creole Annette and her young daughter Antoinette following the Emancipation Act of 1833 which outlawed slavery in Britain and all its colonies. Between 1834 and 1838, former slaves in the colonies were forced to work under a so-called apprenticeship system, thereafter slave-owners were monetarily compensated for each slave even though the slaves themselves received no help, leading to widespread tension in the colonies. Rhys's white Creole characters arc placed in an especially precarious position. Elizabeth Nunez-Harell has described white creole women like Annette and Antoinette as "an outcast, a sort of freak rejected by both Europe and England, whose blood she shares, and by the black West Indian people, whose culture and home have been hers for two generations or more" (281–282). We are told that Annette "still rode about every morning not caring that the black people stood about in groups to jeer at her" (Rhys 10), but when her horse is found dead under the frangipani tree after a series of other incidents, Annette realises that she is indeed "marooned" (Rhys 10), which sets her on a downward spiral to madness. The young Antoinette is unusually perceptive when she declares that "All Coulibri

Estate had gone wild like the garden. Gone to bush. No more slavery – why would *anybody* work?" (11), but the new social marginalisation is really brought home to her when she realises that it has complicated her friendship with her black friend Tia. She was already aware that black people hated the impoverished white Creole minority and dubbed them "white cockroaches", but then Tia tells her "Old time white people nothing but white nigger now, and black nigger better than white nigger" (14), emphasising the fact that people like Antoinette had no place in this new society, and resulting in Antoinette beginning to understand the consequences of this new social environment. And when Tia throws a stone at Antoinette during their escape from Coulibri when it is set on fire, Antoinette knows that things will never be the same again on the island. Amidst the chaos of her teenage years and the death of her mother and brother, Antoinette tries to hold on to the image of Britain as a sanctuary as illustrated in her favourite picture, "The Miller's Daughter," after the popular 1832 poem by Lord Tennyson. So even though she is somewhat hesitant because of a vague sense of foreboding from "what may happen" (46), she agrees to an arranged marriage with an Englishman, fashioned in the image of Bronte's Mr Rochester but purposely denied a name by Rhys to make him a symbol of the coloniser. Rhys's trenchant critique of the ill effects of European colonialism plays out in the second and third sections of the novella through a heart-wrenching portrayal of the disastrous marriage. Antoinette's husband imagines himself to be the victim in this arranged marriage and in true colonial fashion makes no attempt to understand the land and its people or integrate himself into the culture. Instead, he is acutely aware of his own racial superiority over Antoinette and claims that "Creole of pure English descent she may be, but they are not English or European either" (39), emphasising the dominant metropolitan idea that white Creoles in the islands were somehow racially and culturally inferior to pure-bred white European colonisers. His interactions with Antoinette stem out of a purely physical desire for her – "I did not love her. I was thirsty for her, but that is not love. I felt very little tenderness for her, she was a stranger to me, a stranger who did not think or feel as I did" (55) – and even then, he has no scruples about having a dalliance with her maid Amelie in Granbois, or believing malicious rumours about Antoinette and her family's reputation. According to British law, Antoinette's inheritance was written away to her husband as soon as she entered into the marriage, but ironically, in his version, he has been tricked into a disastrous marriage with a lunatic. In a letter to his father, he claims "I have sold my soul or you have sold it, and after all is it such a bad bargain? The girl is thought to be beautiful . . ." (41), and yet he is determined to make Antoinette pay for it.

> They bought me, *me* with your paltry money. You helped them to do it. You deceived me, betrayed me, and you'll do worse if you get the chance . . . If I was bound for hell let it be hell. No more false heavens. No more damned magic. You hate me and I hate you. We'll see who hates best. But first, first I will destroy your hatred. (102)

It is well documented throughout eighteenth- and nineteenth-century literature how slave owners and colonial masters renamed slaves and effectively erased their identities. In Césaire's *A Tempest*, Caliban describes this in very powerful terms: "Call me X. That would be best. Like a man without a name. Or, to be more precise, a man whose name has been stolen. You talk about history . . . well, that's history, and everyone knows it! Every time you summon me it reminds me of a basic fact, the fact that you've stolen everything from me, even my identity! Uhuru!" (Césaire 20). Here Antoinette's husband renames her "Bertha" simply because he likes the name despite repeated protests from her – "Bertha is not my name.

You are trying to make me into someone else, calling me by another name" (Rhys 88). And in a chilling number of pages towards the close of the second section, Bertha, nee Antoinette, devoid of her sense of identity, is hardly anything more than a zombie. In true colonial fashion, Antoinette becomes nothing more than an object in his estimation as he chillingly declares "she's mad but *mine, mine* . . . If she smiles or weeps or both. For *me*" (99), and vows that "she'll not laugh in the sun again . . . vain, silly creature. Made for loving? Yes, but she'll have no lover, for I don't want her and she'll see no other" (99), even as he dominates the narrative in the entire second section. Rhys is not content however with Antoinette's husband having the last word. Antoinette reclaims her agency even as we see her imprisoned in the attic under the watchful eye of Grace Poole. Rhys does not end the novel with Antoinette setting fire to Thornfield; instead, in the final scene, we see her carrying a candle down a dark hallway, having just woken up from a telling dream about Coulibri. She mysteriously states that "Now at last I know why I was brought here and what I have to do" (112) as she carefully shields the candle flame from going out in the draught. As James suggests, "Rhys's superb closure draws the reader away from Antoinette's revenge and self-destruction to the act's inner significance, that of survival and psychic liberation" (39). But perhaps the most haunting aspect of the novel is its nuanced study of the nature of alienation between Europeans and the native people. *Wide Sargasso Sea* once again emphasises that the imperial myth-making rampant in the colonies through colonial education and other such apparatuses did not lead to any improved understanding of each other and in fact often had disastrous consequences. Like in *Heart of Darkness*, both colonial and metropolitan spaces become deeply imbued with meaning, and the characters often become victims of a mythical and false representation of a foreign land where the reality of their experiences do not match their idea of it. As

Judith Raiskin suggests in her essay, "Antoinette and Rochester represent for each other the seductive yet terrifying differences of the Old and New Worlds invented by European literature and art" (254). The idyllic Granbois, the dearly loved honeymoon island to which Antoinette takes her young husband, becomes an anathema to him because the tropical paradise seems to be an extension of her wild beauty, her free spirit and vivacity that he doesn't comprehend, but is desperate to curb and control.

> I hated the place. I hated the mountains and the hills, the rivers and the rain. I hated the sunsets of whatever colour, I hated its beauty and its magic and the secret I would never know. I hated its indifference and the cruelty which was part of its loveliness. Above all I hated her. For she belonged to the magic and the loveliness. She had left me thirsty and all my life would be thirst and longing for what I had lost before I found it. (Rhys 103)

As Emery suggests, "Overwhelmed by what he thinks of as her alien beauty and that of the island she loves, Antoinette's husband feels he has been tricked and seeks revenge by appropriating the mechanisms of illusion and beauty on which she depends" (168). In sharp contrast to this is Antoinette's vision of Britain, culled from the painting of "The Miller's Daughter" and other stories – of Britain being the mother country, a safe space, something that her husband immediately recognises as unreal.

> She often questioned me about England and listened attentively to my answers, but I was certain that nothing I said made much difference. Her mind was already made up. Some romantic novel, a stray remark never forgotten, a sketch, a picture, a song, a waltz, some note of music, and her ideas were fixed. About England and about Europe. (Rhys 56)

But just as the excessive colour of the tropics is disorienting for Antoinette's husband and constantly increases his feelings of estrangement and alienation, Antoinette's vision of Britain as a safe haven morphs into a dream of violence and destruction, so much so that when she is actually in Britain, albeit confined to the attic of Edward's mansion, she refuses to believe it is the same place that existed in her dreams. Raiskin asserts, "The 'dream' each of them seeks in the other embodies within it the nightmare of the strange" (254), as is revealed in the rather telling conversation between Antoinette and her husband:

> "Is it true," she said, "that England is like a dream? Because one of my friends who married an Englishman wrote and told me so. She said this place London is like a cold dark dream sometimes. I want to wake up."
>
> "Well," I answered annoyed, "that is precisely how your beautiful island seems to me, quite unreal and like a dream."
>
> "But how can rivers and mountains and the sea be unreal?"
>
> "And how can millions of people, their houses and their streets be unreal?"
>
> "More easily," she said, "much more easily. Yes, a big city must be like a dream."
>
> "No, this is unreal and like a dream," I thought. (Rhys 47–48)

Rhys's novel then ends up questioning the nature of reality itself and seems to suggest that these dreamscapes that both Antoinette and her husband have constructed about the unknown places will never quite live up to its construction. It is interesting to note that it is only Christophine, the practitioner of obeah in the text, who is the one who recognises that Britain is largely a fantasy. When Antoinette asks her in surprise "You do not believe that there is a country called England?" she replies, in a quite matter of fact way, " I don't say I don't *believe*, I say I don't *know*. I know what I see with my eyes and I never see it" (67). But it is too late when Antoinette realises, if at all, the full import of Christophine's wisdom. The ending of *Wide Sargasso Sea* once again emphasises the perpetual exile that characters like Antoinette find themselves in, "this time not on the frontier, but in the heart of the metropolis" (Raiskin 258).

Following the widespread chaos of the two successive World Wars and the resistance movements that were emerging in Asia, Africa and the West Indies, it was only a matter of time before most countries in Europe, including England, realised they could not hold on to their empires much longer. Once this became clear, most colonised countries witnessed a new-found urgency in their nationalist movements and in their outcries of freedom. After the Quit India movement of 1942 and sustained political pressure, India acquired its freedom from England in 1947, but not without serious consequences, with the country partitioned into the two nations of India and Pakistan. Most of the countries in Africa attained their independence during the 1960s, and it is remarkable to note that by the second half of the twentieth century, England went from being in control of half of the world to a small island nation trying to negotiate its relationship with the hordes of immigrants pouring into the imperial metropolis. These newly formed nation states were not in a state of bliss either; the initial euphoria reflected in Indian Prime Minister Jawaharlal Nehru's "Tryst With Destiny" speech quickly dissipated as the new nation struggled with the challenges of self-governance. Most nations in Africa too continued to wrestle with problems of colonial dependency and effective governance amidst inter-ethnic conflicts. The next chapter will investigate the construction of postcolonial identities through the prism of postcolonial nation-formation.

Works Cited

Achebe, Chinua. *Things Fall Apart*. New York: Everyman's Library, 1958. Print.

———. "An Image of Africa: Racism in Conrad's *Heart of Darkness*." *Heart of Darkness*. Ed. Robert Kimbrough. New York: W. W. Norton & Company, 1988. 251–262. Print.

Anderson, Benedict. *Imagined Communities: Reflections on the Origin and Spread of Nationalism*. London: Verso, 1983. Print.

Boehmer, Elleke. *Colonial and Postcolonial Literature*. Oxford: Oxford UP, 1995. Print.

Bronte, Charlotte. *Jane Eyre*. New York: Penguin Books, 2003. Print.

Césaire, Aimé. *A Tempest*. Trans. Richard Miller. New York: TCG Translations, 2002. Print.

Chatterjee, Partha. *Nationalist Thought and the Colonial World: A Derivative Discourse*? London: Zed Books, 1986. Print.

Conrad, Joseph. *Heart of Darkness*. Ed. Robert Kimbrough. New York: W. W. Norton & Company, 1963. Print.

Daly, Suzanne. *The Empire Inside: Indian Commodities in Victorian Domestic Novels*. Ann Arbor: U of Michigan P, 2011. Print.

Damrosch, David. *Heart of Darkness, "The Man Who Would Be King," and Other Works of Empire*. New York: Pearson Longman, 2007. Print.

Darwin, Charles. *Voyage of the Beagle*. Harmondsworth: Penguin, 1839. Print.

David, Deirdre. "Empire, Race, and the Victorian Novel." *A Companion to the Victorian Novel*. Eds. Patrick Brantlinger and William B. Thesing. Massachusetts: Blackwell, 2002. 84–100. Print.

———. *Rule Britannia: Women, Empire, and Victorian Writing*. Ithaca: Cornell P, 1995. Print.

Desai, Anita. Introduction. *The Home and the World*. By Rabindranath Tagore. London: Penguin Books, 1985. xxi–xxviii. Print.

Dutta, Krishna, and Andrew Robinson. *Rabindranath Tagore: An Anthology*. New York: St. Martin's P, 1997. Print.

Eliot, Charles. *The East Africa Protectorate*. London: Edward Arnold, 1905. Print.

Emery, Mary Lou. "Modernist Crosscurrents." *Wide Sargasso Sea*. Ed. Judith Raiskin. New York: W. W. Norton & Company, 1999. 161–173. Print.

Fanon, Frantz. *Black Skin, White Masks*. New York: Grove P, 1967. Print.

Forster, E. M. *A Passage to India.* London: Harcourt, 1924. Print.

Gopal, Priyamvada. *The Indian English Novel: Nation, History, and Narration.* Oxford: Oxford UP, 2009. Print.

Hochschild, Adam. *King Leopold's Ghost.* Boston: Mariner Books, 1999. Print.

James, Louis. *Caribbean Literature in English.* New York: Longman, 1999. Print.

Kingsley, Mary. *Travels in West Africa.* London: Macmillan & Co. Ltd, 1897. Print.

Loomba, Ania. *Colonialism/Postcolonialism.* New York: Routledge, 1998. Print.

Macaulay, Thomas Babington. *Selected Writings*. Eds. John Clive and Thomas Pinney. Chicago: U of Chicago P, 1972. Print.

Manthorpe, Peter. "London from Sea-Level." *London was Full of Rooms*. Ed. Tully Barnett et al. Adelaide: Lythrum P, 2006. 162–168. Print.

McKay, Claude. *Complete Poems*. Ed. William J. Maxwell. Chicago: U of Illinois P, 2004. Print.

Nunez-Harell, Elizabeth. "The Paradoxes of Belonging: The White West Indian Woman in Fiction." *Modern Fiction Studies*. 31.2 (Summer 1987). 281–293. Print.

Raiskin, Judith. "England: Dream and Nightmare." *Wide Sargasso Sea.* Ed. Judith L. Raiskin. London: W. W. Norton & Company, 1999. 250–258. Print.

Ramamurthy, Anandi. *Images of Africa and Asia in British Advertising*. Manchester: Manchester UP, 2003. Print.

Rhys, Jean. *Wide Sargasso Sea.* Ed. Judith L. Raiskin. London: W. W. Norton & Company, 1999. Print.

Ruskin, John. *Lectures on Art: Delivered before the University of Oxford in Hilary Term, 1870.* New York: John Wiley & Sons, 1888. Print.

Samson, Jane, ed. *The British Empire*. Oxford: Oxford UP, 2001. Print.

Shakespeare, William. *The Tempest*. New York: Dover Publications, 1999. Print.

Stanley, Henry. M. *Through the Dark Continent: Or, The Sources of the Nile Around the Great Lakes of Equatorial Africa and Down the Livingstone River to the Atlantic Ocean*. London: Sampson Low, Marston, Searle, & Rivington, 1880. Print.

Tagore, Rabindranath. *The Home and the World*. London: Penguin Books, 1985. Print.

———. *Gitanjali: Song Offerings*. New York: The Macmillan Company, 1916. Print.

Thackeray, William M. *Vanity Fair*. New York: Barnes & Noble Books, 2003. Print.

Thiong'o, Ngũgĩ wa. *Moving the Centre: The Struggle for Cultural Freedoms*. London: James Currey, 1993. Print.

Viswanathan, Gauri. *Masks of Conquest: Literary Study and British Rule in India*. New York: Columbia UP, 1989. Print.

Williams, John. *A Narrative of Missionary Enterprise*. London: John Snow, 1841. Print.

Notes

1. For a more detailed discussion of Anderson and Chatterjee's discussion on nationalism, see Ania Loomba's *Colonialism/Postcolonialism*.

THREE

RE-IMAGINING THE NATION

Decolonisation, the colonial legacy, and postcolonial writing

Sooner or later they will leave our country, just as many people throughout history left many countries. The railways, ships, hospitals, factories, and schools will be ours and we'll speak their language without a sense of guilt or a sense of gratitude. Once again we shall be as we were – ordinary people – and if we are lies we shall be lies of our own making.

—Tayeb Salih, *Season of Migration to the North*

It can hardly be ignored that the process of decolonisation, primarily in Asia, Africa and the West Indies, was one of the most important global phenomenon in the second half of the twentieth century, and in recent years, there has been a lot of writing that addresses the complex process of the formation of post-colonial nation-states and the chaos and often radical disillusionment that followed soon after. Britain was at the height of its empire in 1914 with 12700000 square miles of land ranging from the Caribbean to Africa to South Asia and South-East Asia under its domain. But by the late 1950s, most of that had disappeared with more independent nations coming into existence throughout the 1960s, especially throughout the African continent. This independence did not come easily. In most cases, it became a reality only after prolonged resistance movements throughout the first four decades of the twentieth century. Europe found itself embroiled in two World Wars and European armies were actively recruiting soldiers from the colonies to fight in their armies, while simultaneously dealing with a series of anti-colonial freedom struggles, often violent ones, across Asia and Africa. Critics like Tamara Sivanandan point out that they ranged from the successive liberation movements in India like Mahatma Gandhi's Satyagraha, the Civil Disobedience Movement and the Quit India movement, to "armed struggle, guerrilla warfare, and revolution, as was the case with the Land and Freedom Armies ('Mau Mau') in Kenya, or the campaigns in Algeria, Indonesia, Malaysia, Vietnam, Angola and Zimbabwe" (Sivanandan 42). Emboldened by the passionate words and revolutionary optimism of Frantz Fanon's *Black Skin, White Masks* and *The Wretched of the Earth*, among others, opposition to colonial rule assumed a new sense of urgency and the year 1952 marked the beginning of a particularly violent phase in the decolonisation process. Though Fanon's writings were specifically aimed at the Algerian struggle for independence, they were influential in a much wider context. Along with the civil war against French colonisation in Algeria, even countries like South Africa, on the other side of the African continent, started witnessing anti-apartheid protests.

The critic Aijaz Ahmad offers a useful periodisation of the formation of independent nation states that came into existence through some kind of organised resistance movement.

> A first phase, occupying the twenty years just after the Second World War, when states acquired independence under the leadership of their respective national bourgeoisies (some radical, other conservative) within the broad context of 'modernization' and integration within the capitalist world system; and a second phase, occupying the period from 1965 to 1975, dominated by wars of national liberation that had a distinctly socialist bearing, despite the possibilities for successful socialist construction being limited due to the 'level of prior economic development and the scale of imperialist devastations.' (Ahmed 30)

According to this periodisation, countries like India, Nigeria and Morocco would fall in the first category, with Vietnam, Laos and the Lusophone African colonies of Mozambique, Angola and others in the second category. India attained its independence in 1947, but not before the mass genocide that followed the partition of the subcontinent into India and Pakistan. Liberia, Egypt and Ethiopia became independent in 1945, but it was through the 1950s and 1960s that decolonisation progressed at a startling speed in Sub-Saharan Africa and in the West Indies. Ghana gained independence in 1957, Guinea in 1958, Nigeria in 1960, Tanzania in 1961, Uganda in 1962, Trinidad and Tobago in 1962, Kenya in 1963, Zambia in 1964, Barbados in 1966 and Zimbabwe as late as 1980. In the Far East, "the Chinese revolution in 1949 was followed by key opening moves in the Cold War: the Korean War, the Suez Canal incident, and the Cuban revolution" (Boehmer 183). Unfortunately, in South Africa, apartheid continued as a state policy until free elections were held in 1994 and Nelson Mandela became the first president of independent South Africa.

Even though the struggle for liberation and the process of decolonisation was far from uniform across the world, one thing seemed fairly constant in all these newly minted sovereign African states – a newfound sense of optimism and naïve belief in potential economic and social development. A lot of postcolonial writers and thinkers initially appear to be ecstatic about the possibilities that would be ushered in by this momentous series of events, and the actual moments of independence were marked by huge crowds, music and dancing, late-night festivities and fiery speeches. In his novel *A Grain of Wheat* (1967), the Kenyan writer Ngũgĩ wa Thiong'o captures the moment when Kenya finally gains its independence. On 12 December 1963, when the Union Jack came down in the darkness and the new Kenyan flag was hoisted in the Nairobi stadium, there was a palpable sense of excitement and expectation. "Everybody waited for something to happen. This 'waiting' and the uncertainty that went with it . . . was a taut cord beneath the screams and the shouts and the laughter" (*Grain of Wheat* 177). But a deep sense of disillusionment quickly set in following the multiple inter-ethnic conflicts in different countries in Africa and quickly wiped out any trace of the earlier celebratory rhetoric. In the Indian subcontinent, the bloodbath that followed the partition of India and Pakistan plunged millions into utter despair. In fact, the celebrated poet Faiz Ahmad Faiz lamented that the much awaited moment of independence had been forever tarnished with the blood of millions who became victims of senseless religious violence. "This stained, spattered light, this/night-bitten break of day/This surely is not the dawn we were waiting for" (Gopal 90). In many of the African nations throughout the 1960s, a sense of fatalism and anger began to emerge as they felt that somehow the newly minted African leaders had failed to deliver on their promise of freedom and prosperity and had betrayed both the "African revolution" and dashed the hopes and aspirations of African people. Nonetheless, the new nation states remained heavily invested in figuring out a new postcolonial identity amidst a lingering colonial legacy, often centred around controversies about the use of the coloniser's language. This chapter will highlight some of those negotiations as reflected in the literature produced at that time.

THE PARTITION OF THE INDIAN SUBCONTINENT

On the eve of Indian independence, a triumphant Indian Prime Minister Jawaharlal Nehru proudly proclaimed:

> Long years ago we made a tryst with destiny, and now the time comes when we shall redeem our pledge, not wholly or in full measure, but very substantially. At the stroke of the midnight hour, when the world sleeps, India will awake to life and

> freedom. A moment comes, which comes but rarely in history, when we step out from the old to the new, when an age ends, and when the soul of a nation, long suppressed, finds utterance. It is fitting that at this solemn moment we take the pledge of dedication to the service of India and her people and to the still larger cause of humanity. (Nehru 25)

Amidst the unprecedented horrors of Partition, Nehru tried to rouse his fellow citizens with this impassioned plea for freedom and glorious self-expression after centuries of British rule. At the same time, he was only too aware that "Freedom and power bring responsibility .... And so we have to labour and to work, and work hard, to give reality to our dreams .... Peace has been said to be indivisible, so is freedom, so is prosperity now, and so also is disaster in this One World that can no longer be split into isolated fragments" (Nehru 24–25). Yet ironically, the story of the post-independence years of one of the largest democracies in the world is one of fragmentation, relentless religious intolerance and deep disillusionment memorably chronicled in the writings of writers like Saadat Hasan Manto, Khuswant Singh, Bapsi Sidhwa, Amitav Ghosh and Salman Rushdie.

In her essay, Leela Gandhi suggests "if Independence narrated the triumphant progress of the national movement, its double, Partition, told an altogether different story – of mutual betrayal, failure, the systematic rift between Congress and the Muslim League, and the estrangement between Muslims and Hindus" (171). The granting of independence to India had been in the works for some time. The significant losses sustained by Britain during the Second World War and the changing nature of Britain's foreign policy, as well as the increasing nationalist uprisings in India, somewhat punctured Britain's sense of superiority and convinced the colonial government that Britain's stronghold on its colonies was fast becoming untenable. So as early as June 1946, almost a year before the actual event, plans to partition the subcontinent were announced. But the "divide and rule" policy followed by the colonial government for years had contributed to a steady decline in the relations between Hindus and Muslims in the subcontinent. This widening mistrust and animosity between these religious groups spilled over into the political sphere, and as early as 1906, the All India Muslim League was founded as a breakaway from the Indian National Congress (INC) to protect the rights of Indian Muslims. In the years that followed, the spirit of independence and demands for political freedom started spreading across the country, and following the successes of the Civil Disobedience and the Quit India movements, the INC, the Muslim League and the British government realised they had to come to a decision about this state of affairs. In 1946, after years of political wrangling, all three agreed on a proposal to partition the Indian subcontinent on religious grounds into the independent nations of India and Pakistan. Such a momentous decision was incomprehensible to ordinary citizens, especially since the INC had stood for Hindu-Muslim unity since its inception. In order to rationalise its role in the partition, the INC tried to shift the blame onto Muhammad Ali Jinnah, the leader of the Muslim League, while the Muslim League held the INC responsible for the decision. As tension between Hindus and Muslims boiled over into violent confrontations all across the subcontinent, the euphoria of political independence from British colonial rule quickly dissipated and the subcontinent witnessed one of the most horrific genocides chronicled in human history. As Priyamvada Gopal points out:

> Over ten million ordinary people – Sikhs, Hindus, and Muslims – were dislocated from their homes and became refugees, at least a million were killed in retaliatory violence undertaken by members of all three communities while thousands of women were abducted, raped, and in many instances, forced to commit suicide to preserve the 'honor' of their communities. Suddenly,

> religious identity seemed to take precedence over all other ways of being and relating to each other. (69)

Contrary to Nehru's claims that the country had found a voice, the horrific carnage and trauma of Partition seemed to stun the intelligentsia into a stupor; very little writing about the partition happened during that period. As Josna Rege points out:

> The experience was too disillusioning, too incomprehensible. For this reason most of the literary outpourings, especially those in the immediate aftermath by people who lived in regions directly affected, were expressions of grief that attempted to relive and thereby relieve the trauma and violence through personal memory, but could account for the Partition only in terms of sin and madness. (82)

And even those accounts were not that many. One of the only notable voices at this time was that of Saadat Hasan Manto (1912–1955). Manto's "Siyah Hashiye" ("Black Margins") was published in October 1948 after he was forced to flee to Lahore, Pakistan. Manto said of his writing: "If you are not familiar with the age in which we live, read my stories. If you cannot endure my stories, it means that this age is unbearable" (53). M. Asaduddin points out: "The areas of human experience and the liminal spaces that he focused on relentlessly, shocked people out of their complacency into a new awareness of reality around them. This is particularly true in the context of his writings about the partition of India" (9). Manto's graphic detailing of Partition violence in stories like "Jelly", "Warning" and "Modesty" were heart wrenching, but did not garner much of an audience because both India and Pakistan, in those post-Independence years, were insistent on creating a national and dominant narrative of the partition which was heavily invested in blaming each other and holding the other accountable for the atrocities. Manto's collection was branded "reactionary" in Pakistan, where he had been forced to relocate from his native

Bombay. His even more controversial story called "Thanda Gosht" ("Cold Flesh") actually got him indicted by the Pakistani judicial system. The story is about a protagonist called Ishwar Singh who returns from the partition carnage to realise that he is unable to make love to his mistress. She predictably suspects him of being unfaithful and in a jealous rage, stabs him with his own dagger. On the verge of death from his stab wounds, Ishwar Singh reveals that during the rampant Partition killings, he had tried to rape a Muslim girl only to find her already dead. This story did not go down well with either the Muslim or Sikh communities, and even though Manto was let off by the court, he admitted that he felt displaced and unmoored, and his writings were a reflection of his despair and fatalism – "Despite my best efforts, I could not dissociate India from Pakistan and Pakistan from India." He asked poignantly: "Now that we were free, had subjection ceased to exist? Who would be our slaves? Thousands of Hindus and Muslims were dying all around us. Why were they dying?" (Sethi). Writers across the subcontinent were unable to wrestle with the topic of Partition till the 1980s, when new narratives mostly written in English finally began to emerge. Two exceptions to this were Khushwant Singh's *Train to Pakistan* (1956), and Attia Hosain's *Sunlight on a Broken Column* (1961). Both narratives evocatively describe the attempt made by the two nation-states to come to terms with the unprecedented brutality of Partition and the new political reality that followed. In Singh's novel, the trains running by the village of Mano Majra in Punjab – transporting passengers culled and grouped together based on their religious affiliations – become a symbol of Partition violence. These trains, often stopped so that passengers are butchered and left as a grizzly cargo of corpses, haunt the once sleepy village of Mano Majra so that whenever flames light up the night sky, the "village was stilled in a deathly silence. No one asked anyone else what the odor was. They all knew. They had known it all along" (Singh

84). Scenes of graphic violence also permeate the pages of Bapsi Sidhwa's novel, *Ice-Candy Man* (1988), made into a film called *1947: Earth* by Deepa Mehta. The novel is narrated from the point of view of a young Parsi girl, Lenny, who lives an idyllic life in Lahore in the 1940s till everything is shattered by the horrors of Partition. The young girl is unwittingly forced to play a role in the rape and eventual prostitution of her beloved Hindu ayah through the machinations of the ice-candy man, a Muslim. Priyamvada Gopal reminds us that even though it was written almost forty years after Partition, Sidhwa's novel is "a powerful rendition of the experience of Partition for a sheltered upper-class child and reminds us that not all children were afforded the luxury of innocence" (76). The haunting partition narratives that emerge almost four decades after the actual event not only remind us of its traumatic legacy, but also indicate that it is only after a significant lapse of time that any fictional representation of one of the most significant events of the subcontinent's history is at all possible.

ALIENATION AND ESTRANGEMENT IN POSTCOLONIAL INDIAN NOVELS

It is worth noting that Jawaharlal Nehru's first invocation to the nation was well-crafted and delivered in English, presumably to immediately establish India on the world stage. Nonetheless, there was considerable uneasiness about writing in the coloniser's language in the first two decades following independence. A lot of postcolonial writers seemed to feel that writing in English would be deemed unpatriotic in view of the recent hard-earned freedom from their oppressors. Still, the voices that dominated the 1930s and 1940s Indian English literary scene like Mulk Raj Anand, R. K. Narayan and Raja Rao continued to write in a post-colonial setting. But in place of the social realist novels of their earlier years, a lot of their later novels deal with a profound sense of alienation and a distaste for modern life. Both of Mulk Raj Anand's post-independence novels, *Seven Summers* (1951), and *The Private Life of an Indian Prince* (1953), are semi-autobiographical, pensive narratives, radically different from his earlier much celebrated novels like *Untouchable* (1935), and *Coolie* (1936). Raja Rao's first post-independence novel *The Serpent and the Rope* (1960) is not even located in India but is more of a global narrative spread across India and Europe. Even though R. K. Narayan's *Waiting for the Mahatma* (1955) does deal with the nationalist struggle and Mahatma Gandhi's assassination, it is also a story about deferred desire and "the making of a reluctant citizen of a new India" (Rege 83). Narayan's celebrated novel *The Guide* (1958), is another tale of personal and spiritual crisis – the helplessness of the individual when pitted against the manifest power of his destiny. This is not to suggest that this feeling of estrangement in postcolonial Indian writing is restricted exclusively to English language writing. While introducing a collection of Hindi short fiction from the 1960s, Gordon Roadarmel writes that in the stories "Major religious, social, and political problems are not of primary concern. Instead, these writers tend to turn inward, portraying loneliness and estrangement, social disruption, urban anonymity, bureaucratic indifference, and a general loss or absence of individual identity" (2–3).[1]

Post-colonial narratives by women writers like Attia Hosain, Nayantara Sahgal, Kamala Markandaya and Anita Desai are rich social documents that offer glimpses into the role of postcolonial women amidst changing notions of family and community. But even in these narratives, the theme of estrangement is omnipresent. Hosain's novel *Sunlight on a Broken Column* is narrated by Laila, a young orphan raised by her uncle and aunt in north India before the momentous events of 1935 to 1947 disrupt their idyllic life. The novel offers an insight into the life of young women growing up in an upper-class Muslim household before the calm domestic atmosphere of the feudal household is shattered by the new political reality. Gopal suggests that writing in the 1960s, "Hosain is able to reflect back on Partition with the benefit of some temporal distance while conveying the remembered immediacy of the personal and political turmoil that marked the division of the subcontinent" (Gopal 143). Sahgal's *Rich Like Us* (1985), is set during the Emergency of 1975 instituted by the then prime minister Indira Gandhi, but the novel also explores the fate of women within conventional marriages and the gradual alienation and slow erosion of values in both domestic and public spheres. Others like Kamala Markandaya in *The Nowhere Man* (1972), and Anita Desai in *Bye Bye Blackbird* (1969), have shifted their attention to the plight of Indians outside the subcontinent. Both their novels are revealing accounts of the racial prejudice and discrimination faced by Indian immigrants in Britain in the second half of the twentieth century, something they had intimate knowledge of given their status as diasporic women.

Remaking the English language in Salman Rushdie's *Midnight's Children*

Some Indian literary critics argued that in the post-independence age, a conscious effort had to be made to reclaim the glorious – albeit Hindu – past, and that meant distancing oneself from the use of the coloniser's language. Writers, including Anita Desai sought to distance themselves from insular views about Indian writing. In a 1989 talk, Desai emphatically asserts "the need to apologize for and defend writing in a particular language can drive a writer into an artistically fatal isolation" (Rege 89). Ironically, Desai seems to be asking for the same kind of artistic freedom that Raja Rao had asked for almost five decades ago. In the foreword to his celebrated *Kanthapura* (1939), Rao speaks of the difficulty of conveying the Indian ethos in the

English language. "One has to convey in a language that is not one's own the spirit that is one's own" (vii). At the same time, he emphasises the expansive nature of the English language and urges re-making it in the same way that the Irish and American have done: "We cannot write like the English. We should not. We cannot write only as Indians. We have grown to look at the large world as part of us . . . The tempo of Indian life must be infused into our English expression, even as the tempo of American or Irish life has gone into the making of theirs" (vii). This controversy about the use of the English language in literary representations of postcolonial India continued well into the 1980s and was invoked with renewed vigour with the publication and ground-breaking success of Salman Rushdie's 1981 novel *Midnight's Children*.

In her first novel, *A Time to be Happy* (1958), Nayantara Sahgal's protagonist Sanad captures the identity crisis of the English-educated urban Indian elite. "I don't belong entirely to India. I can't. My education, my upbringing, and my sense of values have all combined to make me unIndian . . . . Of course there can be no question of my belonging to any other country" (Gandhi 226). Saleem Sinai, Rushdie's protagonist in *Midnight's Children*, becomes the archetypal symbol of alienation in modern postcolonial society; the fragmented individual, caught in a time warp, belonging everywhere and nowhere. Coming at a time when the Indian literary scene was literally languishing, Rushdie's novel was instrumental in reshaping the literary landscape of postcolonial India by diving headlong into the partition narrative and subsequently tracing the growth of a very different kind of post-independence national consciousness. First published in 1981, *Midnight's Children* went on to win the prestigious Booker Prize and subsequently the Booker of Bookers Prize in 1993 and several other literary prizes. The novel, a classic example of "magic realist" literature, is believed to have been influenced by Gabriel Garcia Marquez's *One*

Hundred Years of Solitude (1967) and G. V. Desani's *All about H. Hatterr* (1948). At once a bildungsroman and a political satire, it is narrated by Rushdie's protagonist, Saleem Sinai, one of the thousand-and-one infants born at the exact stroke of midnight on 15 August 1947. In the opening page itself, Saleem famously declares that he "had been mysteriously handcuffed to history, my destinies indissolubly chained to those of my country. For the next three decades, there was to be no escape" (*Midnight's Children* 3). In the novel, the realms of the individual and the nation, the personal and the political, the real and the fictional relentlessly collide to not only tell the story of three generations of Saleem's family, but also to offer a brilliant tapestry of post-independence India, struggling to find its identity. Rushdie configures the individual self/nation dynamic in interesting ways; he resists the notion of a monolithic identity for both and instead advocates the embracing of a chaotic, multifaceted existence. Saleem insists, "I have been a swallower of lives; and to know me, just the one of me, you'll have to swallow the lot as well. Consumed multitudes are jostling and shoving inside me" (4). Even as he disintegrates under the burden of history, he attempts to piece together an epic saga of his family against the backdrop of the emergence of a new nation state. He explains: "I must work faster than Scheherazade, if I am up to end up meaning – yes, meaning – something. I admit it: above all things, I fear absurdity" (4). Saleem's journey flashes back to the story of his grandparents Aadam Aziz and Naseem Ghani in Kashmir and then chronicles the story of his mother Mumtaz/Amina who marries Ahmed Sinai and is forced to flee to Bombay during the years of the freedom movement. On the event of his auspicious birth in Dr Narlikar's Nursing Home, Saleem receives a congratulatory letter from Prime Minister Nehru himself, cementing his destiny with that of the newly born nation. "Dear Baby Saleem, My belated congratulations on the happy accident of your moment of birth! You are the newest bearer of that ancient face of India which is also eternally young. We shall be watching over your life with the closest attention; it will be, in a sense, the mirror of our own" (139). It is Saleem and the other "children of midnight" who can write the history of the new nation, so to speak, and Saleem, a little hesitant as first, gradually embraces his special role. But halfway through the narrative, Saleem's identity is called into question as his upper middle-class privileged life is revealed to be not his at all. Saleem happens to be the illegitimate son of the Englishman William Methwold, switched at birth by his nanny Mary Pereira with Ahmed and Amina's real son Shiva, another child with special powers like that of Saleem. Shiva, in a twist of fate, languishes on the streets of Bombay. Padma, Saleem's loyal companion and occasional interlocutor, is horrified that Saleem turns out to be an impostor, and an Anglo-Indian one at that, but Saleem assures her that when the truth was discovered, it made no difference at all to his family because "in a kind of collective failure of imagination, we learned that we simply could not think our way out of our pasts" (131). As the narrative follows the "children of midnight", especially Saleem, Shiva and Parvati-the-Witch, through their life amidst the monumental historical events shaping the country – like the Indo-China war of 1965, the Indo-Pakistan war of 1971 and especially the dark years of Emergency imposed by Prime Minister Indira Gandhi (referred to as "the Widow" in the novel) – these so-called arbiters of the nation's destiny are revealed to be impotent and powerless in the face of state tyranny, and the initial euphoria and optimism promised by independence appears to be short-lived. But in spite of being keenly aware of his powerlessness and eventual demise, Saleem does not seem to give in to fatalism or disillusionment, contrary to the rhetoric of earlier Partition narratives. As he tells us in the final lines of the novel, "It is the privilege and the curse of midnight's children to be both masters and victims of their times, to forsake privacy and be sucked into the annihilating whirlpool of the multitudes, and to be unable to live or die in peace" (533).

Midnight's Children resists being labelled as a historical novel; instead the novel ponders the malleability of historical truth and the transience of cultural memory in the refashioning of postcolonial national identity. Rushdie himself prefers labelling the novel as a political novel rather than a historical one and maintains that it is simply an individual's version of living through momentous historical events; as such, historical accuracy or the search for authenticity in the novel is counterproductive. The individual version of history, Saleem's in this case, is revealed to be both coherent and untenable at the same time, and Saleem himself is only too aware of it.

> Sometimes, in the pickles' version of history, Saleem appears to have known too little; at other times, too much . . . yes, I should revise and revise, improve and improve; but there is neither the time nor the energy. I am obliged to offer no more than this stubborn sentence: It happened that way because that's how it happened. (530)

In the re-imagination of a new nation, a collection of individual subjective experiences of history (even though fraught with inconsistencies and open to criticism and contradictions) seems to be what is necessary rather than an earlier collective "nationalist" identity. Josna Rege explains, "The individual must either acquiesce to history's grand narratives or be destroyed – swept aside, or crushed underfoot. Rushdie's protagonist Saleem Sinai must also eventually succumb to the relentless march of History, but not before he tells his own story on his own terms" (112).

Rushdie's embracing of this multiplicity of identity and his playful "chutnification" (*Midnight's Children* 530) of language in *Midnight's Children* seemed to open up new vistas for Indian English writers both in the subcontinent and in the diaspora who had long struggled with accusations of inauthenticity levelled against them. In his famous essay "Imaginary Homelands", Rushdie explains the conundrum that Indian English writers face regarding their use of the English language: "Many have referred to the argument about the appropriateness of this language to Indian themes . . . . We can't simply use the language in the way the British did; that it needs remaking for our own purposes . . . . To conquer English may be to complete the process of making ourselves free" (*Imaginary Homelands* 17). Rushdie's words granted a much-needed sense of legitimacy to the use of the language, but it also re-inaugurated a vigorous debate about postcolonial novels and cultural authenticity that continues even today.

Noted Indian critic Makarand Paranjape talks about the enormous influence the Western publishing industry has on postcolonial writing.

> Western media and publishing conglomerates exercise tremendous power over the production and dissemination of images about the Third World. These images not only determine how we are viewed by them, but also how we come to view ourselves. It is not that we are totally helpless or lack the agency to construct our own identities. But the fact is that the strength of these images is so overpowering that few of us can really resist the onslaught. (235)

Indian writers writing in English, especially diasporic writers, become the object of Paranjape's ire as he alleges:

> . . . the positions of such diasporics is akin to that of African middlemen who sold slaves to the white traders. A Naipaul or Ved Mehta comes to India, invades our privacy, interviews us, makes us objects of analysis, captures our reality, then makes a marketable product out of it. When we don't like what he says about us or wish to speak up for ourselves, no one over there is prepared to listen. (239)

According to these critics, women writers are especially guilty of gross misrepresentations by their portrayal of promiscuous men and sexually repressed women as well as tongue-in-cheek presentations of specific Indian traditions like arranged marriage. Paranjape goes on to argue that such representations "may contribute to a continuing 'colonisation' of the Indian psyche by pandering to Western market tastes which see India in a negative light" (238). Paranjape indicts western publishing houses that completely disregard vernacular literature or native literature in translation, which are less popular in the west, and are instead actively involved in creating and preserving an orientalised image of South Asia. But at the same time, critics like Paranjape themselves are often guilty of essentialising Indian writing in English by ignoring the multiplicity of voices that have emerged in the last couple of decades, some of which I will discuss in more detail in the conclusion to this book.

THE TRAUMATIC COLONIAL LEGACY IN POSTCOLONIAL AFRICA

The struggle for authenticity remains a concern in postcolonial African writing as African writers raced to reclaim their agency after the rapid decolonisation that happened in little over two decades. But just like European colonial expansion was erratic and often violent, decolonisation in most of the Sub-Saharan African countries was anything but a smooth transition to independence. In order to understand the trajectory of post-colonial African literature, it is also vital to understand the immense importance that freedom from colonial rule and independent nationhood held for the African people. When Ghana gained its independence on 6 March 1957, Kwame Nkrumah, the first president of independent Ghana, was jubilant. Like Nehru, he urged his countrymen to dream of the untold possibilities that freedom from colonial rule would bring.

> Today, from now on, there is a new African in the world and that new African is ready to fight his own battle and show that the black man is after all capable of managing his own affairs. We are going to demonstrate to the world, to the other nations, young as we are, that we are prepared to lay our own foundation. (Lazarus 1)

This optimism of Nkrumah's speech was captured by one of the main characters in Ayi Kwei Armah's novel, *The Beautyful Ones are Not Yet Born*. "We were ready here for big and beautiful things . . . . The promise was so beautiful. Even those who were too young to understand it all knew that at last something good was being born. It was there. We were not deceived about that . . . . The beauty was in the waking of the powerless" (Armah 84). But this was quickly replaced by disillusionment and despair as most of the African countries in the post-colonial era witnessed severe inter-ethnic conflicts, brutal dictatorial regimes and mass genocides, mostly as a result of widespread economic and social inequalities that had its roots in divisive colonial policy.

Like in Asia, European colonial powers in Africa had maintained their dominance through the policy of "divide and rule," thus playing off the numerous ethnic groups against one another. The Belgians, for instance, encouraged dissension between the minority Tutsis and the majority Hutus by giving the Tutsis more administrative power during their colonial rule in Rwanda. The animosity between these two ethnic groups was so severe that it continued well after independence and culminated in one of the most horrific civil wars and genocides in modern history; over eight hundred thousand people perished in this conflict. The British ruled the predominantly Arab north Sudan and primarily black South Sudan as separate entities, only to combine them when Sudan acquired its independence in 1956. This quite predictably led to a protracted civil war that finally led to the secession and independence of South Sudan in 2011. Some of these conflicts continue even today with countries like Nigeria, Sierra Leone, the Democratic Republic of Congo and the Central African Republic still plagued by political unrest and civil wars. As Neil Lazarus points out, instead of the unity and prosperity that Nkrumah, Thiong'o and others had fervently desired, independence in most cases brought just the opposite – "fragmentation, weakness and social violence . . . . Independence . . . has paradoxically borne witness to stagnation, elitism, and class domination, and to the intensifying structural dependence – economic, political, cultural and ideological – of Africa upon the imperial Western powers" (3).

While reflecting on post-colonial nation formation in Africa, some critics have pointed out that the widespread sense of fatalism in the 1960s was a result of short-sightedness on the part of the Africans, who assumed that independence and the mere transfer of power from the colonisers itself would magically usher in much-awaited freedom and economic and social equality. But such optimism was bound to be fraught with difficulties as political leaders like Julius Nyerere, Tanzania's first prime minister, seemed to suggest as he reflected on the state of affairs in Africa, almost fifteen years after Tanzania gained independence – "I know that we were right in our united demand for freedom from colonial rule . . . Our mistake was not in our demand for freedom; it was in the assumption that freedom – real freedom – would necessarily and with little trouble follow liberation from alien rule" (248–249).[2] Others, like historian Basil Davidson, have suggested that the new African leaders inherited a deeply divided society and it was naïve to expect that this would be an easy or quick fix – "what the new governments were obliged to take over . . . was not a prosperous colonial business, but in many ways, a profound colonial crisis" (182). When Nkrumah took charge of an independent Ghana, he had warned his supporters of the necessity of moral courage given that "bribery and corruption, both moral and factual, have eaten into the whole fabric of our society and these must be stamped out if we are to achieve any progress" (Davidson 163). Still others like Aijaz Ahmad and Tamara Sivanandan have suggested the corrupt indigenous elites who inherited power after decolonisation were often responsible for the widespread dissension that followed. Because of their privileged class position and Western-educated backgrounds, these rulers remained enslaved to a colonial mentality of cultural superiority, albeit in an indigenous form. "These rulers weren't necessarily conscious agents of capitalism from the beginning; they constituted rather a political elite which used state power in order to acquire vast wealth at the expense of the mass of the population, and to turn themselves into a propertied class" (Sivanandan 57). As a result, such rulers often failed to understand the very real social inequalities that plagued their nations, and sometimes even if they did, they hardly tried to alleviate those problems or extend the democratic principles promised by revolutionary leaders during the freedom struggles. In fact, by the late 1960s, a lot of African nations were under some kind of autocratic rule under the pretence that quelling opposition or any kind of localised resistance was necessary for economic development and national advancement. Raymond Betts points out that "some 75 coups d'etat, mostly military in nature, occurred in the former colonial world in the first three decades of independence" (67), notably in Nigeria, Ghana, Zaire, Algeria and even countries like Indonesia and the Philippines. And as we have seen before, through analysis of Rushdie's text, even the bustling Indian democracy went through a gag period with Indira Gandhi's imposition of the Emergency in the 1970s. It is important to underscore that amidst this tumultuous political climate, postcolonial African writers were heavily invested in throwing off the yoke of silence imposed on them by their colonial rulers and emerge as the masters of their own narrative. So even as some writers like Ayi Kwei Armah acknowledged the cynicism and despair resulting from ineffectual post-colonial governance, others like Ngũgĩ wa Thiong'o recognised that they needed to move beyond this cynicism and actively confront the neo-colonialist ideology of the ruling elites if any kind of progress at the level of the masses was to be achieved. In his two best known works, *Black Skins, White Masks* and *The Wretched of the Earth*, Frantz Fanon repeatedly urged his fellow Algerians to not only be part of the active nationalist struggle, but also to go beyond that to interrogate the complex structures of colonial hegemony. With the poignant question "What does the black man want?" (*Black Skin, White Masks* 8), he insisted that colonised subjects must resist and overthrow, albeit violently, the feelings of racial inferiority that they had internalised during decades of colonial domination. As Elleke Boehmer points out:

> Fanon argued that struggle against the colonizer should take as its aims not only complete national autonomy but the transformation of social and political consciousness. The colonized had to 'insult' and 'vomit up' the white man's values. Culture, therefore, was chosen by Fanon, amongst others, as a central area of transformation, the site where psychological and spiritual freedoms might be won. (Boehmer 183)

Heeding Fanon's call, writers across Africa, Asia and the Caribbean started to use their writing as a tool to urge radical cultural transformation and indirectly aid the freedom struggle and nation formation. Writers like Wole Soyinka, Ngũgĩ wa Thiong'o and Caryl Phillips took this role of the writer very seriously as they tried to investigate the legacy of colonialism but also pondered how to decolonise and revitalise a vibrant African culture. "Writers, therefore, were invoked as the beacons, soothsayers, and seers of political movements. It was seen as a writer's role to re-interpret the world, to grasp the initiative in self-definition" (Boehmer 184). Thus Thiong'o reiterated in multiple essays like "Barrel of a Pen" (1983), that "the pen might do the work of the gun; a play might pack the power of a hand grenade" (Boehmer 184), while Caryl Phillips insisted in *The European Tribe* (1987) that a writer "can infuse a people with a sense of their own unique identity and spiritually kindle the fire of resistance" (Boehmer 185). Some African literary scholars have suggested that imperialism doesn't have any direct bearing on African literature and dismissed such writing as political scholarship, an assertion that writers like Thiong'o vehemently dismiss. In his essay on "The Role of the Scholar in the Development of African Literatures", he points out, "Imperialism, both in its colonial and neo-colonial stages, is the one force that affects *everything* in Africa – politics, economics, culture, absolutely every aspect of human life. African literature itself has grown and developed in response to imperialism" (*Moving the Centre* 83).

The most recognised African writers like Chinua Achebe, Wole Soyinka, Ngũgĩ wa Thiong'o, Ayi Kwei Armah and Ama Ata Aidoo set out to navigate the traumatic legacies of colonialism and figure out how to revitalise a stagnant African culture. Books like Camara Laye's *The African Child* (1954), Achebe's *Things Fall Apart* (1958), Soyinka's *Ake: The Years of Childhood* (1981), and Ama Ata Aidoo's *Our Sister Killjoy* (1977) were heavily invested in this project. But fiction wasn't simply the chosen medium through which these African writers negotiated their postcolonial identity. Autobiographies like Peter Abraham's *Tell Freedom* (1954), essay collections like Chinua Achebe's *Morning Yet on Creation Day* (1975) and *Home and Exile* (2000), and Ngũgĩ wa Thiong'o's *Decolonising the Mind: The Politics of Language in African Literature* (1986), and *Moving the Centre: The Struggle for Cultural Freedoms* (1993), are some of the most pioneering texts that have fundamentally shaped the field of postcolonial criticism. In these essays, writers like Achebe and Thiong'o traverse a wide array of topics ranging from the problems with colonialist criticism and racism in literature to linguistic imperialism and the role of African scholars and writers in a colonial, postcolonial and increasingly neo-colonial world. Thiong'o in fact believes that the African writer has gone through three decisive decades: "the age of the anti-colonial struggle; the age of independence; and the age of neo-colonialism" (*Moving the Centre* 60). This revitalisation of postcolonial African culture often crystallised around debates over the use of the coloniser's language in literary representations of postcolonial African culture.

African literature in its entirety is composed of both oral and written literature in languages as varied as Igbo, Kikuyu, Hausa, Somali, Swahili as well as Arab and French, depending on the colonial legacy of a particular nation, and Thiong'o, among others, felt that if things were to be seen from an African perspective, it was vital that literary representations be primarily in an African language and not in that of the former coloniser. In his essay he explains:

> During the colonial stage of Western imperialism in Africa, African languages were suppressed and European languages were deliberately given a status that made them the inevitable vehicle of African peoples' self-definition . . . these language may be the official languages in Africa today but they are not the languages of the majority of people inhabiting Africa. Yet, African writers feel it necessary and natural to write in European languages about African peasants and workers. (*Moving the Centre* 84)

So in October 1968, he and two of his other colleagues, Taban Lo Liyong and Henry Owuor-Anyumba proposed that a new department of African Literatures and Languages replace the English Department at the University of Nairobi. The main purpose of this ambitious endeavour was clear: years of European education had colonised the African mind to the extent that African scholars believed writing in an African language was a non-normative act. "This topsy-turvy vision has been convenient for 'African' literature scholars who have been spared the necessity of having to learn African languages in order to come to terms with the literature produced and the realities embodied in those languages" (*Moving the Centre* 84). If the continent was to reclaim its identity and see things from a distinctly African perspective, it had to be done through one of the native African languages, an argument that Thiong'o later makes in his book *Decolonising the Mind* (1986). Such a move towards the vernacular was hardly new in the postcolonial context – Aimé Césaire had talked about a similar move through his description of "negritude", and Raja Rao had mentioned this in the Indian context. But Africa's other literary giant, Chinua Achebe, while committed to the literary nationalism espoused by Thiong'o, disagreed with him on the use of English. Like Rushdie, Achebe argued that in order to make postcolonial African literature accessible and widely available to a larger audience, it was imperative that some writing be in English because that was the only common idiom among a lot of the African nations. Maybe because of this argument or other unspecified reasons, a large chunk of African vernacular literature is still unavailable or inaccessible to us and so the following section is restricted to the analysis of some of the well-known African novels written in English. It is also important to note that in order to understand the development of modern African literature, attention must be paid to the processes by which the coloniser's language has been largely appropriated by African writers, so much so that some of these languages have effectively become African languages in the same way that English is now the lingua franca in the Indian subcontinent. As Achebe claims in "English and the African Writer" (1965), "I feel that the English language will be able to carry the weight of my African experience. But it will have to be a new English, still in full communion with its ancestral home, but altered to suit its new African surroundings" (349).

THE POSTCOLONIAL AFRICAN NOVELS OF CHINUA ACHEBE, AMA ATA AIDOO AND CHIMAMANDA ADICHIE

As we have seen from the discussion of Joseph Conrad's *Heart of Darkness* in an earlier chapter, African characters in a narrative set in the Congo and ostensibly about Africa don't have a voice, prompting Chinua Achebe, one of the most well-known African writers, to write a trenchant critique of racism in the novel. Yet, in his "English and the African Writer", Achebe admits that Nigeria as it exists today would never have come into existence without British colonial intervention, but is quick to point out that didn't mean the inhabitants of Nigeria were British inventions as well (344). He insists: "The fact remains that Nigeria was created by the British – for their own ends. Let us give the devil his due: colonialism in Africa disrupted many things, but it did create big political units where there was small, scattered ones before" (344), thus emphasising Nigeria's inalienable colonial legacy. Similar to the Indian context, Achebe realises that English-language writers like him are caught in a double bind, trying to capture the African ethos in a language not their own and constantly facing accusations of inauthenticity. But as he explains in another essay "African Literature as Restoration of Celebration", similar to Soyinka's representation of his colonial education in *Ake* (1981), the colonial educational apparatus that causes this split identity is also, paradoxically, responsible for inspiring him to find his own voice.

> I went to a good school modelled on British public schools. I read lots of English books there. I read *Treasure Island* and *Gulliver's Travels* and *Prisoner of Zenda* . . . I also encountered

> Ryder Haggard and John Buchan and the rest, and their 'African' books.
>
> I did not see myself as an African to begin with. I took sides with the white man against the savages . . . The white man was good and reasonable and intelligent and courageous. The savages arrayed against him were sinister and stupid or, at the most, cunning. I hated their guts.
>
> But a time came when I reached the appropriate age and realized that these writers had pulled a fast one on me! I was not on Marlowe's boat steaming up the Congo in *Heart of Darkness*. I was one of those strange beings jumping up and down on the river bank, making horrid faces.
>
> That was when I said no, and realized that stories are not innocent; that they can be used to put you in the wrong crowd, in the party of the man who has come to dispossess you. (*Chinua Achebe: A Celebration* 7)

Achebe, like many of the upper middle-class intelligentsia in Africa and Asia educated in schools established by the colonisers, thus admits that he was also initially guilty of internalising English values and traditions. It is worth mentioning that other writers also address this issue. Rabindranath Tagore relentlessly satirises colonial subjects who bask in their acquired Englishness in a letter written during a visit to London in 1879.[3] Banerrji, a character in G.V. Desani's *All About H. Hatterr*, is reduced to a ridiculous extreme in his adulation of everything English, while Munoo, a character in Mulk Raj Anand's *Coolie*, is positive that the sun cannot burn down the house built by the English because "the sun never set on the British Empire" (Anand 147).[4]

Chinua Achebe also strongly believed in the role of the writer in liberation movements. In an edition of the *Times Literary Supplement*, he categorically asserts, 'Language is our tool, and language is the tool of politicians. We are like two sides in a very hostile game. And I think that the attempt to deceive with words is countered by the efforts of the writer to go behind the words, to show the meaning" (Gikandi 1). Moreover, Achebe was extremely irritated by the Anglo-Irishman Joyce Cary's much-celebrated novel, *Mister Johnson*, published in 1939. In his essay "My Home Under Imperial Fire", Achebe recounts being horrified when the *Time Magazine* of 20 October 1952 described the book as "the best novel ever written about Africa" (*Home and Exile* 22), when all it did was play on existing and bizarre stereotypes – that of a dying and decrepit land peopled by savages who needed to be civilised. For instance, the description of a native African town reads like this.

> Fada is the ordinary native town of Western Sudan. It has no beauty, convenience or health. It is a dwelling-place at one stage from the rabbit warren or the badger burrow; and not so cleanly kept as the latter. It is a pioneer settlement five or six hundred years old, built on its own rubbish heaps, without charm even of antiquity. Its squalor and its stinks are all new . . . All its mud walls are eaten as if by smallpox; half of the mats in any compound are always rotten. Poverty and ignorance, the absolute government of jealous savages, conservative as only the savage can be, have kept it at the first frontier of civilization. Its people would not know the change if time jumped back fifty thousand years. They live like mice or rats in a palace floor; all the magnificence and variety of the arts, the ideas, the learning and the battles of civilization go on over their heads and they do not even imagine them. (Cary 105)

As if the imagery of utter poverty and bestiality was not enough, the Africans themselves are described as grotesque figures, grinning and shrieking as they danced around naked. Quite understandably, it perturbed Achebe, and even though Cary's novel did not make him a writer, it did make him aware that his "home was under attack" (*Home and Exile* 38), and if the story about Africa needed to be told, it had to be told by an African himself. Achebe's novel *Things Fall Apart,* published in 1958, is his attempt to reclaim the African voice, and is widely regarded as having heralded a modern era in African literature. This is not to say that Achebe is the first noted African literary figure; Amos Tutuola's novel *The Palm-Wine Drinkard* was published in 1952 and received significant critical attention. But as Simon Gikandi argues, Achebe is possibly "the first of our writers to recognize the function of the novel not solely as a mode of representing reality, but one which had limitless possibilities of inventing a new national community" (3). In other words, Achebe chooses not to shy away from the colonial project; in fact, one of his main aims is to confront and expose the disastrous effects of colonialism, while simultaneously figuring out a way into the future through a radical re-fashioning of a modern African identity.

In postcolonial African literature, the village is often considered to be the locus around which a vision of African culture and life is constructed. *Things Fall Apart* is thus set in a traditional Igbo community of Umuofia and tells the story of the colonisation of this community through the figures of the traditionalist Okonkwo, his happy-go-lucky father Unoka, and Okonkwo's son Nwoye. Okonkwo, who was "well known throughout the nine villages and even beyond" and whose fame "rested on solid personal achievements" (*Things Fall Apart* 1), is presented at the outset as an embodiment of all the virtues of Igbo life – physical strength, ambition and competitiveness – as he quickly scales the ladder of social mobility with his acquisition of farmlands and becomes a venerable leader in the community. But his rapid rise is curbed when he accidentally kills a boy at a funeral and is exiled for seven years. When he returns to the village, he discovers that Umuofia has been taken over by colonisers who have seized all administrative power. He is troubled by the changes in the village ranging from the imposition of taxes to the conversion of many villagers to Christianity, and is disgusted by the complicity of the village elders with the colonisers. Hoping that his blatant rebellion will provoke a reaction and bring some of the villagers to sanity, he kills one of the court messengers, only to realise that the villagers would not back him up as they had let the rest of the messengers escape; they had "broken into tumult instead of action. He discerned fright in that tumult" (*Things Fall Apart* 176). The novel ends with Okonkwo hanging himself from a tree as the white Commissioner ponders writing this story in a book he plans to title "The Pacification of the Primitive Tribes of the lower Niger" (179). Critics have panned Achebe's apparent pandering to Western stereotypes with his portrayal of traditional Igbo life; they insisted that Achebe is clearly writing for a particular readership that believes Africa is full of blank spaces, waiting to be populated and redeemed by the white man. Contrary to that, as Eckhard Breitinger points out, Umuofia is "an ordered political, religious, cultural cosmos that is based on its own form of a social contract, that follows rational principles and employs standardized rules of conflict mediation" (53). It is the coming of the colonisers that throws everything into disarray and upsets the traditional value systems that have existed over generations. It even forces the archetypal traditionalist male figure of Okonkwo to flout tradition and commit suicide, an act decidedly against Igbo custom and "an offense against the Earth, and a man who commits it will not be buried by his clansmen" (*Things Fall Apart* 178). As Gikandi explains, by placing Okonkwo's narrative against the narrative of his community, Achebe manages to disrupt both dominant discourses – first that "The African has no character because he or she exists solely as the projection of European desire" (27) and second, "the African has no history" (27).[5]

In his introduction to *Things Fall Apart*, Kwame Anthony Appiah mentions that Achebe is acutely aware of the social role of writers and often, in interviews, asserts that his mission is to help his fellow Africans come to terms with their traumatic colonial past and "to escape from those many problems in contemporary African life whose roots can be traced back to the 'moment when we lost our initiative to other people, to colonizers'"(*Things Fall Apart* xi). In the face of the multitude of conflicts plaguing postcolonial Nigeria, including the persecution of writers like Ken Saro-Wiwa and Chris Abani by Nigeria's dictatorial regime, Achebe's comments assume even more significance. Nigerian writer Chimamanda Adichie readily acknowledges Achebe's contribution to African writing and hails *Things Fall Apart* as the novel that gave her permission to write and made her realise that her story is worthy of being told. For the critics who are disillusioned by the political situation in Nigeria, in fact in postcolonial Africa in general, Ifeoma, one of Adichie's main characters in her first novel *Purple Hibiscus*, has some wise words:

> There are people . . . who think that we cannot rule ourselves because the few times we tried, we failed, as if all the others who rule themselves today got it right the first time. It is like telling a crawling baby who tries to walk, and then falls back on his buttocks, to stay there. As if the adults walking past him did not all crawl, once. (Adichie 301)

Even other celebrated African writers like Ama Ata Aidoo emphasise that *Things Fall Apart*, with its reconstruction and reaffirmation of African cultural identity, helped in her own artistic growth. In an interview about African writing, Aidoo says, "[W]hen I read *Things Fall Apart* I said, 'Oh, so? He can do this'" (Pieterese 26), that is, manage to retrieve some of Africa's former glory. That, in turn, spurred her own re-imagination of postcolonial African identity. But writers like Adichie, while acknowledging Achebe's role in bringing postcolonial African literature onto the world stage, are also quick to point out that the Nigeria presented in Achebe's novel is one that is more than a hundred years old, and the modern Nigeria, though still plagued by political uncertainty, has come a long way from the claustrophobic value systems clustered around African villages.

In fact, the conceptualisation of the modern African woman in urban areas provides a significant point of departure for some of the postcolonial African women writers like Ama Ata Aidoo, Nawal El-Saadawi, Buchi Emecheta, Tsitsi Dangarembga and Chimamanda Adichie, among others. Like their male counterparts, these women writers were also invested in recuperating some of Africa's lost glory following the battering from colonialism. But they were also equally motivated to interrogate and expose age-old cultural practices that severely circumscribed African women's lives. Such a move did not sit well with some male literary critics who believed this emergent feminism was being co-opted from the West and was inherently antithetical to the kind of African nationalism necessary to rebuild a postcolonial Africa. Critic Oladele Taiwo argued in his *Female Novelists of Modern Africa* that even though Ama Ata Aidoo was entitled to write about the female experience and put women at the centre of her novel *Our Sister Killjoy*, "It is an error to think that they can live a full life without men . . ." (11). Ugandan writer Taban lo Liyong alleged that he "suspect[ed] that feminism may destroy that which up to now has enabled Africa to withstand all the buffeting from other cultures" (Emecheta 183). But Aidoo, Adichie and other women writers have quickly pointed out that a complete political and social reconfiguration of African identity is virtually impossible if women's voices were deliberately silenced by these faux-nationalist arguments and point out that African women's struggle for more freedom was hardly a new or borrowed Western concept. In fact, in a 1992 article in *Dissent* magazine, Aidoo makes a forceful case for African feminism:

> When people ask me rather bluntly every now and then whether I am a feminist, I not only answer yes, but I go on to insist that every woman and every man should be a feminist – especially if they believe that Africans should take charge of our land, its wealth, our lives, and the burden of our own development.

> Because it is not possible to advocate independence for our continent without also believing that African women must have the best that the environment can offer. For some of us, this is the crucial element of our feminism. (323)

The Nigerian writer Adichie made a similar plea almost twenty years later in a TED talk titled "We Should All be Feminists" delivered to wide acclaim in December 2012 and later published as a book. Like Aidoo, she addresses the accusation that feminism is decidedly un-African – a post-colonial African construct – and emphatically asserts that she is a feminist, which in her definition is "a man or a woman who says, 'Yes, there's a problem with gender as it is today, and we must fix it, we must do better'"(*We Should All Be Feminists* 48). Both these women writers also engage actively with the question of feminism in their work.

Aidoo firmly believed that the "revolutionizing of our continent hinges on the woman question" (Allan 174). Born to a politically active family in Ghana in 1940, Aidoo was made aware of the importance of education for women from a very young age. In her essay "To be a Woman", which can easily be read as a manifesto for African feminism, Aidoo credits her father with helping her develop some of her revolutionary ideas and political fervour. "It was from my father I first heard the rather famous quotation from Dr Kwegir Aggrey: 'If you educate a man, you educate an individual. If you educate a woman, you educate a nation'" (Allan 191). Her commitment to women's education, autonomy and consequently to social change, is apparent in all her major works, including *The Dilemma of a Ghost* (1965), *Our Sister Killjoy* (1977), and *Changes: A Love Story* (1991). *Changes*, which won the 1992 Commonwealth Prize for Literature in Africa, is often hailed as the novel which inaugurated a new tradition of women's writing in Africa. Set in Accra, the novel almost reads like a bildungsroman as it follows a female protagonist, the college-educated, career-minded Esi

Sekyi, and her friend Opokuya Dakwa, as they navigate their need for financial independence along with their roles as wives and mothers within the traditional value-systems that still threaten to cripple women's mobility. Right at the beginning of the novel, Esi, with her Master's Degree in Statistics, her fulfilling job at the Department of Urban Statistics and her frequent travel to national and international conferences to Geneva, Rome, Lusaka and Lagos, is the epitome of the modern woman. But the novel immediately asks whether this modern identity can co-exist with Esi's African one, as her husband Oko wonders "Is Esi too an African woman? She not only is, but there are plenty of them around these days . . . these days . . . these days" (*Changes* 8). The "plenty" of other women emerges in the form of Esi's best friend, Opokuya Dakwa, a licensed nurse and midwife, and Fusena Kondey, the first wife of Esi's second husband Ali Kondey. Though these women have different trajectories in the narrative, their identity crisis primarily centres around marriage, motherhood and financial mobility. All three women are caught between their need for emotional and financial independence and the patriarchal powers that constantly threaten to destabilise that desire. Esi experiences this both in the public and private sphere. Her stuttering old car makes her the subject of cat calls on the streets of Accra, her office secretary's absence means that as a woman she is expected to take over her job responsibilities and help her male colleagues, and her feminist views often mean jeers from a predominantly male audience at conferences. This undermining continues at home. Esi refuses to play the traditional role of nurturer at home by putting her career over her duties as a wife and mother, and Oko, Esi's husband, instigated by friends who he says are laughing at him because he is "not behaving like a man" (8), rapes her in an act of unprovoked aggression. Undeterred by the words of her mother and grandmother who think she is making a mistake, Esi, convinced that her assault is an act of marital rape, divorces her husband, much to the chagrin of Oko's family. They are determined to get Oko married to "an unspoilt young woman, properly brought up, whose eyes have not jumped over her eyebrows with too much education and too much money of her own" (39). Given Esi's bravery and determination to rise above the victimisation that might have been brought on by her rape, Esi's second marriage to the rich, cosmopolitan travel agency owner, Ali Kondey, soon after her divorce, is disturbing to many readers. But it is worth noting that to Esi, fleeing her claustrophobic marriage, Ali's independent attitude is a welcome relief. The England-educated, married, suave Ali seems to initially be the perfect counterfoil to Oko's neediness, but the contrast becomes murky when Ali insists that Esi become his second wife. She is filled with apprehension as she sees the same pattern of patriarchal control re-emerging. When Esi asks Ali why he insists that she wear his ring, Ali claims "To let the rest of the male world know that she is bespoke" (91). Esi is not naïve about his intentions as she retorts, "That she has become occupied territory?" (91), to which Ali replies in the affirmative. Once this territorial control is established, and as Esi had anticipated, marriage changes things. Ali becomes more and more distant from Esi as he realises he is ill-equipped to navigate the challenges of polygamy and his primary loyalties still lie with his first wife, Fusena. Paradoxically, unlike her first marriage, the more Ali pulls away, the more Esi falls in love with him, which almost leads her to having a neurotic breakdown. But in the final pages of the book Esi draws on her innate independence and determination as she quickly realises that Ali's gift of a fancy car is little more than a bribe for her to maintain the sham that is their marriage. "She had known even before Ali actually said the words – that he had brought the car for her, and she had understood the gesture as a bribe. A very special bribe. But a bribe all the same – like all the other things he had been giving her. They were all meant to be substitutes for his presence" (147). Though she is completely "flabberwhelmed" – a Ghanaian neologism that combines "overwhelmed" and "flabbergasted" (149) – she chooses to remain married because to dissolve the marriage would simply be too much work. But it remains a faux-marriage, without expectations on either side, and if Opokuya heard any stories about Ali's womanising, she protected her friend from it. Esi chooses to keep Ali's expensive gift and sells her old rickety car to her friend Opokuya, who had long wanted it.

In the novel, cars become the site through which conflicts about women's mobility are played out. The bright, beautiful Fusena, Ali Kondey's first wife, is forced to abandon her promising career as a teacher to make way for Ali's flourishing one. Fusena is relegated to the role of nurturer to the couple's children; her career is limited to running a small business, and her two-door unpretentious vehicle is quite fit for these little runs. But Fusena always worries that her lack of education might one day drive Ali away, and her worst fears are confirmed when Ali tells her about his intentions to marry the college-educated divorcee, Esi. The first thing Fusena asks him "before the words were properly out of his mouth, 'She has a university degree?'" (*Changes* 99). Fusena had occasionally checked in on her husband at his office, just to make sure he was not having an affair, so this declaration catches her completely unaware and makes her explode with jealousy and anger. However, because of her social position, she is unable to express herself except through her actions and her car. Fusena immediately stomps out of her house, into her vehicle. Her "car screeched to life, and Fusena backed out so roughly, she nearly scraped one side of her husband's rather elegant and capacious chariot, and also nearly hit the family dog" (99). Though Fusena is such a crucial character in the narrative, she is not given much of a voice and remains restricted to eight short sentences, mostly after she hears the news of Ali's remarriage. But, as the critic Tuzyline Allan points out in the novel's afterword, "Fusena's silence, therefore, bespeaks not the absence of an inner life but rather her double isolation within the dominant society and, in particular, her own restrictive Muslim culture. She appears silent because she is 'not being heard'" (Allan 181). It is the same silence that Esi had worried about when Ali insisted on marriage, and even in spite of the isolation she feels at the end of the novel, she is able to resist it primarily because of her financial independence. Sissie, Aidoo's protagonist in *Our Sister Killjoy,* talks about this restrictive aspect of marriage. "Here . . . they let a girl grow up as she pleases until she is married. And then she is like any woman anywhere: in order for her man to be a man, she must not think, she must not talk" (*Our Sister Killjoy* 112). Fusena and Esi in this novel seem to embody Sissie's words.

Opokuya and her husband, Kubi, incessantly bicker about the one car they own, and one that Kubi insisted should be primarily used to serve his needs as a Civil Servant. Opokuya, a "good woman" (*Changes* 9) according to Oko, initially seems to be less discontented with traditional gender roles except when it came to the use of the car, which would have served her needs better as a full-time nurse and primary caregiver to the couple's four children. But even as Opokuya is uncertain of Esi's choices, her mistrust of Kubi is quite apparent in their conversations and in the final pages her apprehensions are legitimised when Kubi tries to force himself upon Esi, which she immediately resists primarily out of her loyalty to her old friend. Just as Opokuya tries to protect Esi by not telling her of her husband's infidelities, Esi too spares her dear friend any knowledge of this assault. But by selling her car to Opokuya, Esi gives her friend much-needed mobility. As Esi is determined to forge her own destiny without either man in her life, so can Opokuya symbolically, through her own vehicle. In fact the novel seems to offer the suggestion that strong female friendships are the only thing that can resist or combat male patriarchal oppression. As Allan points out, female bonding triumphs over heterosexual love in the novel. "Theirs [Esi and Opokuya] is the novel's preferred model of love, a strong, nonoppressive current of feeling that flows between two women. Both Ali's spasms of affection and Oko's domineering passion fail the test" (Allan 184).

Chimamanda Adichie's debut novel, *Purple Hibiscus* (2003), also presents female friendship and solidarity as a way of combating postcolonial patriarchal oppression. The Nigeria of Adichie's novel is far removed from that of Achebe's, but it is still a country fraught with political unrest and social inequality. Nigeria, like many other African countries like Sudan and Sierra Leone, had seen relentless political turmoil since its independence from Britain in 1960 with the bloody civil war (1967–1970) and the secession of the short-lived Republic of Biafra (the subject of Adichie's second novel). *Purple Hibiscus* is set in the 1990s when Nigeria was under the rule of the dictator Sani Abacha, who maintains his control over the country through repression and tyranny. Thiong'o offers more insight into the post-colonial bourgeoisie and the ruling elites who had not been able to dissociate themselves from the unequal power structures of colonialism.

> The African bourgeoisie that inherited the flag from the departing colonial powers was created within the cultural womb of imperialism . . . So even after they inherited the flag, their mental outlook, their attitudes towards their own societies, toward their own history, toward their own languages, toward everything national, tended to be foreign; they saw things through eyeglasses given to them by their European bourgeois mentors.
>
> As a consequence, the economic, political and cultural structures of colonialism have more or less remained intact. There has been no dismantling of the colonial state. The result has been the gradual political alienation of the ruling elite in these countries. And the way they have responded to this political alienation has

> been by repression. They have been making sure that all centres of democratic expression or opposition are crushed, for this is the only way they can maintain themselves in power. (*Moving the Centre* 84–85)

The novel is narrated through the point of view of fifteen-year-old Kambili Achike as she tries to navigate her identity in both private and public spheres. Kambili's father Eugene is a wealthy man, the owner of the newspaper *Standard* that is outspoken in its resistance against the oppressive dictatorial regime of General Big Oga. We are told that he "used the *Standard* to speak the truth even though it meant that the paper lost advertising" (*Purple Hibiscus* 5). Eugene had been graced with a human rights award from Amnesty World for standing up for freedom and free speech and is well respected in his parish because of his unlimited generosity to his parishioners. His title in the village is "omelora, The One Who Does for the Community" (56). Yet he is a tyrant at home, beating his wife to the point of her having multiple miscarriages and breaking his children's bones if they dared to defy him. Eugene is clearly meant to be an embodiment of Nigeria's traumatic colonial legacy, and he himself asserts that Christian missionaries irrevocably shaped his identity. As Julie Mullaney points out, "The damage to the body politic in postcolonial Nigeria mapped in Adichie's attention to state corruption, censorship and torture is mirrored in Eugene's tyrannical approach to family and both are tied in part to the forms of damage inculcated in colonial encounter" (55). Eugene becomes the archetypal "mimic man," the class of middlemen created by the British administrators to serve as interpreters between them and the natives. As we have seen earlier in the chapter, some of these native elites seized power in many African countries after decolonisation. Others, like Eugene, internalised the values of the coloniser and, because they lacked any real political authority in the face of dictatorial regimes, often morphed into tyrants and unleashed domestic violence as that was the only sphere in which they could assert any semblance of control. Eugene's actions show the disastrous effects of colonialism on the culture of the colonised, where European culture is privileged over indigenous religions and belief systems. Eugene forbids the use of the traditional Igbo language at home and insists that his children only speak English as that is the "civilized" language. He demands excellence in grades from Kambili and her brother Jaja, and prevents them from visiting his father Papa-Nnukwu because he is a heathen who insists on practicing his pagan religion as opposed to the strict Catholicism espoused by Eugene. "We had to sound civilized in public, he told us; we had to speak English. Papa's sister, Auntie Ifeoma, said once that Papa was too much of a colonial product. She had said this about Papa in a mild, forgiving way, as if it were not Papa's fault" (*Purple Hibiscus* 13).

Auntie Ifeoma, Eugene's sister and University professor, a widowed mother of three, provides the foil to Eugene's oppression and tyranny. When Jaja and Kambili go to stay with her in Nsukka for a few weeks, she tears up the schedule that Eugene had given them and urges them to be spontaneous and outspoken, even defiant, in their interactions with their cousins. Coming from a household in which they would only speak when spoken to, and that too in measured and hushed tones, Auntie Ifeoma's boisterous household opens up a whole new horizon for Kambili. "Laughter floated over my head. Words spurted from everyone, often not seeking and not getting any response. We always spoke with a purpose back home, especially at the table, but my cousins seemed to simply speak and speak and speak" (120). Ifeoma, like Eugene, practices Christianity, but her attitude to religion "represents the development of an inclusive set of beliefs and values empowered not endangered by its encounters with other cultures" (Mullaney 56). She points out to the young, impressionable Kambili that "Papa-Nnukwu was not a heathen but a traditionalist, that sometimes what was different was just as good as what was familiar, that when Papa-Nnukwu did his itu-nzu, his declaration of innocence, in the morning, it was the same as our saying the rosary" (*Purple Hibiscus* 166). They break into uplifting Igbo songs in the middle of the rosary and Kambili is bewildered by such unorthodoxy and openness, so very different to the restrictive and stifling lifestyle she is accustomed to. "Aunty Ifeoma prayed for the university, for the lecturers and administration, for Nigeria, and finally for peace and laughter today. As we made the sign of the cross, I looked up to seek out Jaja's face, to see if he, too, was bewildered that Aunty Ifeoma and her family prayed for, of all things, *laughter*" (127).

A visit to Aunty Ifeoma's church is even more startling. To Kambili, used to the strict sexist traditions of her father's parish, women with uncovered heads or wearing jeans was confounding. "Papa would be scandalized. A woman's hair must be covered in the house of god, and a woman must not wear a man's clothes, especially in the house of God, he would say" (240). Thus begins Kambili's emotional, spiritual and sexual awakening. Aided by her rambunctious cousin Amaka and Auntie Ifeoma's parish priest Father Amadi, Kambili emerges from a shy, frightened person into a young girl who does not hesitate to stand up for her own beliefs. At the beginning of the novel, Papa, angry at Jaja's defiance when he refuses to go to communion, throws a missal and breaks Mama's étagère of glass figurines. Kambili, as sorry as she was for her mother, couldn't bring herself to accuse her father. She tells us "I meant to say I am sorry Papa broke your figurines, but the words that came out were 'I'm sorry your figurines broke Mama'" (10). But later on, after she is relentlessly beaten up by Eugene for refusing to give up the portrait of Papa-Nnukwu that Amaka gave her, she admits to Amaka that it was indeed her father who was responsible for her being in the hospital: "'It was Uncle Eugene who did that to you, *okwia*?' she asked . . . 'Did Aunty Ifeoma tell you?' I asked. 'No, but I guessed so.' 'Yes. It was him,' I said, and then headed for the toilet. I did not turn to see Amaka's reaction'" (220). Kambili, who was initially flabbergasted that Jaja had told some of the stories of domestic violence to Auntie Ifeoma, incidents that were meant to stay within the high walls of Eugene's house, now hardly misses a beat in indicting her beloved father.

Like in Aidoo's novel, female bonding in *Purple Hibiscus* is at the core of the resistance to patriarchal oppression. While Ifeoma tries to empower Kambili and carefully manipulate tradition within the structure of the Church, Ifeoma's daughter Amaka is more radical in her approach and challenges the limits of the Church's adaptation to its African milieu. As Mullaney points out, Amaka's refusal to "observe those practices that continue to devalue Igbo culture, like the taking of an English confirmation name, is an indictment of the Church's extant failures to cherish women and Igbo culture equally" (57). Kambili and Amaka don't get along initially as Kambili believes that Amaka treats her as a unique specimen and is condescending. Kambili wishes that she "would not keep looking at me as if I were a strange laboratory animal to be explained and catalogued" (*Purple Hibiscus* 118). But she slowly gains the confidence to interact with Amaka, bond over the Igbo music of Fela and Osadebe and Onyeka that Amaka is fond of, and even confides in her, which culminates in her final confession in the hospital. Amaka, along with Father Amadi, becomes the main catalyst for Kambili's emotional growth even as Nsukka becomes the site of Kambili's radical change. In contrast to the pensive, fearful Kambili of the beginning of the novel, in the final pages we see a Kambili laughing loudly "above Fela's stringent singing . . . Because Nsukka could free something deep inside your belly that would rise up to your throat and come out as a freedom song. As laughter" (299).

Ifeoma's friendship with her brother's wife Beatrice is also one of the mainstays of the novel. Ifeoma is not unaware of the treatment meted out to her by Eugene, and she constantly urges Beatrice to leave him, especially after a brutal beating sends Kambili to the hospital. Ifeoma insists that "When a house is on fire, you run out before the roof collapses on your head" (213). She wants Kambili and Jaja to come to Nsukka when Kambili is released from the hospital so "it will be easier for you [Beatrice] to leave when they are not there" (214). It is Beatrice who constantly refuses to leave, claiming that "a husband crowns a woman's life" (75) and that she is grateful that Eugene didn't leave her to take another wife, when his social standing could very well grant him that opportunity. Though she often dismisses Ifeoma's urgings as "University talk" (75), it is unmistakable that Ifeoma's words offer her comfort as it is to Ifeoma's house she flees when Eugene breaks a side table on her belly, causing yet another miscarriage. Though she dismisses Ifeoma's pleas to stay there by claiming that "Where would I go if I leave Eugene's house? Tell me, where would I go? . . . Do you know how many mothers pushed their daughters at him?" (250), it is safe to say that Ifeoma's support gives her courage as she finally avenges years of abuse by slowly offering Eugene poisoned tea. Though Beatrice's final act is hotly debated on grounds of Christian morality, it is clear that female friendships offer succour to these postcolonial African women as they battle abuse and neglect in both the private and public spheres. But even as Kambili and Beatrice are able to stand up to the patriarchal abuse, Ifeoma's forced relocation to America casts a shadow on female empowerment in the novel.

As this analysis demonstrates, the process of decolonisation and postcolonial nation-formation was uneven and fraught with difficulties to say the least. Political turmoil continues even today in some of the sub-Saharan countries, while others in Africa and Asia try to figure out how to resist and combat the process of neo-colonialism even as they deal with a traumatic colonial legacy. Some of the concerns about neo-colonialism and globalisation, albeit driven by market forces and corporations based in the United States rather than European countries, have become ubiquitous in the twenty-first century and will be discussed in some detail in the final chapter.

Works Cited

Achebe, Chinua. "African Literature as Restoration of Celebration." *Chinua Achebe: A Celebration*. Eds. Kirsten Holst Petersen and Anna Rutherford. Oxford: Heinemann, 1991. Print.

———. "English and the African Writer." *Transition* 75/76 (1997): 342–349. Print.

———. *Home and Exile*. Oxford: Oxford UP, 2000. Print.

———. *Morning Yet on Creation Day: Essays*. London: Heinemann, 1975. Print.

———. *Things Fall Apart*. New York: Everyman's Library, 1958. Print.

Adichie, Chimamanda. *Purple Hibiscus*. New York: Anchor, 2003. Print.

———. *We Should All Be Feminists*. New York: Anchor, 2012. Print.

Ahmad, Aijaz. *In Theory: Classes, Nations, Literatures*. London: Verso, 1992. Print.

Aidoo, Ama Ata. *Changes: A Love Story*. New York: The Feminist Press, 1991. Print.

———. *Our Sister Killjoy: or, Reflections from a Black-Eyed Squint*. London: Longman, 1988. Print.

———. "The African Woman Today." *Dissent* 39 (1992): 319–25. Print.

———. "To be a Woman." *Sisterhood is Global*. Ed. Robin Morgan. New York: Anchor, 1985. 258–265. Print.

———. "To be an African Woman Writer – An Overview and a Detail." *Criticism and Ideology*. Ed. Kirsten Holst Petersen.

Uppsala, Sweden: Scandinavian Institute of African Studies, 1988. 155–72. Print.

Allan, Tuzyline Jita. Afterword. *Changes: A Love Story*. By Ama Ata Aidoo. New York: The Feminist P, 1991. Print.

Anand, Mulk Raj. *Coolie.* New Delhi: Penguin Books, 1993. Print.

Armah, Ayi Kwei. *The Beautyful Ones are Not Yet Born*. Toronto: Macmillan, 1969. Print.

Asaduddin. M. Introduction. *Black Margins*. By Saadat Hasan Manto. New Delhi: Katha, 2003. 1–43. Print.

Betts, Raymond. *Decolonization*. London: Routledge, 1998. Print.

Boehmer, Elleke. *Colonial & Postcolonial Literature*. Oxford: Oxford UP, 1995. Print.

Breitinger, Eckhard. "Sub-Saharan African Literature." *Companion to the New Literatures in English*. Ed. Christa Jansohn. Berlin: Erich Schmidt Verlag, 2002. 47–75. Print.

Cary, Joyce. *Mister Johnson: A Novel.* New York: Harper & Brothers, 1951. Print.

Davidson, Basil. *Modern Africa*. London: Longman, 1983. Print.

Desani, G. V. *All About H. Hatterr: A Gesture*. London: Aldor, 1948. Print.

Emecheta, Buchi. "Feminism with a small 'f.'" *Criticism and Ideology*. Ed. Kirsten Holst Petersen. Uppsala, Sweden: Scandinavian Institute of African Studies, 1988. 173–185. Print.

Fanon, Frantz. *Black Skin, White Masks*. New York: Grove P, 1967. Print.

———. *The Wretched of the Earth*. New York: Grove P, 1963. Print.

Gandhi, Leela. "Novelists of the 1930s and 1940s." *An Illustrated History of Indian Literature in English*. Ed. Arvind Krishna Mehrotra. Delhi: Permanent Black, 2003: 168–192. Print.

Gikandi, Simon. *Maps of Englishness: Writing Identity in the Culture of Colonialism*. New York: Columbia UP, 1996. Print.

Gopal, Priyamvada. *The Indian English Novel: Nation, History, and Narration.* Oxford: Oxford UP, 2009. Print.

Hosain, Attia. *Sunlight on a Broken Column.* New Delhi: Penguin, 1961. Print.

Isichei, Elizabeth. *A History of the Igbo People.* London: Macmillan, 1976. Print.

Lazarus, Neil. *Resistance in Postcolonial African Fiction.* New Haven: Yale UP, 1990. Print.

Manto, Saadat Hasan. "Adab-e-Jadeed." *Dastavez.* Ed. Balraj Manra. New Delhi: Modern Publishing House, 1986. Print.

———. *Black Margins.* Ed. M. U. Memon. Trans. M. Asaduddin. Delhi: Katha, 2003. Print.

Mullaney, Julie. *Postcolonial Literatures in Context.* London: Continuum, 2010. Print.

Nehru, Jawaharlal. *Jawaharlal Nehru's speeches.* Vol 1. Bombay: Publications Division, Government of India, 1949. Print.

Nkrumah, Kwame. *I speak of Freedom: A Statement of African Ideology.* New York: Frederick A. Praeger, 1962. Print.

Nyerere, Julius. "The Process of Liberation (1976)." *Politics and State in the Third World.* Ed. Harry Gouldbourne. London: Macmillan, 1979: 248–258. Print.

Paranjape, Makarand. "What About Those Who Stayed Back Home? Interrogating the Privileging of Diasporic Writing." *Shifting Continents/Colliding Cultures: Diaspora Writing of the Indian Subcontinent.* Ed. Ralph J. Crane and Radhika Mohanram. Atlanta: Rodopi, 2000. 225–245. Print.

Petersen, Kirsten H. and Anna Rutherford. *Chinua Achebe: A Celebration.* Oxford: Oxford UP, 1991. Print.

Pieterese, Cosmo and Dennis Duerden, eds. *African Writers Talking.* New York: Africana Publishing, 1972. Print.

Rao, Raja. *Kanthapura.* New York: New Directions, 1963. Print.

Rege, Josna. *Colonial Karma: Self, Action, and Nation in the Indian English Novel.* New York: Palgrave, 2004. Print.

Roadarmel, Gordon. Introduction. *Modern Hindi Short Stories.* Berkeley: U of California P, 1974. Print.

Rushdie, Salman. *Imaginary Homelands: Essays and Criticism 1981–1991.* London: Granta Books, 1991. Print.

———. *Midnight's Children.* New York: Random House, 1981. Print.

Sahgal, Nayantara. *A Time to be Happy.* London: Gollancz, 1958. Print.

———. *Rich Like Us.* London: Heinemann, 1985. Print.

Salih, Tayeb. *Season of Migration to the North.* Trans. Denys Johnson-Davies. New York: New York Review Books, 1969. Print.

Sethi, Ali. "The Seer of Pakistan." *The New Yorker.* 20 August 2012. Web. 4 December 2015. <http://www.newyorker.com/online/blogs/books/2012/08/the-seer-of-pakistan.html>

Sharma, Meenakshi. *Postcolonial Indian Writing: Between Co-option and Resistance.* New Delhi: Rawat Publications, 2003. Print.

Sidhwa, Bapsi. *Ice-Candy Man.* Oxford: Heinemann, 1988. Print.

Singh, Khushwant. *Train to Pakistan.* New York: Grove P, 1961 Print.

Sivanandan, Tamara. "Anticolonialism, National Liberation, and Postcolonial Nation Formation." *The Cambridge Companion to Postcolonial Literary Studies.* Ed. Neil Lazarus. Cambridge: Cambridge UP, 2004: 41–65. Print.

Tagore, Rabindranath. "Letters and Notes." *Away: The Indian Writer as an Expatriate.* Ed. Amitava Kumar. New York: Routledge, 2004. 73–86. Print.

Taiwo, Oladele. *Female Novelists of Modern Africa.* London: Macmillan, 1984. Print.

Thiong'o, Ngũgĩ wa. *A Grain of Wheat.* London: Heinemann, 1980. Print.

———. *Decolonising the Mind: The Politics of Language in African Literature.* Oxford: James Currey, 1986. Print.

———. *Moving the Centre: The Struggle for Cultural Freedoms*. London: James Currey, 1993. Print.

Notes

1. For more on this "inward-turn" and feelings of alienation in postcolonial Indian novels, see Josna Rege's insightful discussion in *Colonial Karma*.

2. For more on this, see page 55 of Sivanandan's essay, "Anticolonialism, National Liberation, and Postcolonial Nation Formation".

3. In a letter excerpted from Krishna Dutta and Andrew Robinson's anthology of some of Tagore's works in Amitava Kumar's book, Tagore calls the "England-worshipping Bengali" as "ingabanga" (75). Tagore mentions certain traits that characterise an ingabanga: "An ingabanga sitting with an Englishman, whether he be talking or listening, will appear in every gesture and facial movement to be the acme of humility. But catch him with his own countrymen in his own sphere, and he will display genuine temper" (Tagore 5).

4. In Desani's novel, Banerrji asserts: "I also love England. And Englishmen, women and children. I often wish I could change my maiden name 'Nath' to 'Noel.' I have recently formed several English connexions myself, and I like dogs too. If you require a proof of my sincerity, I am a member of the English Tail Waggers, although I had the clear nationalist choice to join the Kennel Club of India" (197). For the quote on Coolie, see page 147 of Anand's novel. For more of a discussion on this, see pages 250 to 253 of Meenakshi Sharma's book on postcolonial Indian writing.

5. Gikandi refers to Elizabeth Isichei's book *A History of the Igbo People*, where she mentions that the British imperial historian Margery Perham, in her study of Lord Lugard and the invention of Nigeria, had claimed that the Igbos and other ethnic groups in the South East of Nigeria "have no history before the coming of the Europeans" (Isichei 3).

FOUR

Into the Heart of the Empire
Colonial migration to England in the eighteenth and nineteenth century

> I am the little Colonial walking in the London garden patch – allowed to look perhaps, but not to linger.
>
> —*Journal,* Katherine Mansfield[1]

In an essay "Africans and Afro-Caribbeans: A Personal View", the West Indian writer C. L. R. James emphasises the importance of Britain's black community in the history of the nation.

> Those people who are in western civilization, who have grown up in it but yet are not completely part [made to feel and themselves feeling that they are outside] have a unique insight into their society . . . . What such persons have to say, therefore, will give a new vision, a deeper and stronger insight into both western civilization and the black people in it. (James 63)

James was talking about the influx of West Indian, African and Indian immigrants to Britain after 1948 that fundamentally altered the racial demographics of Britain. Britain's post-1948 immigration conundrum has been studied widely and will be covered adequately in the next chapter. But these outsiders, that is, the colonial migrants and travellers that James so succinctly articulates, had routinely started appearing right from the beginning of the European imperial expansion and slave trade.

Not much material was to be found on the early migrants and travellers till a few years back when scholars like Peter Fryer, C. L. Innes and Rozina Visram tried to address this lacuna by exploring the representation of black people in literature in the one hundred and fifty years prior to the watershed mid-twentieth-century moment of decolonisation.[2] Peter Fryer draws attention particularly to the group of Africans who were seized from a Portuguese ship and brought to the court of James IV of Scotland at the beginning of the sixteenth century (Fryer 3–4). There are also records of a black trumpeter in the court of Henry VII and a group of Ghanaians who were brought to England in 1555 in order to be taught English and then sent back to Africa so that they would then be able to act as interpreters between the natives and British merchants engaged in the trade of ivory and spices on Africa's West Coast (4–5). The flourishing slave trade also led to the increase in the number of black people in England. Not only did they come on ships as servants of British merchants, but they also followed their masters when they visited their homeland and were often traded or gifted to friends and family. David Dabydeen points out that in popular paintings, cartoons and advertisements, including those of the legendary Hogarth, black people were engaged in a variety of occupations and roles – "footmen, coachmen, page-boys, soldiers, sailors, musicians, actresses, prostitutes, beggars, prisoners, pimps, highway robbers, street-sellers, and other similar roles" (19–20). With this steady rise in immigration, Britain was suddenly faced with the practical problem of framing the increasing number of black and brown bodies within the British body politic. But as Dabydeen's quote illustrates, black people in Britain were almost always in servile positions, if not outright objectified and pushed to the margins of society. EIC officials often made huge fortunes in India and when they came back to England, they brought back the servants and maids or ayahs whom they had hired in India. As

Visram points out, the servants or ayahs were brought back for a variety of reasons. "A reluctance to leave behind a favourite, faithful servant; a wish to recreate the nostalgic splendor of Indian life in England; to minister to the needs of the family and children during the long arduous sea voyage back – an ayah was considered to be an expert at this; or merely as a status symbol or curiosity" (*Ayahs* 12). For instance, Warren Hastings, one of the Governor-Generals of India, brought back two Indian boys as well as four ayahs when he returned at the end of his tenure. So did William Hickey, the "gentleman attorney" of Calcutta who brought back with him a "little pet boy, Nabob" (*Ayahs* 12). But often, if they did not perform their service well, these servants were either deported back to their home country or left destitute on the streets, and in some cases even sold as slaves. Advertisements selling slaves and sometimes looking for runaway slaves and stowaways began to appear with startling regularity. An advertisement in Steele and Addison's *Tatler* in 1709 read – "A Black Indian Boy 12 years of Age, fit to wait on a Gentleman, to be disposed of at Denis's Coffee-house in Finch-Lane near the Royal Exchange" (*Ayahs* 14). Visram mentions two others, one asking for a "Run-away Bengal Boy" which appeared in 1743 and one for a lost "East India Tawney Black" (*Ayahs* 14), which appeared in 1737.

Rozina Visram also points out that along with servants, Indian sailors, who were either hired or kidnapped to serve as the crew of British trading ships, were mistreated and often forced to flee once the ships docked in England. Joseph Salter, appointed Missionary to the Orientals and Africans, talks about some brutal treatment that was meted out to the lascars aboard the ships, including being mercilessly beaten and forced to eat pork, which of course was sacrilege for them. Salter claims that he was amazed that "the coloured part of mankind exists only to be used like brute beasts, and to have the most insulting names language can supply heaped upon them"

(150). In fact, the treatment was at times so savage that some of the lascars would disappear during the voyage or abandon their ship as soon as they docked. Travelers like Mirza Abu Taleb Khan also mentions this in his narrative – "Sixteen of our best lascars being much disgusted by the treatment received on board this ship, deserted and hid themselves in the woods; and it was discovered that the remainder of the crew only waited the approach of the night to follow the example of their comrades" (33–34). This was becoming such a problem that in 1786, a committee was set up to help these destitute sailors by either finding them employment or repatriating them back to the colonies. This committee alone had located about 320 people in need of aid. Eventually in June 1857, the Strangers Home in West India Road was officially opened to temporarily house destitute sailors, but also to aid in repatriation and to spread the message of Christianity among them. Even though the exact number of black people living in Britain in the late eighteenth century is not known, it is believed to be between ten and twenty thousand.

At the same time, on the heels of England's increasing mercantile prowess and the culture of consumption that followed, black and brown bodies became yet another exotic commodity that served as a status symbol for their owners. This trend became more pronounced in the early nineteenth century when material objects like precious gemstones and cashmere shawls were highly coveted for their exotic appeal, but so were Indian bodies engaged in the service of colonial "nabobs".[3] In his book, Sukhdev Sandhu notes that these brown bodies "served as human equivalents of the porcelain, textiles, wallpapers, and lacquered pieces that the English nobility was increasingly buying from the East" (4). So in paintings and portraits, black or brown bodies in all their exotic finery often accompanied their wealthy colonial masters or mistresses. C. L. Innes points out that Hogarth's *Taste in High Life* "shows a small African boy dressed in turban and plumes, as much an exotic pet as the little poodle in coat and bonnet in a room bedecked with images and objects from China, India, France, and other worlds" (Innes 10–11). The oriental garb was a necessary part of this tableau as it helped the colonial nabobs showcase the authenticity of their colonial experience and also re-affirmed their wealthy status in British society. As Innes points out, "Such pages were often dressed in exotic livery, featuring turbans and robes which might have little to do with their ancestral cultures, and much more to do with an orientalist perception of those regions. In such outfits, they were an adornment like the ostrich and peacock feathers, the paisley shawls, the silks, which adorned their mistresses" (14). Queen Victoria herself had several Asian servants, and two of them, Mohammed Bux and Abdul Karim, achieved particular prominence. In fact, Abdul Karim became such a favourite of the Queen that she started learning Hindustani from him and was delighted with it. She is quoted in Visram's book as saying, "I am learning a few words of Hindustani to speak to my servants. It is a great interest to me for both the language and the people. I have naturally never come into real contact with before" (*Ayahs* 31). The Queen's patronage of her Indian "munshi" Karim did not sit well with her court and her ministers, who did everything they could to put him in his "proper place" by emphasising his humble background to the class conscious Victorian public. This ensured the divide between royalty and their native servants remained markedly distinct.[4]

On the one hand, the demographic in Britain throughout the eighteenth and nineteenth century was shaped by the increasing number of black/brown servants and sailors. On the other hand, there was a steady influx of royalty as well as wealthy native travellers and migrants, doctors, merchants and teachers of Asian languages who offered a unique perspective on native life to the British public. If the working class natives were just about tolerated in the heart of the empire, the aristocratic visitors were often a source of wonder and amazement and treated as exotic objects. In other words, racial prejudice took different forms depending on the wealth and social status of the visitors and immigrants. Queen Victoria's, and subsequently the Prince of Wales's (later Edward VII) fondness for Indian maharajahs caused some serious consternation in administrative circles. During his tour of India in 1875, Edward VII is said to have asserted "because a man has a black face and a different religion from our own, there is no reason why he should be treated as a brute" (*Ayahs* 174). This did not sit well with the administrative officials in the colonies. That the treatment of princes in England during the late nineteenth century rattled some nerves among colonial officials is evident from a scathing letter sent to Lord Hamilton by Lord Curzon, the Viceroy of India from 1899 to 1905. Curzon complains about the reception given to the Rajah of Kapurthala by stating that "at home every man with a turban, a sufficient number of jewels and a black skin, is mistaken for a miniature Akbar, and becomes the darling of drawing rooms, the honoured guest of municipalities and the hero of newspapers" (*Ayahs* 175).

This chapter, focusing on literature from pre-1850 Britain, explores the early black presence in the imperial metropolis. First, it investigates the role that Olaudah Equiano's narrative played in the abolitionist movement in the eighteenth century. Later, it reads the British fascination with exotic objects as a euphemism that masks the undercurrent of xenophobia already palpable in metropolitan attitudes towards an increasing foreign presence in the eighteenth and the first half of the nineteenth century. In the absence of a solidly defined discourse of scientific racism, reaction to black and brown bodies manifested itself through blatant objectification – an attitude that climaxed in the Great Exhibition of 1851.[5] Surprisingly, early immigrants and travellers did very little to resist such objectification; in fact, the first Indian writer in English, Dean Mahomed, actively promoted the exotic nature of his "shampooing" techniques in order to gain economic and social stability. But at the same time, immigrant narratives, like that of Mahomed or Olaudah Equiano, are characterised by a peculiar resistance to unquestionably accept British social and cultural hegemony. Instead, they embrace a multiplicity of roles. As Innes emphasises:

> Such authors found little difficulty in presenting themselves as black *and* British, or African and English, or Indian and English, or Caribbean and Scottish, or various combinations of these identities. Their works assert a sense of core humanity and selfhood at the same time as they demonstrate their flexible performance of roles, emphasising possibility and potentiality rather than fixed definitions. (2)

So while Equiano "presents himself as an African while he is an Englishman named after a Swedish king" (Innes 2), Mahomed, dressed in oriental attire, draws attention to his Indian identity while simultaneously canvassing for British patronage. So it is worth noting here that what emerges from the following analysis of select pre-1850 migrant writing is not any sort of homogenous literary tradition or any essentialised migrant identity over the course of a century, but rather a preoccupation with motifs like multiple identities and performativity.

Black Voices in England in the Eighteenth Century

As C. L. Innes points out in her book, "During the eighteenth-century enlightenment period, the equation between writing, civilization and humanity became established, and the question as to whether black people were capable of writing and literary creation became crucial to the debates surrounding the abolition of slavery" (17). Eighteenth-century and early nineteenth-century narratives by African writers are therefore not only important because of the perspective they provide into the early black presence in England, but also because they are valuable in understanding the immediate political impact they had on the abolitionist movement that was rapidly gathering steam in the second part of the eighteenth century. Quite predictably then, one of the main issues that plagues early African writing like that of Olaudah Equiano or Ignatius Sancha was whether these narratives were written by the authors themselves or through some kind of an amanuensis. Several testimonials tagged on to the main narrative were often explicit proof of their authenticity. So, for instance, in her foreword to *The Letters of Ignatius Sancho*, the editor, Miss Crewe, categorically states that the main reason for this effort was "to show that an untutored African may possess abilities equal to an European, and the still superior motive, of wishing to serve his family" (Innes 23). Sancho's letters, written between 1766 and 1780 to friends and family, preceded the more well-known narrative by Equiano. The letters proved to be extremely popular and the first edition, published in 1782, had at least 12,000 subscribers – a substantial number in that day and age. Sancho, born on a slave ship and baptised "Ignatius", was first given at the age of two to three sisters from Greenwich who gave him his last name, and was then adopted by the Duke and Duchess of Montagu and eventually became their butler. Sancho's letters are an astonishing document about the social and political mores of late eighteenth-century England and are now widely hailed by critics as one of the earliest examples of black British writing. Critics like David Dabydeen, Paul Edwards and others have also been quick to point out that even Sancho is by no means the first African to produce narratives in English. Sancho's and Equiano's narratives were preceded by Ukawsaw Gronniosaw, whose forty-nine page narrative titled *Narrative of the Remarkable Particulars in the Life of James Albert Ukawsaw Gronniosaw, An African Prince, Related by Himself* was published in 1772, and Ottobah Cugoano's *Thoughts and Sentiments on the Evil of Slavery* was first published in 1787.

But in spite of these early narratives, *The Interesting Narrative of the Life of Olaudah Equiano, or Gustavus Vassa, the African,* first published in 1789, is crucial because of the role it played in the anti-slavery movement in England.

When the abolition of slave trade was being debated in the British Parliament, Equiano's narrative was submitted along with a long list of prominent subscribers and anti-slavery activists that included the Prince of Wales, Thomas Clarkson, Josiah Wedgwood and others. This is not the only achievement of this narrative, structured in the form of a memoir. Critics like Robert Steptoe and Houston Baker credit it with being a combination of a picaresque novel and an African trickster tale; a tradition that would be later picked up by writers like Mark Twain and Ralph Ellison. Others emphasise the importance of the slave narrative in the African American literary tradition and its far-reaching influence on writers like Frederick Douglass, Richard Wright, Harriet Jacobs and others. Still others, like the African novelist Chinua Achebe, hail Equiano as the first Igbo novelist who provides the reader with an insight into native Igbo customs and cultures.[6] Needless to say, this text with its amalgam of ethnographic document and harsh indictment of the brutality of slavery was one of the most important literary texts to be produced in the eighteenth century.

Even though there are some discrepancies in the dates mentioned in the narrative, Equiano gives a detailed account of his childhood in Africa and his subsequent nightmarish experience aboard a slave ship till his eventual journey into England. Born around the year 1745 in Nigeria, Equiano was captured when he was around eleven and brought by slave ship first to Barbados, then to a plantation in Virginia where he was bought by a British Naval officer called Lieutenant Pascal. After he served with Lieutenant Pascal in the Seven Years War, Pascal sold him back into slavery to Robert King, a Philadelphia merchant, who eventually helped him buy his freedom. After a few more voyages to the Mediterranean and Central America, he made his way to England, where three years after the publication of his book, he married Susanna Cullen in Cambridgeshire in 1792 and had two daughters – Ann Maria and Johanna. He continued to live in England till his death on 31 March 1797. Equiano's 1789 book about his multiple adventures went through nine editions in English and was even translated into Dutch, German and Russian. This narrative was instrumental in shaping the discourse of the abolitionist movement not just because it was a harsh indictment of the horrors of slavery, but also because of the emotional power of an eyewitness account of someone who had been exposed to its horrific brutalities first hand on a slave ship. What is most interesting to note here is that Equiano, like Mahomed after him, is adroit in negotiating his African and British identity. He repeatedly talks about his suffering African countrymen and prides himself on his African identity, even referring to himself as "The African" in the title of the memoir. In the beginning pages of the text, he constructs a picture of a lush and peaceful Africa, quite contradictory to the savage, uncivilised Africa of the European imagination that was used to justify slavery in the first place. On the other hand, much of the narrative, as well as the letters that precede it, unequivocally assert his claim as a British subject, a nation which not only introduced him to Christianity but which, "by its liberal sentiments, its humanity, the glorious freedom of its government, and its proficiency in arts and sciences, has exalted the dignity of human nature" (Equiano 7).

Equiano's birthplace of Essaka in Nigeria is described as a veritable Garden of Eden where the land was fertile and verdant and people were simple, industrious and actively engaged in building their community. He emphasises Africa's natural resources time and again:

> Our land is uncommonly rich and fruitful, and produces all kinds of vegetables in great abundance. We have plenty of Indian corn, and vast quantities of cotton and tobacco . . . We have spices of different kinds, particularly pepper; and a variety of delicious fruits which I have never seen in Europe; together with gums of various kinds, and honey in abundance. All our industry is exerted to improve those blessings of nature. (24)

He also emphasises the industriousness and integrity of the natives, in stark contrast to the deliberate European stereotypes of Africans as savage and indolent people. Equiano repeatedly points out that they are "all habituated to labour from our earliest years . . . and as we are unacquainted with idleness, we have no beggars" (25). Addressing the popular idea of Africans as grotesque and somewhat sub-human, Equiano maintains that "deformity is indeed unknown amongst us, I mean that of shape", and that women were graceful and comely and indeed "cheerfulness and affability are two of the leading characteristics of our nations" (25). Moreover, native Africans were not only incredibly accomplished in warfare and the use of weaponry, but "even our women are warriors, and march boldly out to fight along with the men" (26). At the same time, they are not lacking in culture as they "are almost a nation of dancers, musicians, and poets. Thus every great event, such as a triumphant return from battle, or other cause of public rejoicing is celebrated in public dances" (22). Equiano's objective here is unmistakable; he is not only interested in demystifying all the European stereotypes about Africa, but he also wants to emphasise the fact that the rationale used to justify slavery was, in fact, untenable. In other words, as critics point out, the argument that the slave trade was designed to ameliorate the depravity of African living conditions sounds hollow in the face of the thriving African civilisation that Equiano paints in his narrative. Equiano also doesn't hesitate to dispute the other popular rationale used to justify slavery; that Africans are inferior because of their skin colour. He points out that tropical climates often have an effect on skin colour and insists that Spaniards "who have inhabited America under the torrid zone, for any time, are become as dark coloured as our native Indians of Virginia; of which I *myself have been a witness* . . . Surely the minds of Spaniards did not change with their complexions" (Equiano 30–31). And it is here that he makes the most impassioned case against slavery by reminding Europeans that they share a common ancestor with Africans.

> Let the polished and haughty European recollect that his ancestors were once, like the Africans, uncivilized and even barbarous. Did Nature make *them* inferior to their sons? And should *they too* have been made slaves? Every rational mind answers, No. Let such reflections as these melt the pride of their superiority into sympathy for the wants and miseries of their sable brethren, and compel them to acknowledge, that understanding is not confined to feature or colour. (Equiano 31)

By a very clever appeal to the rationality of the European mind, Equiano thus manages to successfully argue against the brutality of the slave trade.

In fact, Equiano even turns the trope of the cannibalism and savagery of African natives – often marshalled with a great deal of alacrity in travel narratives – on its head. When he is kidnapped and brought aboard the slave ship, he is terrified by the savagery of the European merchants and asks "if we were not to be eaten by those white men with horrible looks, red faces, and loose hair" (39). When the ship docks in Bridgetown, Barbados, and merchants came aboard to examine the slaves, his fear of being eaten alive resurfaces. As the men examine their movements to make sure they are hardy workers, "we thought by this we should be eaten by these ugly men, as they appeared to us" (42) which causes them much trembling and apprehension till they are told next morning that they are not to be eaten, but in fact sent to work on the mainland. Later in the narrative, he employs another popular Western literary trope when, following a shipwreck, he becomes a Robinson Crusoe figure who is able to save the lives of his white shipmates through his quick thinking and resourcefulness. As Innes points out, "Equiano draws on and refashions a number of literary traditions to his own purposes; he redeploys the travel narrative to draw on the anthropological observing mode of European travellers reporting back 'home,' but at the same time he resituates the European observer as the observed" (Innes 42). Equiano thus proves himself to be remarkably well versed in Western modes of thinking. Instead of ending the narrative at the moment when he gains his freedom, he continues to show how he stakes claim to his adopted country of England and to an English identity by pursuing Methodism, marrying an Englishwoman and establishing himself as a spokesperson on behalf of the black community in England, but never at the cost of his African identity. One of the remarkable aspects of the narrative is Equiano's consummate ability to juggle these multiple perspectives, that of "the eye-witness of Igbo life and of the slave ship; the extoller of primitive man; the writer, reader, and Protestant convert; the political abolitionist and economic free-trade advocate" (Sollors xxii). Yet, the most significant achievement of this narrative undoubtedly remains the strong advocacy of the anti-slavery movement. As Sonia Hofkosh points out, "Being a true relation of occurrences which had taken place, and of sufferings which he had endured, it produced a degree of humane feeling in men's minds, to excite which the most animated addresses and the most convincing reasoning would have labored in vain" (334–335).

Exoticism and xenophobia in nineteenth-century England

The discourse of "exoticism" has been widely theorised in postcolonial studies and multiple books have been published on the subject. The Oxford English Dictionary defines the word "exotic" as "coming from or typical of a distant foreign country" or "strikingly colourful or unusual" (249). In her introduction to a book called *"New" Exoticsms*, Isabel Santaolalla draws on the OED definition and points out that though the OED dates the word "exotic" only to the end of the sixteenth century, the fascination for foreign objects can be traced further back in time (Santaolalla 9). She emphasises that "It was indeed the lure of the exotic that led to the appropriation of Egyptian decorative motifs in early Greek architecture, or to the embrace of eastern cults like those of Isis and of Mitra in Rome . . ." (9). Pia Pal-Lapinski mentions that in the mid-eighteenth century, Samuel Johnson in his *Dictionary* (1755) defined the "'exotick' primarily in terms of what it was *not*: as 'foreign, not produced in our own country; not domestick'" (Pal-Lapinski 1). She further points out that in Samuel Richardson's novel *Clarissa, Or, The History of a Young Lady* (1747), Clarissa's seduction by the inveterate rake Robert Lovelace "transforms her into an exotic being, a 'foreigner' who has no place in English society, whose only option is an extravagantly staged death" (Pal-Lapinski 1), thus highlighting a complicated, gendered relationship between foreign-ness and immorality and decadence. From the middle of the eighteenth century then, a word that was previously associated with something new or unfamiliar assumed negative connotations and began to be associated with ideas of fear and contamination; anything exotic was perceived as a palpable threat to English racial and sexual identity. This discourse gathered steam with the onset of high imperialism in the nineteenth century, even as exoticism became synonymous with cultural appropriation. Clara Gallini points out that the "Great Exhibitions (London, Paris, Philadelphia, Turin . . .) which concretely, in their great 'national pavilions', constructed the exotic in order to suggest it as practice for domestic use" (214). Graham Huggan further elaborates on the construction of the discourse of exoticism.

> For the exotic is not, as is often supposed, an inherent *quality* to be found 'in' certain people, distinctive objects, or specific places; exoticism describes, rather, a particular mode of aesthetic *perception* – one which renders people, objects and places strange even as it domesticates them, and which effectively manufactures otherness even as it claims to surrender to its immanent mystery. (13)

Huggan rightly points out that the word "exotic" doesn't necessarily indicate an inherent difference in people or places, but is a carefully constructed discourse that is skilfully marshalled in the politics of global consumption. Huggan's arguments are bolstered by Stephen Foster, who argues that the concept of culture and that of the exotic functions in comparable ways:

> Both terms label and thereby initiate the 'control' of social phenomena which, being at the outset remote and unknown, may for those reasons appear chaotic, threatening, bizarre, ineluctable. These terms begin the domestication of the foreign and unpredictable, so that once the labelling is imposed, the phenomena to which they then apply begin to be structured in a way which makes them comprehensible and possibly predictable, if predictably defiant of total familiarity. (Foster 21)

Foster's formulation of the exotic is strikingly similar to Louise Kaplan's definition of a "fetishism strategy." "Fetishism strategy", as defined by Kaplan, is the "need to transform something unfamiliar and intangible into something familiar and tangible" (1).[7] In an effort to understand why certain people, objects and cultures are coded as "exotic" within Western aesthetics, Deborah Root points out the following:

> Exoticism in its commodified form appears as a sophisticated appreciation of other cultures or as an aestheticized nostalgia for a different place or time, but the content of exotic images links it closely to colonialism and to contemporary systems of economic and cultural domination. The process of exotification is another kind of cultural cannibalism . . . Differences clearly do exist between cultures, and the issue is not that these are noticed but how these come to be aestheticized and by whom . . . This aestheticization is dependent on a mechanism whereby differences are abstracted from their cultural context and rendered strange or curious (a process that seems to relate to the fascination with cultural difference as display of grotesquerie in early museums). (30)

Drawing on Huggan, Foster, Root and Kaplan's theorisations of exoticism and fetishism strategy, and focusing on Anglo-Indian encounters in the first half of the nineteenth century, this section reads the discourse of exoticism both as an euphemism that masks the xenophobia latent in Britain's perception of the "foreign", and as a mode of control that is mobilised for the cultural appropriation of the "other", that endeavours to make the unfamiliar, familiar and safe. Nineteenth-century Anglo-Indian interactions in the imperial metropolis witness an ebb and flow of exoticism and xenophobia, while in the twentieth century the discourse of exoticism morphs into the state-sponsored discourse of multiculturalism and xenophobia translates into blatant racism against South Asians.[8]

British Commodity Culture and Immigrant Identity in the Nineteenth Century

In the early decades of the nineteenth century, Britain was preoccupied with its own growing supremacy as a mercantile nation. Industrial and technological advancement following the Industrial Revolution and unprecedented revenues generated by trade with Asia and Africa produced in the early nineteenth-century British mind-set a sense of economic and cultural superiority. The construction of a commodity culture organised around the production and circulation of consumer goods reached a climax with the Great Exhibition of 1851. As discussed briefly in the first chapter, Prince Albert, on the opening day of the exhibition, declared that "the products of all quarters of the globe are placed at our disposal, and we have only to choose which is the best and cheapest for our purposes" (Richards 28). His statement not only proclaimed Britain as the leader in the global market, but immediately situated the British consumer within a network of commodity exchange where he could pick the most useful object from a vast array of products, even those brought from distant parts of the world. Eastern commodities like tea had been anglicised and domesticated into a British ritual as early as the middle of the eighteenth century, and Britain's fascination with curry was steadily on the increase in the nineteenth century. Living in London at a time when the city was one of the major trading centres in the world – with products ranging from tea, coffee, sugar and cotton to spices and tobacco being ferried into it through the Thames and other waterways from Africa and Asia – Indian travellers and immigrants could scarcely have failed to recognise the value of Eastern commodities in British metropolitan life. Once immigrants started making an appearance on Britain's shores in the nineteenth century, it was almost unavoidable that they figured a way to tap into the money economy heralded by the Industrial Revolution.

In his book on commodity culture in Victorian England, Thomas Richards argues that in the Victorian mind-set, the word "Empire" was synonymous with Britain's economic expansion and it was generally believed that imperialism would be contingent on the effective outward-bound movement of surplus capital and commodities (120). Richards points out that "It did not matter whether one was for or against Empire: it was an article of faith among jingoes and liberals and radicals alike that, in Marx's words, 'it becomes necessary for capital progressively to dispose ever more fully of the whole globe . . . so as to find productive employment for the surplus value it has realized'" (120). Richards also suggests that while Britain was always on the lookout for new markets in its empire to dispose of the excess or "surplus" commodities from its burgeoning industrial production, it was also scouring the globe for raw materials and commodities to feed the endless demand of countless mills and factories that had sprung up all over Britain. In this context, both commodities and surplus commodities acquired a new sense of value.

Even though Richards's argument is specific to Victorian Britain, I think it is particularly helpful in understanding the incipient commodity culture of late eighteenth and early nineteenth-century Britain. Both the raw materials and commodities that were used in industrial production, as well as the finished products, drove Britain's imperial ambitions in the early decades of the nineteenth century. In other words, the need to circulate commodities necessitated the establishment of a network of exchange between Britain and other countries around the globe and directly resulted in the establishment and prosperity of the EIC. Within such an economic matrix, failure to partake of the network of exchanges and to generate money would indicate that non-productive people were a burden to society and hence would be promptly relegated to the underclass – a class elaborately categorised in Henry Mayhew's compendium on London's street life – or even to the far-flung colonies along with surplus commodities. In an essay, Deirdre David rightly points out that in line with several of his contemporaries, "Dickens finds the colonies of white settlement to be convenient repositories for characters difficult to integrate into English society" (87). Hence, in *Hard Times*, Tom Gradgrind, who has disgraced himself in the eyes of all around him, is shipped off to one of the distant lands and Mr Micawber, at the end of *David Copperfield*, sails with his family to Australia (David 87). Dickens does not indicate the reason for the marginalisation of these characters at the end of his narratives other than suggesting they were morally suspect, and David doesn't elaborate on this economic angle. But it seems fairly apparent that, among other things, failure to generate money through bodily labour and hence to contribute to Britain's material wealth necessitated their withdrawal from metropolitan society. While both Mayhew and Dickens refer to Victorian London, it is worth noting that this commodity-oriented economy was already in place in the beginning of the nineteenth century. The economic regime and fear of being denoted as surplus commodities and being relegated to the underclass made South Asian travellers and immigrants engage in self-orientalisation to gain economic and social mobility.

Early colonial travellers to England – The *Travels of Mirza Abu Taleb Khan*

In this cultural climate of rampant consumerism, when Eastern objects were quite a rage, South Asians themselves were regarded as little more than exotic objects and elicited curiosity and wonder anywhere they went. In the last decades of the eighteenth century, several South Asians travelled to the heart of the empire and some of them, like Mirza Itesa Modeen and Mirza Abu Taleb Khan, constantly talked about the attraction of the British public to these exotic brown bodies. Quoted by Visram, Mirza Itesa Modeen, a South Asian traveller to Britain in 1765, believed "even the mere company of an Indian dressed in Oriental clothes could add to the reputation of a man" (*Asians in Britain* 8). Mirza Abu Taleb Khan, an official in the administrative division of the EIC in India, travelled all over Europe in the late eighteenth and early nineteenth century and in 1810, published a translated volume of his travels. The *Travels of Mirza Abu Taleb Khan in Asia, Africa, and Europe* records an extremely interesting incident.

> One day, a great crowd having assembled about me, a shopkeeper advised me to walk into his house, and to sit down till they should disperse. I accepted his kind invitation, and went into the shop, where I amused myself looking at some penknives, scissors, etc. The people however thronged so about his windows, that several of the panes were broken; and the crowd being very great, it was in vain to ask who had done it. (Khan 143)

In his book, *Novels Behind Glass*, Andrew Miller demonstrates how the invention of plate glass in the mid-1830s revolutionised the whole business of selling in nineteenth-century Britain. The commodities displayed behind the shop window both elicited desire and created a distance between the object and the consumer with the very material presence of the plate glass between them (Miller 5). Unaware that he was being perceived as an object himself, Khan goes inside the shop to see the products of Britain's newfound industrial prowess. Once his body is more clearly framed among indispensable commodities, but is simultaneously distanced by the material presence of the transparent glass, the crowd can barely control its acquisitive desire, resulting in the shattering of glass windows. This incident quite literally draws attention to the violence in the "contact zone" that accompanies the fetishisation of the brown body. Louise Kaplan's brilliant definition of "fetishism strategy" (1) is particularly useful in understanding this phenomenon. Kaplan declares that "fetishism is a mental strategy or defense that enables a human being to transform something or someone with its own enigmatic energy and immaterial essence into something or someone that is material and tangibly real, a form of being that makes the something or someone controllable" (5). In a commodity-obsessed society, the move to establish the Eastern bodies as exotic entities transforms the "other" into dehumanised commodities and becomes an effective mode of exerting control over them. In nineteenth-century Britain, the exoticisation of brown bodies was a mode of control. But the fear of being relegated to the margins of British metropolitan society prevented travellers like Abu Taleb Khan and some immigrants like Dean Mahomed from resisting rampant objectification. Rozina Visram comprehensively demonstrates that the ayahs and lascars who were employed in the service of the EIC and left destitute on the streets of London after being discharged from active service were treated with contempt and loathing by the British public. Abu Taleb Khan and Mahomed therefore not only indulged in self-exoticisation but also tried to figure out ways by which they could trade their skills and their ethnicity to contribute to the market–centric economy of Britain and, in the process, gain access to mainstream society. Khan, at one point, reveals his desire to be of more practical use in British society by teaching foreign languages to the British public.

> When I first arrived in London, it had been my determination to have opened a Public Academy to be patronized by Government, for instructing such of the English as were destined to fill important situations in the East, in the Hindoostany, Persian, and Arabic languages . . . . By these means I expected to have passed my time in England in a rational and advantageous manner; beneficial both to myself, and to the nation I came to visit. (Khan 163)

Khan's intentions here are strikingly similar to Thomas Macaulay's formulation of the "mimic men" in his infamous "Minute on Indian Education" (1835) – "We must at present do our best to form a class who may be interpreters between us and the millions whom we govern; a class of persons, Indian in blood and colour, but English in taste, in opinions, in morals, and in intellect" (249). Though Macaulay conceptualises this idea almost thirty years after Khan, attitudes like this might have alerted Macaulay to such a possibility. Khan clearly accepts the administrative dominance of the British in colonial India, thus tangentially contributing to the imperial process. He was of course followed in this by other immigrants like Monshee Mahomet Saeed from Bengal who "could speak and write English tolerably" and who, in 1777 advertised himself as a teacher of "Persian and Arabick" (*Ayahs* 63). Another linguist, Syed Abdoollah, was a Professor of Hindustani at the University College, London in the 1850s, and presented himself as someone who was invested in the welfare of the South Asian community in Britain. He was even present at the opening of the Strangers Home for Asiatics and Africans in 1856 (*Ayahs* 63). Ganendra Mohan Tagore, a Bengali who had been educated in Britain, was also a Professor of Hindu Law and Bengali Language at University College in the 1860s.

So even as the EIC was engaged in furthering British mercantile interests in India, some imperial subjects were, as Visram states, "demonstrating their resourcefulness and adaptability" (*Asians in Britain* 357) in the heart of the imperial metropolis by engaging in "cultural entrepreneurship"(42), that is, making a livelihood out of "selling culture" to Englishmen with a voracious appetite for anything Oriental. As such, these nineteenth-century travellers and migrants can be held accountable for what I term "ethno-pornography", along the lines of Sau-ling Cynthia Wong's use of the term; that is, the move to highlight one's ethnicity in order to get a foothold in white society.[9] Aware of this, and in an effort to downplay accusations of "selling themselves" under economic pressure, immigrant narratives, like those of Mahomed, make an attempt to establish the indispensability of the brown body in healing the British body politic, portrayed as damaged by the onslaught of industrialisation and colonial expansion.

Dean Mahomed, the first Indian writer in English

Dean Mahomed's life was distinguished by the sheer diversity of his experiences. Mahomed was born in Patna, Bihar in 1759 and started his career as a soldier in the EIC's Bengal army under Godfrey Baker, an Irish cadet. He served the army from 1769 to 1782, but when Captain Baker decided to return to Ireland, a desire "of seeing that part of the world" and a conviction that he would suffer "much uneasiness of mind" in the absence of his patron and best friend prompted Mahomed to take the decision of immigrating to Europe. According to Michael Fisher, he arrived at Dartmouth in England in September 1784, at the age of 25 (*Travels* 124). His early years as a migrant were spent in Ireland under the patronage of the Baker family, who lived in a prosperous part of Cork, but his exact position within the household is not known. Records indicate that he was engaged in some kind of managerial position and it is during his stay in Ireland that he married Jane Daly and in 1793–1794 wrote *The Travels of Dean Mahomed*, recounting his experiences as a soldier in the EIC's army. Widely celebrated as the first book to be written and published in English by an Indian, *Travels* was undoubtedly an attempt by Mahomed to situate himself within the Western literary world. Written as a series of letters to an imaginary friend, William A. Bailie, a colonel in the service of the EIC, and possibly influenced by Equiano's narrative, it is an attempt to provide an insider's perspective on the Indian colonial landscape with graphic portraits of native people and places. Michael Fisher has done some pioneering work on Dean Mahomed in his two books, so this chapter will focus on his lesser known but equally fascinating text.[10] First published in 1822, Mahomed's lesser known text, *Shampooing, or Benefits Resulting from the Use of The Indian Medicated Vapour Bath, As Introduced into This Country, by S. D. Mahomed (A Native of*

India), can be read as a classic example of an early nineteenth-century advertising success story.

In the same vein as Equiano before him, Mahomed's deft manipulation of available socio-economic and literary conventions of the time to construct a self that is simultaneously a "much obliged, and devoted, humble servant" to his British patrons and a proud Indian who believes, after having observed the contrasting lifestyle in Ireland, that his countrymen have "still more of the innocence of our ancestors, than some of the boasting philosophers of Europe" (*Travels* 32–34) makes *Shampooing* a fascinating and complex read. Rozina Visram tells us that a significant number of South Asian immigrants were engaged in self-employment, "as keepers of lodging-houses and cafes, as purveyors of Indian culture, playing music or hawking Indian cures and wares, reminding us that earning a living catering for compatriots or 'selling culture' was as important in the nineteenth century as in the twentieth, and did not begin with the post-war generation of migrants" (*Asians in Britain* 357). A lot of working-class Indians, in the nineteenth century, marketed their own ethnicity as a means of survival and worked as itinerant traders selling textiles or other Oriental merchandise door to door. Others were engaged in the restaurant business. Curry was already much in demand in Britain; by 1784, curry and rice had become a specialty on the menus of a lot of fashionable eateries in London's Piccadilly (*Asians in Britain* 6). Dean Mahomed had moved to London with his family around 1807 and had found temporary employment with Sir Basil Cochrane in his vapour-bath establishment in Portman Square. But his shrewd business sense convinced him that there was money to be made in the restaurant business and accordingly he set up the Hindoostanee Coffee-House in 1810 at 34 George Street, Portman Square. There were around 550 coffee houses in London by the second decade of the eighteenth century. So in order to distinguish himself, Dean Mahomed chose to highlight his ethnicity to create a consumer base and cater to the palate of the India-returned "nabobs" who were still wallowing in the nostalgia of their experiences in the East.

Visram mentions that this business venture was probably the first instance of "economic survival through ethnic 'cultural-entrepreneurship'" (*Asians in Britain* 39) among the early South Asian immigrants in Britain. According to Janet Freeman, one earlier attempt had been made to market Indian food in London by "'the Mistress of Norris street Coffee-House, Haymarket', who advertised in 1733 that she not only sold 'true Indian curey paste', but would 'at the shortest Notice, [send] ready dressed Curey and Rice, also India Pilaws, to any Part of Town' (*Public Advertiser*, 6 December)" (110). But Dean Mahomed's establishment is widely credited, and the original site even marked in 2005 by the Westminster City Council with a plaque as "London's first Indian restaurant" (Freeman 110). Anthony Clayton mentions that an advertisement in *The Times* on 27 March 1811 emphasised the uniqueness of Mahomed's coffee house in terms of presenting an authentic "Oriental" experience (121). The note mentions that the coffee house was available "for the entertainment of Indian gentlemen, where they may enjoy . . . the real Chilm tobacco, and Indian dishes, in the highest perfection, and allowed by the greatest epicures to be unequalled to any curries ever made in England; with choice wine and every accommodation" (Clayton 121). The emphasis here is clearly on the "real", the authentic dining experience that only a native of India could provide. This emphasis on the "native" is probably because there are indications that British women often used their curry-making skills to cater to different East Indian families settled in London. Visram mentions Sarah Shade, who was apparently able to make a living for over a year and a half by selling curry to different families in London (*Asians in Britain* 6). It is also important to underscore here that the allusion to "Indian gentlemen" was a reference to the

British "nabobs" and not people of Indian origin per se. Such fashionable establishments would probably be inaccessible to the lascars and ayahs of South Asian origin who crowded the streets of London.

Mahomed, by recreating an Indian setting in his coffee house and serving authentic Indian dishes, aspired to cater to a particular section of nineteenth-century society. His strategy worked to the extent of getting him a substantial mention in the nineteenth-century version of the *Good Food Guide*, that is, in *The Epicure's Almanack*, but not enough to make it a lasting career for him. The entry itself in *The Epicure's Almanac* gives us a better idea of Mahomed's intent.

> At the corner of George Street, there was until very lately an establishment on a novel plan. Mohammed, a native of Asia, opened a house for the purpose of giving dinners in the Hindustanee style, with other refreshments of the same genus. All the dishes were dressed with *curry-powder, rice, Cayenne, and the best spices* of Arabia. A room was set apart for smoking from *hookahs with Oriental herbs . . . Chinese pictures and other Asiatic embellishments,* representing views in India, oriental sports, and groups of natives decorated the walls (Freeman 110–11; emphasis added).

This graphic portrayal alerts us to the extent to which Mahomed went to create an Oriental atmosphere in order to distinguish his coffee house from the host of coffee houses mushrooming all over London. Mahomed deliberately fuses Chinese, Indian, Arabic identities to construct an Oriental tableau and actually uses objectified "native bodies", probably portraits displaying Indian scenes, to adorn the walls of his coffee house. But Mahomed could not sustain this Oriental fantasy for too long and for various reasons that are not completely clear, he was forced to declare bankruptcy in the *London Gazette* in 1812 (*Asians in Britain* 40).

The entrepreneurial streak in Mahomed would not let him quit even after he had to file for bankruptcy. Around 1814, he arrived in Brighton to establish himself as a "Shampooing Surgeon". Brighton, made more accessible by the railway connection from London, was fast becoming a fashionable sea-side resort primarily because of the virtues of sea-bathing in curing ailments, a medical view popularised by Dr Richard Russell and by the patronage of King George IV (*Asians in Britain* 40–41). Even before the arrival of Mahomed, Brighton already had a variety of bathing establishments which professed various cures, and it is amidst such an environment that Mahomed set up his shampooing establishment and bath. As with his coffee house, Mahomed knew that the only way he could survive amidst severe competition was by marketing his ethnicity. He had to find a way to emphasise that he was "different" and what he offered was both unique and superior to all the existing establishments in Brighton. Visram suggests that the reason Mahomed's bath was so successful was because he was at the right place at the right time (*Asians in Britain* 42). Brighton's Royal Pavillion, modelled on an Oriental mode of architecture and commissioned by King George IV, was completed by 1821 and Mahomed's baths, "with its associations of oriental luxury, would have blended in with such associations" (*Asians in Britain* 42). Though such a view cannot completely be disregarded, Mahomed's baths were a stupendous success primarily because of the shrewd business acumen of its proprietor. Mahomed draws on two prominent social and cultural conventions of the time to create a specific clientele for his establishment; his self-construction as an Eastern sage and "Shampooing Surgeon" is possible because of the lack of a well-organised medical system in Britain at the time. Moreover, his emphasis on commodification – ranging from presenting the immigrant body as an ethnic commodity to attract consumers and packaging the shampooing method as a successful medical procedure, to the publicity of the establishment through a narrative that is an extended advertisement in itself – is well aligned with the exotic commodity fetish of early nineteenth century Britain.[11] As Innes emphasises, "his dual presentation of himself as drawing on both the ancient arts of Hindu medicine and the modern science of Europe is illustrated in the advertisements for the baths, as well as the portraits of himself in European and 'exotic' oriental mode" (55).

Shampooing was a practice that was widely prevalent in India; it involved the massaging of the whole body with aromatic oils and was primarily believed to be helpful in increasing blood circulation and reducing stress. Mahomed invests this traditional practice with medical benefits while claiming that shampooing along with the vapour bath is "in all cases of violent exercise . . . a quick and delightful restorative" (17) compared to the traditional warm bath. He is quick to emphasise in his frontispiece that he alone is responsible for introducing this particular Indian method of shampooing, distinguished by its medical benefits, to Britain.

> Shampooing; or Benefits Resulting From the Use of The Indian Medicated Vapour Bath, As introduced into this country, by S. D. Mahomed, (A Native of India) containing a brief but comprehensive view of the effects produced by the use of the Warm Bath, in comparison with Steam or Vapour Bathing. Also A detailed account of the various Cases to which this healing remedy may be applied; its general efficacy in peculiar diseases, and its success in innumerable instances, when all other remedies had been ineffectual. To which is subjoined An Alphabetical List of Names (Many of the very first consequence,) subscribed in testimony of the important use & general approval of The Indian Method of Shampooing. (29)

Even though this text is clearly meant to be a promotion for his establishment, Mahomed cunningly structures it around testimonials by satisfied patrons in order to avoid allegations that he is blowing his own trumpet. Mahomed thus adopts a publicity stunt akin to the modern day money-back guarantee; he is so confident of his abilities that he would rather let his patrons do the talking.

In order to distinguish himself both from itinerant Oriental peddlers who sold medicinal drugs and from other quacks, Mahomed needed to adopt a title to somewhat legitimise his establishment as something which was indeed offering a medical cure for serious ailments, and he did this by calling himself a "Shampooing Surgeon". Even though the organisational structure of the medical profession was in near chaos before the passage of the Medical Act of 1858 and "quacks," "empirics," and "drug peddlers practiced freely with no legal sanctions against them" (Petersen 5), Mahomed did his best to document his medical credentials by claiming that he "was educated to the profession of, and served in the Company's Service, as a Surgeon" (vii). There is no concrete evidence of Mahomed ever getting a medical degree or a university education in India. So he cleverly decided to stick with the epithet of surgeon rather than physician, because having lived in Britain for a considerable time before setting up the vapour bath, he knew that a university education was what distinguished physicians from other orders of medical practitioners like surgeons and apothecaries.[12] This apparent deception did not sit well with the medical faculty who, Visram quotes, called him "a cheat and a Hindoo juggle" (*Asians in Britain* 41). But Mahomed took great pains in his preface to protect himself against such ridicule by relying on his ethnicity and presenting himself as a pioneer in this field. But as with all new discoveries, he acknowledged that there would be some amount of scepticism. The desire to present "indisputable evidence" (Mahomed ix) of the effectiveness of his practices is what ultimately resulted in his compilation of testimonials from satisfied patrons.

Even as he struggled with charges of inauthenticity, Mahomed's text managed to forge new grounds. In a world obsessed with boundaries and a desire to keep the realms of the coloniser/colonised, native/immigrant and Hindu/Muslim markedly distinct, Mahomed not only literally disrupted boundaries between brown and white bodies by bringing them in close proximity to each other in the enclosed space of the vapour bath, but also blurred religious distinctions between Hindus and Muslims. He stated that "to the hindoos, who are the cleanest and the finest people in the East, we are principally indebted for the Medicated Bath, in cases of disease and bodily infirmity" (15). His religious identity as a Muslim doesn't prevent him from claiming allegiance to a distinctly Hindu tradition and he draws his conviction from a popular discourse dating from the Mughal age that identified Hindus simply as inhabitants of the land of Hindustan.

The text itself is divided into several chapters devoted to particular ailments like asthma, contractions, paralysis, rheumatism and sprains and each is prefaced by a brief introduction followed by a comparative analysis of why the medicinal vapour bath is more effective than the warm bath, as prescribed by the traditional medical faculty in Britain. This is followed by testimonials from grateful patrons who have been cured of their respective ailments by the magical properties of the vapour baths. Mahomed had already emphasised that he was an innovator of this method and that "the herbs and essential oils with which my Baths are impregnated, are brought expressly from India, and undergo a certain process known only to myself, before they are fit for use" (17). Throughout the text, he reiterates his claims and constantly warns against imitators who might try to usurp his credibility. In fact, so confident is he of his methods that he even proudly announces "*I challenge competition from the cures which I have performed*" (37).

Each testimonial is structured in a similar way; it highlights the failure of traditional remedies in curing the ailment, mentions the initial scepticism that surrounds the experimentation of a new form of treatment and finally expresses the profound gratefulness which generally accompanies a complete cure. Mahomed's remedies produced glowing reviews from his patrons; in most cases, they expressed a sincere desire to spread the word about the efficacies of the cure so that more people could benefit from the magical transformative power of the vapour bath. The language in most of the letters is strikingly utilitarian. Following their recovery, Mahomed's patrons wished to share their exultation with the general mass so "that it may give hope and confidence to the afflicted" (Mahomed 30), and they do so even more willingly because they "desire the good of others; it being a pity that such a valuable remedy should not be made public" (22).

The letters also make constant comparisons between traditional medical practices and the curative power of Mahomed's methods. The text includes a letter to the *Brighton Gazette*, dated 27 September 1821, that explicitly explains why Mahomed's method is infinitely better than conventional medical practices. "It is not generally known, that the celebrated comedian, Mathews, whose surgical attendants pronounced him *incurable*, and stated that he would be a cripple for life, in consequence of a dislocation from the hip, occasioned by the accident of his being, some time ago, thrown out of his gig, was completely and effectually cured by Mahomed's process of shampooing" (Mahomed 92). This passage is particularly fascinating because it effectively sums up all of Mahomed's strategies. It establishes that Mahomed's methods produce better outcomes, that an ailment which had been earlier pronounced "incurable" (he even italicises the word to emphasise it) has been healed, and that a "cripple," that is, a dysfunctional white body, has been made whole by the intervention of this Eastern medical man. What is also worth emphasising here is that the process of shampooing is never described in great detail. Aside from one letter from F. Carter which mentions the use of a particular medicine – "tobacco leaves steeped in a particular liquid" (Mahomed 78) – the minimal description of the actual shampooing process manages to preserve the mysterious allure of the exotic East in the public imagination. The focus is constantly redirected to the transformative power of the process that heals the afflicted white body into wholeness with a symbolic dropping of the crutches, an image that is reiterated throughout the text.

The image of the crippled white body plagued by different diseases ranging from rheumatism to gout and sprains is one of the central tropes in the text. The letters repeatedly emphasise that after constant interventions of Mahomed's shampooing and vapour bath, the white body is restored to health and any kind of external support, like crutches, are completely discarded. For example, this was mentioned in a letter from Stephen Robinson, "after three of your Medicated Indian Vapour Baths, Mrs. R. was enabled to lay aside her crutches and walk a considerable distance" (Mahomed 29) and "after coming out of the Bath the third time, Lady Louisa walked across the room without support" (56). The space of the bath is marked as a healing space where the brown body, through its knowledge of healing practices, salvages the diseased white body and nurses it back to health. The implication here is that rapid industrialisation and Britain's preoccupation with its imperial expansion had fundamentally damaged the British body politic. Britain had gained substantial economic prosperity but fissures had started to develop in the social fabric, as evident from the chaotic nature of the medical system. Mahomed's narrative suggested that intervention by immigrants like him was vital for the well-being of the British body politic. His claims were bolstered when he was hailed the "star of the east" by one of his patrons, W. M. Hart, who hoped that he would "be the means of guiding thousands from the bed of affliction, to the comforts of ease, health, and happiness" (Mahomed 31). An excerpt from a letter from a patron published in the *Brighton Gazette* similarly emphasises that having experienced "the invigorating and healing effects of this Eastern remedy, we shall be among its greatest advocates" (80).

Mahomed's grand claims are given further credence by an ode published in the *Brighton Gazette* on 8 October 1822. This mysterious patron, who is initialled as M. W., hailed Mahomed as his Muse and "*Indian sage*" (Mahomed 88) and launched into a glorious eulogy about Mahomed's steam baths. Addressed to both Mahomed and a Mr Bolton, who we are told "first employed steam-engines in coining" (87), it insisted that the true achievement or potential of "steam" was not to be found in the harnessing of steam boats or steam engines which are at the heart of Britain's mercantile economy but instead in Mahomed's use of steam as a restorative and salutary agent, for "What use are honours, plenty, wealth, / without the best of treasures, health?" (87). In the true spirit of the industrial capitalist economy, health is equated with money, but what is more interesting to note is the deflation of the very symbol of Britain's industrial and imperial ambitions, the steam engine and steam boat, to a state of nothingness. As if that wasn't enough, the ode ends with a powerful admonishment to Bolton to make way for the Eastern sage – "Bolton! Give place – the *Indian sage*/ Doth all my Muse's powers engage; / *Thou* giv'st the uncertain treasure, wealth, / But *He Heaven's richest blessing, Health*" (88). There is little chance of ascertaining the identity of the contributor, but by including this ode among other things in his text, Mahomed both engages in self-promotion and succeeds in somewhat legitimatising his, and by extension, the presence of other Indian immigrants in the imperial metropolis.

Dean Mahomed thus succeeds in doing what many would have deemed impossible for an immigrant struggling to negotiate his identity in an alien space. He undoubtedly engages in "ethno-pornography" by self-orientalising for commercial gains. But what is remarkable is that he mobilises and embellishes existing stereotypes about the "other" (the reification of physical differences, the immigrant/colonised body as an object, the lure of the exotic East) and yet manages to make them work in his favour. The ostentatious décor of his bath, his flamboyant Oriental outfits, especially during royal visits, the constant emphasis of his ethnic identity, were all part of his strategy to make the Oriental body hyper-visible and make his bathing establishment more appealing to consumers in a highly competitive market. Visram writes of how local newspapers in Brighton repeatedly mentioned Mahomed as one of its local celebrities remembered as "'gorgeous in Eastern costume, with his pretty wife by his side, and a dagger in his girdle" (*Asians in Britain* 43). At the same time, by being economically viable, he effectively resisted social marginalisation and, in fact, successfully argued for the indispensability of foreign presence on the British mainland. As Kate Teltscher emphasises:

> Shampooing, with its celebration of Dean Mahomed's skill in healing the sick and its reference to his 'introduction' of the benefits of Indian medicine, provides a 'potent counter to the familiar trope of the East as the source of the nation's infection,' . . . [he thus] becomes one of the most striking instances of the ability of some Asian and black writers to draw upon their cultural heritage and their double identity as loyal subjects and 'outsiders' to offer themselves as pathologists, able to redeem the ills which will make Britain a whole and healthy body. (413)

ENGLAND IS NOT THE PLACE FOR ME

As the preceding analysis demonstrates, there was a significant black/brown presence in England throughout the eighteenth and the nineteenth century that has often been overlooked in British national history. Alongside the hundreds of black immigrants and travellers who were promptly relegated to the margins on their arrival or when their utility diminished, there were plenty of others who were actively engaged in defying all odds and finding a foothold for themselves in an inhospitable society, even at the cost of somewhat compromising their ethnic identity. In the second half of the nineteenth century and the first half of the twentieth century, Britain saw an increasing number of visitors and migrants from the colonies and there was a profusion of narratives that emerged during this period. Ruvani Ranasinha points out that even at the most conservative estimate, at least eighty different South Asian writers published over 180 books between 1870 to 1950 (147). The number is obviously considerably more if we include writers from Africa and the West Indies. Many of them were part of the urban elite who came to England for education. Others stayed in England for several years. And others divided their time between England and their home country. Most of them wrote insightful accounts about their observations of British society and customs and, because of their perspective as outsiders looking in, their contribution is invaluable to British colonial history. But with the publication of Charles Darwin's *Origin of Species* in 1859, the discourse of exoticism became unmistakably tinged with reified notions of difference and racial superiority and even educated, middle-class natives were prone to prejudice and bigotry. The Jamaican writer, Mary Seacole, spoke of her disappointment at the stereotypes she faced in England in her *The Wonderful Adventures of Mrs Seacole in Many Lands* (1857). When she came to England, she was quite confident that her healing powers were superior to European doctors, as her competency had been well documented in New Granada and Jamaica, where she was successfully able to treat cholera and yellow fever. But "in England all her attempts to put her gifts and understanding to the service of the British are dismissed with barely disguised contempt or indifference ... She realized that it is her colour that prevents them from taking her seriously" (Innes 128). Cornelia Sorabji, who came to England to study medicine in the 1890s, did not fare any better. She recalls in her autobiography *India Calling* (1934) that in spite of her being Christian, her sari-clad appearance on the streets would often lead to random urgings to convert to Christianity. "Indian boys and men had long been coming in respectable numbers. But their clothes had not the same allure or suggestion of foreignness. Dear old ladies were always trying to convert me – for instance – the heathen at the gates" (Sorabji 52). The social reformer Behramji Malabari was also disappointed at the reception he got in England. He came to England in 1890 to garner support for his crusade against Hindu marriage customs and brought with him a pamphlet entitled *An Appeal from the Daughters of India.* Even though he believed that Indian women would benefit from continued British presence in India, everything about life in London irked him no end and he made his impressions of England abundantly clear in *The Indian Eye on English Life* (1893). In language that is strikingly similar to English travel narratives about India, Malabari comments on the frenzied pace of life in the metropolis:

> People live in a whirlwind of excitement, making and unmaking their idols almost every day. They seem to be consumed by a mania for novelty; everything new serves to keep up the fever of excitement. Today they will set up a fetish, anything absurd, fantastic, grotesque, and worship it with breathless enthusiasm ... In a word, the English seem to be as fickle as their weather. Flit about poor butterflies of a brief season, and drink your fill of the poisoned nectar you so madly crave. (Malabari 40)

Such observations would become quite standard in post-1948 narratives about postcolonial Britain as the new wave of immigrants from the colonies tried to find a place for themselves in an increasingly openly xenophobic society. These narratives will be explored in greater detail in the next chapter.

Works Cited

Banton, Michael. "The Cultural Determinants of Xenophobia." *Anthropology Today* 12.2 (1996): 8–12. Print.

Clayton, Antony. *London's Coffee Houses: A Stimulating Story*. London: Historical Publications, 2003. Print.

Dabydeen, David. *Hogarth's Blacks: Images of Blacks in Eighteenth-Century English Art*. Kingston-upon-Thames: Dangaroo P, 1985. Print.

David, Deirdre. "Empire, Race, and the Victorian Novel." *A Companion to the Victorian Novel*. Eds. Patrick Brantlinger and William B. Thesing. Massachusetts: Blackwell, 2002. 84–100. Print.

Equiano, Olaudah. *The Interesting Narrative of the Life of Olaudah Equiano, or Gustavus Vassa, the African, Written by Himself*. Ed. Werner Sollors. New York: Norton, 2001. Print.

Fisher, Michael. *The First Indian Author in English: Dean Mahomed (1759–1851) in India, Ireland and England*. Delhi: Oxford UP, 1996. Print.

———, ed. *The Travels of Dean Mahomet: An Eighteenth-Century Journey through India*. Berkeley: U of California P, 1997. Print.

Foster, Stephen. "Exoticism as a symbolic system." *Dialectical Anthropology* 7. 1982–1983: 21–30. Print.

Freeman, Janet Ing, ed. *The Epicure's Almanack: Eating and Drinking in Regency London*. London: The British Library, 2012. Print.

Fryer, Peter. *Staying Power: The History of Black People in Britain*. London: Pluto P, 1984. Print.

Gallini, Clara. "Mass Exoticisms." *The Postcolonial Question: Common Skies, Divided Horizons*. Eds. Ian Chambers and Lidia Curti. New York: Routledge, 1998. 212–20. Print.

Hofkosh, Sonia. "Tradition and *The Interesting Narrative.*" *Romanticism, Race, and Imperial Culture, 1780–1834.* Eds. Alan Richardson and Sonia Hofkosh. Bloomington: Indiana UP, 1996. 330–44. Print.

Huggan, Graham. *The Postcolonial Exotic: Marketing the Margins.* New York: Routledge, 2001. Print.

Innes, C. L. *A History of Black and Asian Writing in Britain.* Cambridge: Cambridge UP, 2002. Print.

James, C. L. R. "Africans and Afro-Caribbeans: A Personal View." *Writing Black Britain: 1948–1998: An Interdisciplinary Anthology.* Ed. James Procter. New York: St. Martin's P, 2000. 60–63. Print.

Kaplan, Louise J. *Cultures of Fetishism.* New York: Palgrave Macmillan, 2006. Print.

Khan, Abu Taleb. *Travels of Mirza Abu Taleb Khan in Asia, Africa and Europe.* Trans. Charles Stewart. London: Longman, Hurst, Rees, and Orme, 1810. Print.

Macaulay, Thomas Babington. *Selected Writings.* Eds. John Clive and Thomas Pinney. Chicago: The U of Chicago P, 1972. Print.

Mahomed, S. D. *Shampooing, or Benefits Resulting from the Use of the Indian Medicated Vapour Bath, As Introduced into this Country, by S. D. Mahomed (A Native of India).* Brighton: Creasy and Baker, 1826. Print.

Malabari, Behramji M. *The Indian Eye on English Life; or Rambles of a Pilgrim Reformer.* Westminster: Archibald Constable, 1893. Print.

Miller, Andrew. *Novels behind Glass: Commodity Culture and Victorian Narrative.* Cambridge: Cambridge UP, 1995. Print.

Mohr, Dunja. M. *Embracing the Other: Addressing Xenophobia in the New Literatures in English.* Amsterdam: Rodopi, 2008. Print.

Pal-Lapinski, Pia. *The Exotic Woman in Nineteenth-Century British Fiction and Culture: A Reconsideration.* New Hampshire: U of New Hampshire P, 2005. Print.

Peterson, Jeanne, M. *The Medical Profession in Mid-Victorian London*. Berkeley: U of California P, 1978. Print.

Porter, Roy. *Bodies Politic: Disease, Death and Doctors in Britain, 1650–1900*. Ithaca: Cornell UP, 2001. Print.

Ranasinha, Ruvani. "Textual Culture and Reception: 1870–1950." *South Asians and the Shaping of Britain, 1870–1950: A Sourcebook*. Ed. Ruvani Ranasinha. Manchester: Manchester UP, 2012. 147–206. Print.

Richards, Thomas. *The Commodity Culture of Victorian England*. New York: Verso, 1991. Print.

Root, Deborah. *Cannibal Culture: Art, Appropriation, and the Commodification of Difference*. Boulder, Colorado: Westview P, 1996. Print.

Salter, Joseph. *The Asiatic in England: Sketches of Sixteen Years' Work Among Orientals*. Seely, Jackson & Halliday, 1873. Print.

Sandhu, Sukhdev. *London Calling: How Black and Asian Writers Imagined a City*. London: Harper Collins, 2003. Print.

Santaolalla, Isabel. "Introduction: What is 'New' in 'New' Exoticisms?" *"New" Exoticisms: Changing Patterns in the Construction of Otherness*. Ed. Isabel Santaolalla. Amsterdam: Rodopi, 2000. 9–17. Print.

Seacole, Mary. *The Wonderful Adventures of Mrs Seacole in Many Lands*. Ed. Ziggy Alexander and Audrey Dewjee. Bristol: Falling Wall P, 1984. Print.

Sollors, Werner. Introduction. *The Interesting Narrative of the Life of Olaudah Equiano, or Gustavus Vassa, the African, Written by Himself*. By Olaudah Equiano. Ed. Werner Sollors. New York: Norton, 2001. ix–xxxi. Print.

Sorabji, Cornelia. *India Calling*. London: Nisbet, 1934. Print.

Teltscher, Kate. "The Shampooing Surgeon and the Persian Prince; Two Indians in Early Nineteenth-century Britain." *Interventions 2*, no. 3 (2000): 409–23; 413. Print.

The Epicure's Almanack or Calendar of Good Living. London: Longman, Hurst, Rees, Orme & Brown, 1815. Print.

Visram, Rozina. *Asians in Britain: 400 Years of History*. London: Pluto P, 2002. Print.

——. *Ayahs, Lascars and Princes: Indians in Britain 1700–1947*. London: Pluto P, 1986. Print.

Waite, Maurice, ed. *Paperback Oxford English Dictionary*. Seventh Edition. Oxford: Oxford UP, 2012. Print.

Wong, Sau-Ling Cynthia. *Reading Asian-American Literature: From Necessity to Extravagance*. Princeton: Princeton UP, 1993. Print.

Notes

1. See Judith Raiskin's essay "England: Dream and Nightmare" in *Wide Sargasso Sea*.
2. I draw heavily from Fryer, Innes and Visram's two books for the historical details documented in this chapter.
3. Several EIC officials came back to Britain having amassed a fortune in India and, having assumed the epithet of a "nabob", set up lavish establishments in London. Indian servants were an integral part of such establishments.
4. For a detailed account of the relationship of Queen Victoria with Abdul Karim, see pages 30 to 33 of Visram's book *Ayahs, Lascars and Princes: Indians in Britain 1700–1947*.
5. I am using Anne McClintock's term here. In *Imperial Leather*, she makes a distinction between scientific racism and commodity racism.

> I am doubly interested in the Pears' Soap ad because it registers an epochal shift that I see having taken place in the culture of imperialism in the last decades of the nineteenth century. This was the shift from scientific racism – embodied in anthropological, scientific and medical journals, travel writing and ethnographies – to what I call commodity racism. Commodity racism – in the specifically

> Victorian forms of advertising and photograph, the imperial Expositions and the museum movement – converted the narrative of imperial Progress into mass-produced consumer spectacles. (McClintock 33)

6. For a detailed description of the significance of the book, see pages 36 to 46 of Innes's book, *A History of Black and Asian Writing in Britain.*
7. For more on this, see Louise J. Kaplan's *Cultures of Fetishism.*
8. In her introduction to a collected edition, Dunja M. Mohr has an elaborate footnote on the etymology of the word xenophobia and its various connotations. Xenophobia is translated as "fear of strangers" (Mohr x). She quotes Michael Banton's essay, "The Cultural determinants of Xenophobia" from *Anthropology Today*, where he explains the distinction between xenophobia and racism – "Racism can then be the name for that dimension by which persons assigned to another group are kept as a distance because they are considered racially inferior. Xenophobia can designate the way that others are kept at a distance because they are considered different" (Banton 8). Drawing on Banton, Mohr concludes that "racism implies hostility and extreme hatred, presupposing the superiority of the Self over the Other, whereas xenophobia is chiefly associated with fear of the Other – often fear of the Other within the Self" (Mohr x). It is in this sense that I use the word "xenophobia" in this chapter.
9. I am using this term in the sense that Sau-ling Cynthia Wong defines Frank Chin's use of "food pornography". Wong defines the term as a form of self-orientalisation used by Asian American writers that "translates to reifying perceived cultural differences and exaggerating one's otherness in order to gain a foothold in a white-dominated social system . . . . superficially, food pornography appears to be a promotion, rather than a vitiation or devaluation of one's ethnic identity" (Wong 55). Though Wong specifically uses this term in the context of alimentary culture in Asian American literature, I think it has striking parallels to Dean Mahomed's self-exoticisation in the early nineteenth century.

10. Fisher conducts a comprehensive study of Mahomed's life in his two books, *The Travels of Dean Mahomed* and *The First Indian Author in English*.

11. In his book on medical practices in Britain, Roy Porter emphasises that "though in recent times the medical profession has energetically massaged its own public image, identity-management is not unique to the modern era of spin doctors and public-relations consultants – indeed it dates back to the very first medical professionals" (129). Dean Mahomed does this "identity management" extremely effectively in the preface of this fascinating text. He presents himself as an authority on the shampooing practice in India but claims that his experiments have led him to believe that the process "which in India is used as a restorative luxury, would, with certain improvements, operate in this country also, as a most surprising and powerful remedy for many cases of disease"(Mahomed viii).

12. As Jeanne Peterson confirms, unlike physicians who had to have a university degree to practice medicine, surgeons were not university-educated men in early nineteenth-century Britain: "As was traditional among craftsmen, surgeons learned their skills by apprenticeship. Their training was necessarily practical and not at all classical or theoretical as the physicians' training reputedly was . . . . In order to make a living, most members of the surgeons' corporation had to prescribe and dispense drugs as well" (10).

FIVE

STRANGERS IN A STRANGE LAND

Assimilation, multiculturalism and the re-evaluation of national identity in postcolonial Britain

This has been the century of strangers, brown, yellow, and white. This has been the century of the great immigrant experiment. It is only this late in the day that you can walk into a playground and find Isaac Leung by the fish pond, Danny Rahman in the football cage, Quang O'Rourke bouncing a basketball, and Irie Jones humming a tune. Children with fast and last names on a direct collision course. Names that secrete within them mass exodus, cramped boats and planes, cold arrivals, medical checkups. It is only this late in the day, and possibly only in Willesden, that you can find best friends Sita and Sharon, constantly mistaken for each other because Sita is white (her mother liked the name) and Sharon is Pakistani (her mother thought it best–less trouble). Yet, despite all the mixing up, despite the fact that we have finally slipped into each other's lives with reasonable comfort (like a man returning to his lover's bed after a midnight walk), despite all this, it is still hard to admit that there is no one more English than the Indian, no one more Indian than the English. There are still young white men who are *angry* about that; who will roll out at closing time into the poorly lit streets with a kitchen knife wrapped in a tight fist.

—Zadie Smith, *White Teeth*

On 22 June, 1948, the *S. S. Empire Windrush* docked at the English port of Tilbury, heralding what many critics facetiously refer to as the beginning of a "colonisation in reverse" (Dawson 1). This is not to suggest that the presence of foreigners in Britain was an anomaly up to this point. As we have seen in the earlier chapter, there was a significant black presence in England in the eighteenth and nineteenth century. In fact, the late nineteenth century saw an increase in the rise of colonial migrants and travellers to the imperial metropolis. More often than not, these travellers came from a privileged background and were treated with more curiosity than anything else; if anything, their fluency in their master's language was a source of constant amazement. In "Africans and Afro-Caribbeans; A Personal View" (1984), the writer C. L. R. James tells us that native Britons were extremely confused by his command of the English language when he first came to Britain in 1932. "What surprised them most was that I had read more and had absorbed more of English literature and history than almost every English person I met. My knowledge astonished them and I was astonished too because I thought I had been reading what the average educated person in England read" (Procter 60). But other, less privileged migrants, like the ayahs and lascars who were brought to Britain in the service of colonial officers, were not so lucky to be just an object of wonder. They were often left to fend for themselves after they were discharged from service and led extremely hard lives on the margins of society, as Rozina Visram so elaborately documented in her books and as we have seen in the preceding chapter.[1] But the arrival of four hundred and ninety-two West Indian immigrants on the *Empire Windrush* and the mass migration from the former colonies that followed changed the course of British history in such significant ways that a thorough re-evaluation of what it meant to be British became inevitable in post-war Britain. Standing on the deck of the *S. S. Empire*

Windrush, Calypso singer Lord Kitchener performed a paean to the immigrant dream of England as a land of possibility. Sung in English instead of the more popular Trinidadian Creole, Lord Kitchener's song "London is the Place for Me" captures the optimism and hope that was felt by this initial group of West Indian immigrants.

> Well believe me, I am speaking broad-mindedly
> I am glad to know my mother country
> I've been traveling to countries years ago
> But this is the place I wanted to know
> London, that's the place for me.[2] (Dawson 1)

This utopian vision of the mother country as a welcoming place in Lord Kitchener's song was a result of the steady indoctrination of colonial subjects that happened during colonial rule in the West Indies, as well as in Africa and South Asia. Most colonial subjects truly believed that when they did undertake the journey to the mythical England, they would be welcomed with open arms. In his "Journey to an Expectation" (1960), George Lamming tells us, "England lay before us, not a place, or a people but as a promise and an expectation" (Procter 57). As Ashley Dawson explains, "Schoolchildren in Britain's many tropical colonies had been fed a diet of British literature for a half-century or so . . . . According to colonial ideology, Britain originated democracy, the rule of law, and the ethics of good sportsmanship. How could she fail to provide an adequate welcome to her colonial sons and daughters?" (Dawson 2). Stuart Hall also corroborates Dawson's words as he explains the haloed vision of England in the colonial imaginary:

> When finally Britain convinced itself it had to decolonize, it had to get rid of them, *we all came back home*. As they hauled down the flag, we got on the banana boat and sailed right into London . . . they had always said that this was really home, the streets were paved with gold and, bloody hell, we just came

to check out whether that was so or not. (Hall 24; emphasis added)

This naïve optimism felt by immigrants in the late 1940s was not out of place, especially since the arrival of the *Windrush* was to some degree facilitated by the passage of the Nationality Act of 1948. After the loss of Britain's jewel in the crown following Indian Independence in 1947, and after some restlessness and political uncertainty even in settler colonies like Australia and Canada, Britain's Prime Minister Clement Attlee and the government passed the Nationality Act – which promised colonial subjects formal equality throughout the Empire – in order to somewhat placate the rising discontent in the remaining colonies. At first glance, this piece of legislation seemed to encourage colonial migration to the metropolis because of an implicit understanding that formerly colonised subjects would be on par with British citizens. But even as the *Windrush* arrived, Britain's latent xenophobia and anxieties about racial purity began to re-surface. Not only was little effort made to successfully assimilate the immigrants into British society, a member of Attlee's cabinet even suggested that the passengers aboard the *Windrush* be transported to "East Africa, where they might be of economic utility without sullying the blood of Britain's white population" (Dawson 9). For these West Indian immigrants and the successive groups of immigrants thereafter, the naïve optimism and hope of a better life in the mother country soon turned into disillusionment and despair as they realised that the streets of gold they had imagined were far from reality. Furthermore, rampant discrimination in access to public service jobs, housing opportunities and even successive incidents of racial violence and rioting marked the black British experience in the second half of the twentieth century. Lord Kitchener's optimism gave way to the reality of his experiences as this poem from 1956 illustrates:

My Landlady's too rude,
In my affairs she likes to intrude.
This is how she start
A lot of restrictions to break your heart.
After ten o'clock
Tenants must know my front door is lock,
And on the wall she stick up a notice
'No lady friends not even a Princess.' (Procter 20)

This chapter then will explore black British writing that charts some of the experiences of colonial immigrants. Interestingly, at the same time, most postcolonial black British writing also argues for an evaluation of British national identity based on the rapidly changing demographics, and this emerges as a dominant theme in most writings from post-war Britain.

BRITAIN IN THE COLONIAL IMAGINATION

In the footsteps of Edward Said's influential book *Orientalism*, postcolonial critics have continuously engaged with the different ways in which Western discourse invented and mobilised imaginings of the "Other", and how that became inextricably linked with English self-representation. But as Simon Gikandi suggests in *Maps of Englishness*, not many theorists dwell on how the "Other" gazes at Europe. "Colonial culture is as much about the figuration of the metropolis in the imagination of the colonized themselves as it is about the representation of the colonized in the dominant discourses of the imperial center" (Gikandi 20). Priya Joshi's book, *In Another Country: Colonialism, Culture and the English Novel in India*, attempts to fill this void in different ways and is crucial in establishing how colonial/post-colonial migrants/immigrants are actively involved in their representation in the West. It is well documented by Thomas Macaulay's infamous declaration in the "Minute on Indian Education" (1835) that creating a class of "mimic men" was one of the official objectives of the imperial educational policy (Macaulay 249). But it was also the colonial desire to "familiarize themselves with the language, style, and manners of the ruling race" (Varma 6) that aided the imperial mission of producing a class of anglophiles and was also responsible for a utopic vision of England in the minds of colonial subjects. In her book, Joshi works through a rich colonial archive to trace the reading patterns of Indians during the nineteenth century. She demonstrates that contrary to common British perception garnered from the Orientalist narratives of Forster, Kipling or Orwell, Indians did not just "travel in trains, deliver and receive mail, play cricket and polo, bargain, dissemble, squat, spy, eat, shout, sleep, talk, hunt, and then talk some more" (Joshi 35), but were in fact voracious readers who consumed just about anything that was made available to them through the imperial machinery. Joshi reveals how less popular British novelists like G. W. M. Reynolds and Marie Corelli had devoted readerships in India perhaps because "Indian readers would have discovered a symbolic affinity between their struggles against the colonial machinery and those of Reynolds' oppressed masses in London against the ruling classes" (82). It is not surprising then that a lot of postcolonial novels talk about the weight of Britain's colonial education apparatus. In fact, Bharat, a character in Yasmine Gooneratne's *A Change of Skies*, is not exaggerating when he says: "Long before I saw Britain for the second time (as a postgraduate student), I knew London . . . I knew, long before I ever ate one, what muffins tasted like" (Lokuge 12). In his autobiographical novel, *To Sir, With Love*, the Caribbean writer E. R. Braithwaite remembers his childhood in British Guiana – "As a boy I was taught to appreciate English literature, poetry and prose, classical and contemporary, and it was absolutely natural for me to identify myself with the British heroes of the adventure stories against the villains of the piece who were invariably non-British and so, to my boyish mind, more easily capable of villainous conduct" (40). To Amitav Ghosh's young narrator in *The Shadow Lines*, London is very much an imaginative space shaped by the stories that his friend Ila and his Uncle Tridib have told him. It is glorious in all its halo, it signifies all that he yearns to achieve, it helps him go through his mundane life in Calcutta before he realises that expectations never match up to reality. "It was easy enough on the A to Z street atlas of London that my father had brought me. I knew page 43, square 2, by heart: Lymington Road ought to have been right across the road from where we were. But now that we had reached the place I knew best, I was suddenly uncertain" (*Shadow Lines* 57). Little did the colonial establishment realise that their administrative and educational policies in the colonies would backfire. Propelled by years of imperial myth-making, colonial subjects would be ready to undertake a steady immigration from the colonies into the heart of the imperial metropolis in the hope of a better life.

THE REALITIES OF POST-WAR BRITAIN

As early as 1907, the writer Jean Rhys, arriving as Gwen Williams at Southampton, recalls the shock of arrival in her first novel, *Voyage in the Dark* (1934):

> It was as if a curtain had fallen, hiding everything I had ever known. It was almost like being born again. The colours were different, the smells were different, the feelings things gave you right down inside were different. Not just the difference between heat, cold; light, darkness; purple, grey. But a difference in the way I was frightened and the way I was happy. (James 37)

V. S. Naipaul, on his arrival in London, was surprised to find that the city of his imagination did not exist. In *An Area of Darkness* he recalls, "It [London] had become the centre of my world and I had worked hard to come to it. And I was lost. London was not the centre of my world. I had been misled; but there was nowhere else to go" (42). In Caryl Phillips's *A Distant*

Shore (2003), Gabriel/Solomon, a refugee from an unnamed war-torn country in Africa, makes his way to England amidst countless hardships and difficulties. He had always been told that British people were good and kind and, like other people in the colonies, he was under the impression that England would always welcome its colonial subjects with open arms, especially those fleeing any form of persecution. One of his fellow refugees, Bright, insists that he too is an Englishman and well respected by white people – "Only the white man respects us, for we do not respect ourselves. If you cut my heart open you will find it stamped with the word 'England.' I speak the language, therefore I am going to England to claim my house and my stipend" (Phillips 119). Gabriel is apprehensive about this optimistic vision of Bright's, but he lets himself follow through with the journey only to realise that the England in which he finds himself is teeming with immigrants like him struggling to get a foothold and who are thwarted in their attempts at every point. This was nothing like the England he had envisioned – "This is not the England that he thought he was traveling to, and these shipwrecked people are not the people that he imagined he would discover. Under this sad roof, life is stripped of ambition and it is broken" (155). Other writers talk about similar experiences. Following an incident on the city bus where a white female passenger refuses to sit beside him, E. R. Braithwaite – in *To Sir, With Love* – expresses his dismay and disillusionment with London's discriminatory attitude towards immigrants after facing the ravages of war.

> I suppose I had entertained some naively romantic ideas about London's East End, with its cosmopolitan population and fascinating history. I had read references to it in both classical and contemporary writings and was eager to know the London of Chaucer and Erasmus . . . . But this was different. There was nothing romantic about the noisy littered street bordered by an untidy irregular picket fence of slipshod shopfronts and gaping

bomb sites . . . . There was rubble everywhere and dirt and flies. And there were smells. (9)

In Hanif Kureishi's *The Buddha of Suburbia*, Haroon and his friend Anwar arrived in Britain with their heads stuffed with images of daffodils and the Lake country from their colonial education. They were in for a rude awakening: "London, the Old Kent Road, was a freezing shock to both of them. It was wet and foggy; people called you 'Sunny Jim'; there was never enough to eat, and Dad [Haroon] never took to dripping on toast" (24) because he had "thought it would be roast beef and Yorkshire pudding all the way" (24). Kureishi emphasises that the image Haroon had of England was a myth: "He'd never seen the English in poverty, as roadsweepers, dustmen, shopkeepers and barmen. He'd never seen an Englishman stuffing bread into his mouth with his fingers, and no one had told him the English didn't wash regularly because the water was so cold – if they had water at all" (24). [3]

Moreover, when Haroon "tried to discuss Byron in local pubs no one warned him that not every Englishman could read or that they didn't necessarily want tutoring by an Indian on the poetry of a pervert and a madman" (*Buddha* 25). Like C. L. R. James quoted before, Haroon's knowledge of English literature is astonishing to Britons and they look at him not simply with wonder but almost as an object of ridicule. This profound alienation and disillusionment that immigrants experienced was further exacerbated by the discrimination and prejudice they encountered while seeking employment or housing. In his *Postcolonial London: Rewriting the Metropolis*, John McLeod suggests "Several postcolonial writers bear witness to the racism, violence and torment they and others experienced during the decade, and offer a bleak, sombre view of the city that demythologizes the colonial myth of London as the heart of a welcoming site of opportunity and fulfilment for those arriving from the colonies" (27). Writers like Sam Selvon in *The Lonely Londoners* (1956), Colin MacInnes in his *City of Spades* (1957), and *Absolute Beginners* (1959), V. S. Naipaul in *The Enigma of Arrival* (1987) and George Lamming in *The Emigrants* (1954) captured the angst of immigrants as they struggled to find a place in an alien society. Jobs were also hard to come by and as Moses, Selvon's protagonist in *The Lonely Londoners,* points out, "They send you for a storekeeper work and they want to put you in the yard to lift heavy iron. They think that is all we good for, and this time keeping all the soft clerical jobs for them white fellars" (Selvon 36). In *To Sir, With Love*, E. R. Braithwaite recounts how he too learnt this the hard way. He had come to England for post-graduate study in 1939 with the naïve belief that England was the "hub of fairness, tolerance and all the freedoms" (39). He didn't hesitate to volunteer for the Royal Air Force because he was just serving his mother country. Yet after six years, when he has to find a stable job, he realises that nobody would hire him based on the colour of his skin. When he makes an appearance before prospective employers who had been courteous before seeing him, he is immediately told that the position has miraculously been filled. He is repeatedly denied employment and housing till he is completely exasperated with the racial politics that he sees playing out – "Disillusionment had given place to a deepening, poisoning hatred; slowly but surely I was hating these people who could so casually, so unfeelingly deny me the right to earn a living. I was considered too well educated, too good for the lowly jobs, and too black for anything better" (Braithwaite 44).

Wole Soyinka, the Nigerian writer who came to England in 1954 to study at the University of Leeds, also had several encounters with racism. He recalls one such encounter in his poem "Telephone Conversation" written in 1960. The poem is structured as a telephone conversation between a black African of unspecified nationality and a prospective landlady from whom he hopes to rent an apartment in London. The conversation occurs in one of the iconic red London telephone booths while a "Red double-tiered/Omnibus squelching tar" (78) glides by. Like Braithwaite, who had decided to call his remaining two prospective employers and tell them that he was black in *To Sir, With Love*, Soynika's narrator decides to make the woman aware about his ethnicity before he actually goes to look at the property – "I hate a wasted journey – I am African" (78). The result of this revelation is predictable as there is a sharp intake of breath after which she proceeds to interrogate him on the shade of his skin colour – light, dark, very dark, etc. The narrator, stupefied by this open demonstration of racism, realises the stories he has heard before about instances like this were real after all. But instead of being rattled, the narrator turns this into an opportunity for satire as he slowly exposes the deep-seated prejudices that linger in postcolonial England. The "lipstick coated, long gold-rolled/Cigarette-holder pipped" (78), ostensibly middle-class voice doesn't know the meaning of words like "sepia" or "brunette". Her ignorance is exposed and she is reduced to a laughable caricature as the narrator proceeds to narrate the different shades of his body parts. The poem ends on a sombre note with the narrator asking, "'Madam,' I pleaded, 'wouldn't you rather/See for yourself?'" (78) before the telephone receiver is slammed down on him. The narrator's question remains unanswered, but the silence beautifully highlights the daily prejudices and humiliation to which colonial immigrants were exposed in England. As Braithwaite points out acerbically while reflecting on his very British upbringing in British Guiana, "It is wonderful to be British – until one comes to Britain" (39).

This active discrimination and atmosphere of racial intolerance soon led to active violence against immigrants. In Kureishi's *The Buddha of Suburbia*, Anwar and his wife Jeeta had transformed a toy shop in South London into a relatively successful grocery business, but their everyday existence was threatened by the spectre of racial violence. The area they lived in was economically impoverished and full of neo-fascist groups who, at night, "roamed the streets, beating Asians and shoving shit and burning rags through their letter-boxes. Frequently the mean, white, hating faces had public meetings and the Union Jacks were paraded through the streets, protected by the police" (*Buddha* 56). In Phillips's *A Distant Shore*, the character Mahmood had worked steadily to be in charge of one of his brother's restaurants, The Khyber Pass, in Leicester, and was hoping to even start a new business with his wife Feroza. But like in Kureishi's novel, the spectre of race-related bigotry and violence was omnipresent even in such a small Midland town and Feroza worried that it was leading to the premature aging of her husband.

> The sight of fat-bellied Englishmen and their slatterns rolling into The Khyber Pass after the pubs had closed, calling him Ranjit or Baboo or Swamp-Boy, and using poppadoms as Frisbees, and demanding lager, and vomiting in his sinks. And threatening him with his own knives and their beery breath, and bellowing for mini-cabs and food that they were too drunk to see had already arrived on the table in front of them, was causing Mahomed to turn prematurely grey. (Phillips 180)

It was becoming increasingly clear to colonial immigrants in the 1950s that the Nationality Act of 1948 had been something of a hogwash. The idea of equality for all colonial subjects was tenable as long as they and the British citizens remained geographically separate. As long as there was material distance between the English and the "Other", it was possible to control them using various discursive practices, but "the influx of immigrants from the former colonies ensures that blackness is not simply a semantic or performative category but a real presence and cultural threat to the pastoral image of England as an island" (Gikandi 70). As soon as this new wave of immigrants in the metropolis started demanding their rights as guaranteed by the Nationality Act, all of the rhetoric about racial hierarchy that was mobilised to establish colonial rule began to resurface in Britain and new nationalistic policies had to be formulated in order to control the pace of immigration. In other words, when there was a threat of the destabilisation of English identity, there was the need for both new state regulations and a new set of discourses that would curb the growing presence of immigrants within the physical confines of England. Yet, as McLeod asserts, in the work of some of these writers "despite the cruelty of urban life experienced by newcomers, London is also daringly imagined as making possible a utopian social blueprint where the prejudices and hostilities encountered on the street might be conquered" (27). For instance, in *Colour Bar* (1954), Learie Constantine talks about the initial racial segregation that took place in terms of housing which then spread to other port cities like Liverpool, Glasgow, Hull, Newcastle and even London, but downplays any racial violence. "Coloured residents in Britain, despite the fact that they are unable to choose freely where they will live and find themselves virtually obliged to reside in a recognized 'black area' which is often a slum area, have won general respect from Police and city authorities for living quietly, soberly and lawfully" (Procter 65).

POLICING BLACK BRITAIN: RACIAL POLITICS AND BRITISH NATIONAL IDENTITY FROM THE 1950S TO 1980S

In Selvon's 1956 novel, *The Lonely Londoners*, Moses, at the beginning, talks about the increasing number of West Indians in the streets of London but naïvely assumes that nothing will be done to control them – "In fact, the boys all over London, it ain't have a place where you wouldn't find them, and big discussion going on in Parliament about the situation, though the old Brit'n too diplomatic to clamp down on the boys or to do anything drastic like stop them from coming to the Mother Country" (Selvon 8). But this illusion of diplomacy did not last long. Even though the government initially hesitated to introduce a formal policy to curb immigration out of a desire to maintain whatever semblance of imperial power it still had in parts of the world, in the early 1950s, immigration into England was actively discouraged and colonial officials were asked to be far more discerning and even restrictive in the number of passports given to immigrants at the point of embarkation. When that did not have much of a noticeable effect, members of the British Parliament floated a discourse about the nature of British identity quite naturally predicated on a racial model. As Dawson points out, "In March 1954, a small number of Tory members of Parliament began a debate by alleging that 'immigrants' were abusing the welfare state and that 'virile young men' from the colonies posed a threat to law and order" (11), reigniting debates around colonial criminality and sexual miscegenation. Following the Notting Hill riots of 1958, black and Asian immigrants in England were beginning to encounter a "growing politics of racial intolerance expressed at an official, institutional level" (Procter 95). Even though the government officially criticised the perpetrators of the riot, Prime Minister Macmillan argued for the need for legislation that would control immigration from the Caribbean and South Asia, thus effectively holding immigrants responsible for the violence. Critics like Dawson and Procter point out that it was the cuts in spending for housing and education and a general scarcity of jobs post 1948 that led to competition and antagonism between colonial immigrants and the white working class, leading, in some degree, to these race riots. But by introducing new controls and "by portraying the Caribbean residents of British cities as the catalysts of racial conflict, the government conveniently brushed over its own role in fostering the social conditions that helped generate conflicts such as the Notting Hill riots" (Dawson 12). Thus, in striking contrast to the Nationality Act of 1948, which encouraged immigration from England's former colonies, the Commonwealth Immigration Act of 1962 started distinguishing between British passport holders born in the UK and those born in the colonies or former colonies, effectively reducing the status of Britain's immigrant population to that of second-class citizens. Amidst this backdrop, Conservative Party MP Enoch Powell delivered his controversial "Rivers of Blood" speech at a Conservative Association meeting in Birmingham on 20 April 1968, in which he ominously stated that the expanding immigrant population was a legitimate threat to Britain's unsullied racial identity and called for the mass repatriation of immigrants. As McLeod points out, "Keen to frighten his white British audiences into a sense of apocalyptic doom, Powell was not immune from deploying incendiary images in his proleptic vision of a Britain destroyed by immigration" (129–130). In this speech, Powell engages in rampant fear-mongering as he points out the consequences of colonial migration. He claimed that it was "like watching a nation busily engaged in heaping up its own funeral pyre"(Powell 283). The tone gets more ominous as he sounds the warning bells:

> As I look ahead, I am filled with foreboding; like the Roman, I seem to see 'the River Tiber foaming with much blood.' That tragic and intractable phenomenon which we watch with horror on the other side of the Atlantic but which there is interwoven with the history and existence of the States itself, is coming upon us here by our own volition and our own neglect. Indeed, it has all but come. (289)

McLeod rightly emphasises that "Powell's declarations of race and nation sadly granted political respectability to racism and attracted instant popular support, the effects of which were immediately felt on London's streets (and elsewhere)" (129). There were numerous reports of openly racist incidents where immigrants would be declined service at restaurants and were subject to racist name-calling and violence on the streets of London. Powell's apocalyptic words led to the adoption of more policing strategies and more calls for repatriation of black British subjects over the 1970s. And in 1981, British Prime Minister Margaret Thatcher "formally rescinded the provisions of the 1948 act. British national identity, long based on exclusionary informal parameters, at last became a matter of blood belonging. While explicit talk of repatriation died down following Thatcher's politically astute co-option of the fascist vote, exclusionary definitions of national identity had been codified that sanctioned myriad forms of racist denigration, harassment, and inequality" (Dawson 13).

Simon Gikandi points out that "Empire gave England power and prestige but left its national character untouched; even at the height of its empire, England remained an island untouched by the landscapes and subjects it dominated; now with post imperial migration, the blacks have come to contaminate the realm" (86). Along with the new state policies and regulatory measures, new discourses were also introduced in Britain that were based on a monolithic, racialised conception of national identity where, inevitably, being English was placed at the top of the totem pole. One among these was the discourse of cultural nationalism or cultural assimilationism. Bart Moore-Gilbert points out that during the 1960s "whereas the far Right seeks the expulsion of 'aliens,' 'cultural assimilationism' advances the ostensibly more moderate position that immigrants can, indeed, belong to British society – provided that they surrender the cultural identities which they have brought with them and adopt the norms, values and social practices of the host society" (131). So assimilation into English society would require a complete disavowal of immigrants' racial and cultural identity. But as Avtar Brah points out, from a frequently cited 1966 speech by the then Home Secretary Roy Jenkins, in order to project the

British state as more inclusive, the discourse of assimilationism was soon replaced by that of integration, which Jenkins claimed "should be viewed, not as a 'flattening process of assimilation but as equal opportunity, accompanied by cultural diversity, in an atmosphere of mutual trust'" (Brah 25). However, such a policy, with its emphasis on cultural diversity, is inherently problematic not only because it obscures the economic and political realities of immigrant life, but also because it veers towards the currently in-vogue concept of "multiculturalism". In both America and England, discourses of "multiculturalism" were mobilised as an antidote to fears of cultural miscegenation from immigrant communities within the nation state. By forcing immigrant communities into specific ethnic enclaves, the discourse of multiculturalism, in its existing form, insists on celebrating difference, thus effectively othering such communities.

For Stuart Hall, this reformulation of English national identity was institutionalised when Margaret Thatcher came into power in 1979; when "Englishness", variously referred to as "Thatcherism", equated national community with the white race. Hall points out "This nationalist discourse eschews the openly racist language of biological superiority and uses instead the more coded language of cultural difference to promote an English nation that is culturally homogenous and exclusively white" (Chrisman 107). Ziauddin Sardar elaborates – "Multiculturalism comes chronologically after 'assimilation' and 'integration' . . . . Multiculturalism focused on 'celebrating difference' . . . . Difference is a hot commodity in our art galleries and museums where it is regularly constructed, fabricated and paraded as a sign of enlightened plurality" (138). It is amidst this changing racial and cultural climate that writers like Hanif Kureishi, Zadie Smith, Meera Syal, Monica Ali, Caryl Phillips and David Dabydeen actively engage with the question of Black British-ness and urge a re-evaluation of British national identity.

Black British writers have been actively engaged in debunking the exclusionary notion of British identity that came into the forefront of British politics and culture during Margaret Thatcher's tenure. Unlike the United States, where "black" refers exclusively to people with origins in Africa, in Britain the term "black" came to refer to people from Africa, Asia and the Caribbean. It became a political signifier, used more as a term of political solidarity against the discrimination of the white Britisher rather than as an indicator of biological difference. Ashley Dawson explains: "As the contributors to *The Empire Strikes Back* pointed out, it made little difference whether immigrants to Britain were called 'blacks, browns, darkies, nig-nogs, or Pakis.' The goal of such derogatory labels was the same; to represent non-whites as outsiders, an invading force of dangerous aliens who threatened British identities that were conceived as pure and perpetual" (19). The term "Black-British" then became an important tool for activists and writers like Kureishi, Monica Ali and Meera Syal who used it to argue for a more inclusive definition of British identity.[4] Through their novels, these writers puncture the discourse of happy multiculturalism that insisted on celebrating cultural co-existence while deliberately ignoring the uncomfortable realities of immigrant life. At the same time, writers like Kureishi often mocked the naïveté of immigrants who held on to the idea of Britain as a land of possibility and, not unlike their ancestors in the nineteenth century, were only too happy to engage in self-exoticisation in the hope of economic viability and increased social acceptance. Also, by portraying immigrant life in all its complexity, contemporary British writers argue for a reconfigured, more inclusive idea of Englishness and advocate a new form of multiculturalism that, as Kureishi states, is "not a superficial exchange of festivals and food, but a robust and committed exchange of ideas" (*The Carnival of Culture*).[5] In other words, while these writers attempt to resist the imposition of a specific ethnic identity – fostered by discourses like multiculturalism – and record the plurality of immigrant responses to a xenophobic society, they simultaneously underscore the fact that British-Asian immigrants are not passive subjects from whom culture is appropriated. Instead, their work highlights the ways in which South Asian immigrants are also active participants in the process of cultural consumption, or as Sunaina Maira puts it "not only on the receiving, or rather giving, end of cultural appropriation" (331).

Home and Belonging in Late Twentieth-Century Immigrant Narratives

As we repeatedly see in novels by Black British writers, postcolonial England was an extremely hostile environment, hardly conducive to the fulfilment of the immigrant dream of a land of unimagined possibilities. In spite of the burgeoning immigrant population, the imperial metropolis remained a very segregated place, where a cross-pollination of cultures was actively discouraged. In an essay titled "On Cultural Diversity", published as part of a collection on the future of British cities in 1991, West Indian writer David Dabydeen paints a pretty bleak picture of London.

> A city packs people in. They live on top of each other, alongside each other, sideways to each other. The city is a hive in this sense, but there are no inevitable passageways between one cell and another. And this has been the problem for West Indian culture in London – the white people who come to the West Indian cells for a while, to attend a carnival or to taste curried goat, return afterwards to their own cells. They don't spend long enough in the West Indian cells to appreciate the syntax, metre, chords, daubs, noises and smells created in these cells.
>
> And they don't invite West Indians to visit their cells (called universities, banks, concert halls, theatres, arts councils, art galleries, Houses of Parliament, television studios) for a

> prolonged period either, or in any great numbers. The city is culturally diverse, but there is little cross-fertilization of cultures taking place. White people remain incarcerated in their own cells, afraid to venture out in case they are mugged by West Indians. ("On Cultural Diversity" 104)

Critics like John McLeod have pointed out that Dabydeen's pessimism possibly resulted from the underlying tension that he witnessed between the white British public and the black immigrant population in the wake of the race riots of the 1980s and the Rushdie Affair (159). But similar representations of London abound in the works of other postcolonial writers like Andrea Levy, Hanif Kureishi, Atima Srivastava, Meera Syal, Bernardine Evaristo and Monica Ali. Ali's *Brick Lane,* published in 2003, tells the story of the Bangladeshi, particularly the Sylheti, community inhabiting an area of East London. Ali has been panned by critics for portraying Brick Lane as something of an urban ghetto jostling with ethnic shops and Bangladeshi restaurants, with very little interaction with the wider world of London. Nazneen, Ali's female protagonist, finds herself in an alien world when she dares to venture out of Brick Lane:

> Every person who brushed past her on the pavement, every back she saw, was on a private, urgent mission to execute a precise and demanding plan: to get a promotion today, to be exactly on time for an appointment, to buy a newspaper with the right coins so that the exchange was swift and seamless, to walk without wasting a second . . . Nazneen, hobbling and halting, began to be aware of herself. Without a coat, without a suit, without a white face, without a destination. (*Brick Lane* 40)

In contrast to the languid pace in the Tower Hamlets where she lives, surrounded by other Bangladeshi immigrants and engaged in the menial work of a seamstress, this frenzied world outside terrifies Nazneen. But the frisson of apprehension/excitement quickly dissipates when Nazneen realises that in spite of being markedly distinct in her sari, she is as good as invisible to the people around her. In an epiphany, she notes, "They could not see her any more than she could see God. They knew that she existed (just as she knew that He existed) but unless she did something, waved a gun, halted the traffic, they would not see her" (40). In a single moment, Nazneen learns that in this postcolonial London, immigrants like herself would, at the most, be just tolerated, and this thought ironically frees her so she can fade into the background and turn her gaze on them. Confined to her home and burdened with her duties as wife and mother, the ice-skating that she watches on television becomes a symbol of her freedom and empowerment. So quite fittingly at the end, when Nazneen makes the decision to not return to Bangladesh with her husband even though she had longed for it all her life, she goes ice-skating with her daughters and her close friend Razia. As she hesitates to skate in a sari, Razia reminds her, "This is England . . . You can do whatever you like" (415). This optimism at the end of the novel is less about the possibilities England seems to offer the immigrants, but more about Nazneen emerging from the shadows of the patriarchal power exerted both by her husband Chanu and her lover Karim. She is able to voice her own desires and do right by her daughters in a comparatively less conservative British society. Nazneen, like Alsana in Zadie Smith's *White Teeth*, appears to be more sane and clear-eyed than her husband as she heeds her friend Mrs Azad's earlier words about assimilation – "Assimilation this, alienation that! . . . Fact: we live in a Western society. Fact: our children will act more and more like Westerners, Fact: that's no bad thing. My daughter is free to come and go. Do I wish I had enjoyed myself like her when I was young? Yes!" (89). As Nick Bentley points out, "Implicit in Mrs Azad's celebration of her daughter's freedom is recognition of what she sees as empowerment of women in contemporary Western society.

Throughout the novel, it tends to be the women who gain most by accepting British culture" (Bentley 92).

Chanu, Nazneen's husband, is less perspicacious. He seems to have a naïve belief in the possibilities that London can offer immigrants till he realises that his degree in English from Dhaka University is not much valued in England, and when it comes to promotions, his intellectually inferior white colleague will always be ahead of him. He is troubled by the fact that his little daughter Shahana acts like a "memsahib" and knows nothing about the history of her own country. "In the sixteenth century, Bengal was called the Paradise of Nations? These are our roots. Do they teach these things in the school here? Does Shahana know about the Paradise of Nations? All she knows about is flood and famine. Whole bloody country is just a bloody basket case to her" (*Brick Lane* 148). Chanu conveniently forgets that Shahana was born in England, was technically English, was learning plenty about her country in her history class and had no desire to know anything more about her roots.

> Shahana did not want to listen to Bengali classical music. Her written Bengali was shocking. She wanted to wear jeans. She hated her kameez and spoiled her entire wardrobe by pouring paint on them. If she could choose between baked beans and dal it was no contest. When Bangladesh was mentioned she pulled a face. She did not know and would not learn that Tagore was more than poet and Noble Laureate, and no less than the true father of her nation. Shahana did not care. Shahana did not want to go back home. (*Brick Lane* 144)

In fact, Shahana doesn't miss any opportunity to claim that she is from London when the family is out in a public place. On a tourist bus to see the city, Chanu stumbles over Bangladesh in a response to a question from the tour-guide, while Shahana rolls her eyes and says "I'm from London" (244). Alienated from his children, emotionally distanced from his wife as she embarks on a secret love affair with the young radical Karim, and in the face of an increasingly inhospitable workplace, Chanu is forced to leave his job and take up the job of a taxi driver. His disillusionment is complete as he laments that the life of an immigrant is inherently tragic.

> This is the tragedy. When you expect to be so-called integrated. But you will never get the same treatment. Never . . . I myself have struggled for a long time. But now I am simply taking the money out. 'Every rupee of profit made by an Englishman is lost forever to India.' That is how I am playing them at their own game now. (*Brick Lane* 202)

As Nick Bentley points out, Chanu's "initial celebration of English culture and learning show him at first to be an appropriated colonial subject. His later position, however, represents colonisation in reverse as he is now satisfied by taking money from the nation that had exploited his people in the days of Empire" (91). Eventually, completely disillusioned with immigrant life, Chanu chooses to return to Bangladesh and his love of English literature that can be nurtured fruitfully in the former colonies, even as Nazneen chooses to stay back in England.

All of these themes appear in varying degrees in the works of Hanif Kureishi, one of the most well-known British-Asian writers. In one of his early plays, *Borderline,* one of Kureshi's characters, the investigative journalist Susan, asserts, "I want to show how things are changing under the skin of England. I want to chart the pricking of a certain kind of imperial inflation" (Moore-Gilbert 4). This demythologising of England remains a dominant motif, particularly in his early work. *My Beautiful Laundrette* (1985), directed by Stephen Frears, tells the story of the unlikely friendship between Pakistani Omar and white Johnny while they embark on the successful renovation of a launderette in strife-torn, racist London. The film subverts some of the prevalent racial stereotypes by showing Omar and his rich uncle Nasser as wielders of economic power while Johnny is clearly in a subservient role as he assists in the renovation. Yet none of the characters can escape their place on the fringes of society; Omar and Nasser are marked by their race while Johnny and his skinhead buddies are marked by their working class status. The imperial metropolis is shown in an even more unflattering light in *Sammy and Rosie Get Laid* (1988). The film chronicles the racial and sexual encounters that ensue when Rafi, a politician presumably from Pakistan, visits his son Sammy and his partner Rosie in London, and scenes of idyllic London are interspersed with scenes of metropolitan police in riot gear. Susie Thomas points out, "During the making of the film, Thatcher was elected for a third term: homophobia, homelessness, ruthless enterprise capitalism and racist police brutality turn London into a 1980s version of 'The Waste Land' by T.S. Eliot (1888–1965)" (Thomas 45). This picture of London as a place of profound hardship and alienation continues in *London Kills Me* (1991), *The Buddha of Suburbia* (1990), and *The Black Album* (1995). It has earned Kureishi the ire of right-wing English critics who irritably ask, " . . . why show a semi-derelict London, riddled with unemployment, poverty and racist violence?" (Thomas 26). But Kureishi refuses to play the role of "the writer as public relations officer" (Moore-Gilbert 45) and maintains that even though most of his protagonists are from the lower echelons of England's race and class hierarchy, they rarely lack agency. Omar in *My Beautiful Laundrette* is "a 'wog' to the white fascists and an 'in-between' to his Pakistani relatives; but far from feeling himself a misfit, he is confident that he can make it in Britain" (Thomas 26).

Like Shahid in Kureishi's *The Black Album*, Karim in *The Buddha of Suburbia* is initially more secure in his claim to Englishness as a second-generation immigrant. In the famous opening lines of the novel, he proudly proclaims:

> My name is Karim Amir, and I am an Englishman born and bred, almost. I am often considered to be a funny kind of Englishman, a new breed as it were, having emerged from two old histories. But I don't care – Englishman I am (though not proud of it), from the South London suburbs and going somewhere. (*The Buddha of Suburbia* 3).

The word "almost" from the opening sentence becomes the key to Karim's self-fashioning throughout the novel as he constantly oscillates between distancing himself from and embracing his racial and sexual identity. Initially, as this sentence demonstrates, Karim's South Asian lineage makes him uncomfortable and he staunchly insists on staking a claim to Englishness as his national identity. He is sure his lighter skin aids his self-representation, but as he realises soon enough, xenophobia is rampant in English schools towards immigrant kids or kids with biracial identities. As someone born in England, Karim is justified in feeling a sense of belonging to England, but like Haroon, Karim realises that even though he was supposed "to be English, . . . to the English we were always wogs and nigs and Pakis and the rest of it" (53). Being biracial does not grant him any special privilege. The constant racial discrimination doesn't stop Karim from holding on to the possibility of London being a more inclusive space for people like him, as opposed to the narrow-minded suburbs. When a move to London is in the works, Karim reveals that he "fantasized about London and what I'd do there when the city belonged to me . . . there were thousands of black people everywhere, so I wouldn't feel exposed" (121). But his experience with Thomas Shadwell's theatre group, where he is forced to enact the role of boy-hero Mowgli from Kipling's *Jungle Book* simply because he looks the part, jolts him into the reality of his position in London's society.

In Meera Syal's novel *Anita and Me* (1996), a semiautobiographical novel about a young girl growing up in the mining town of Tollington in the late 1960s and early 1970s, Meena is initially very confident that England is her home. Her family is an atypical immigrant family; though her mother remembers her old home often, there is an unspoken understanding that England is their new home now. The novel does not gloss over the hardships that her parents and other relatives faced initially when they tried to make a home in England. Meena often overhears conversations about what her family had to endure. "You remember, walking round Swiss Cottage, trying to find a boarding house that did not have that sign 'No Irish, Blacks or Dogs?' . . . Hai, the letters I wrote home, so many lies about the jobs we had, the money we were making. My mamaji still thinks I am a college lecturer . . . You know that old trick, you ring up and get an interview in your best voice, then they see your face and suddenly the job is gone" (Syal 165). Like the protagonists in some of Kureishi's works, in this novel too, the colour of their skin prevents immigrants from having fair access to either housing or jobs. But Meena, unlike other children in immigrant narratives, has a lot of freedom; she is not religiously constrained, as is evident from her visits to Sunday school. And, as she herself contemplates, her parents are still deeply in love, unlike the dysfunctional English families she sees all around her. It is only her parents' perpetual concern that she might be led morally astray without the right kind of influence that suffocates her, and she looks for succour in the wild, carefree Anita Rutter. Her increasing correspondence with Anita however makes her defensive about her cultural baggage. As a growing adolescent with limited social mobility, her desire to be accepted within her peer group is not extraordinary. But the desire to belong triggers musings about racial and cultural differences and the thought that the reason Anita prefers fat Sally or Sherrie is because of her race takes shape. This is when the trappings of Indian culture start becoming intolerable to her. She wants fish fingers and chips instead of home-cooked dal and sabzi, and would rather wear flared jeans than be caught in a flashy Indian outfit.

Meena's veneer of self-confidence begins to crack as she contemplates the possibility of a hypothetical interracial relationship. She is aware on some level that she will always be different and she teeters between the classic immigrant conundrum of visibility and invisibility.

> For some reason, I wanted to shed my body like a snake slithering out of its skin and emerge reborn, pink and unrecognizable. I began avoiding mirrors, I refused to put on the Indian suits my mother laid out for me on the bed when guests were due for dinner. I hid in the house when Auntie Shaila bade loud farewells in Punjabi to my parents from the front garden, I took to walking several paces behind or in front of my parents when we went on a shopping trip, checked my reflection in shop windows, bitterly disappointed it was still there. (Syal 146)

Like Zadie Smith's second-generation character of Magid Iqbal in *White Teeth* – who conveniently changes his name and identifies himself as Mark Smith to his English friend, much to the wrath of his father Samad Iqbal – Meena here is clearly wishing for something that wouldn't mark her as different and would earn her the closeness that she craves with Anita. Yet she feels sick to her stomach when she hears Anita gloat about skinheads attacking an Indian bank manager:

> . . . we went Paki bashing, it was bosting! This Paki was standing at a bus stop, he was in a suit, it was dead funny! Nah, I only watched, the lads like did it, you know, and us wenches, we just shouted and held their lager . . . They really did him over and you know what, the stupid bastard didn't do nothing back! (277)

Meena realises she will clearly be just another Paki to Anita. Even when Sam, one of the perpetrators of that violent attack, tells her later on that she is different and not another Paki, she doesn't believe him one bit and emphasises her Indian-ness in a way she had never done before.

> 'When I said them,' he rasped, 'I never meant you, Meena! It was all the other, not you!'...
>
> 'You mean the others like the Bank Manager?'
>
> Sam looked confused.
>
> 'The man from the building site. The Indian man. I know you did it. I *am* the others, Sam. You did mean me.' (314)

Her final act of grace, refusing to indict Sam and Anita in the accident involving Tracey, raises her above her white peers; by absolving their guilt and giving them a chance to reform themselves, she stakes a firmer claim to her adopted land, symbolised by the family's actual physical move to a bigger house away from the suburb that had been her home for many years. As the narrative draws to a close, Meena confidently asserts: "I now knew I was not a bad girl, a mixed-up girl, a girl with no name or no place. The place in which I belonged was wherever I stood and there was nothing stopping me simply moving forwards and claiming each resting place as home" (Syal 303).

Questions of home and belonging are not as easy for Zadie Smith's protagonists in her brilliant debut novel, *White Teeth* (2000). England isn't a welcoming place for Samad Iqbal, Smith's one-armed protagonist, originally hailing from Bangladesh who had served in the British army during the Second World War. Samad had idolised his ancestor, the mythical Mangal Pande, who is often credited for starting the Indian Mutiny of 1857, and had hoped to follow in his legendary footsteps by earning glory for himself and his country through his military exploits. When his dreams did not manifest, he finds himself stuck in a dead-end job as a waiter in a London restaurant. He is forced to wrestle with his identity and his place in the bigger scheme of things.

> I'm a cripple . . . And my faith is crippled . . . What am I going to do, after this war is over, this war that is already over – what am I going to do? Go back to Bengal? Or to Delhi? Who would have such an Englishman there? To England? Who would have such an Indian? They promise us independence in exchange for the men we were. But it is a devilish deal. (Smith 93)

Samad here articulates the classic schizophrenia characteristic of the immigrant condition – a state of perpetual un-belonging. But as he rightly recognises, he is, like other immigrants, fundamentally damaged, not just physically but emotionally and psychologically as well. This metaphor of being split, fractured, damaged is reiterated throughout the text. Samad recognises this as he says to Mad Mary, "We are split people. For myself, half of me wishes to sit quietly with my legs crossed, letting the things that are beyond my control wash over me. But the other half wants to fight the holy war. Jihad!" (150). Samad's wife Alsana tells Archie's wife Clara while they are both pregnant that their kids would have " . . . daddy-long-legs for fathers. One leg in the present, one in the past. No talking will change this. Their roots will always be tangled" (68), while Irie, Archie and Clara's daughter, horrified to learn that her mother had a set of false teeth most of her life, realises "Millat was right; these parents were damaged people, missing hands, missing teeth. These parents were full of information you wanted to know but were too scared to hear" (314). The implication here is unmistakable; Britain, in some way or the other, has been unable to fulfil the needs of its immigrant subjects, leaving them psychologically damaged and unable to function in a meaningful way.

Cultural confusion and stereotyping in immigrant narratives

In a 1967 speech quoted by Kureishi in his essay "The Rainbow Sign", British Conservative Party member Duncan Sandys emphatically asserted, "The breeding of millions of half-caste children would merely produce a generation of misfits and create national tensions" (6). Hanif Kureishi refers to this quote and to Enoch Powell's "Rivers of Blood" speech to illustrate the effect such rampant xenophobia and constant calls for repatriation was having on immigrants, including himself: "I wasn't a misfit; I could join the elements of myself together. It was the others, they wanted misfits; they wanted you to embody within yourself their ambivalence" ("The Rainbow Sign" 6). Zadie Smith's second-generation characters in *White Teeth* graphically capture this feeling of in-betweenness. English by birth, but marked as foreign by their appearance, they struggle equally with the burden of history and their own in-between identity. Like Karim and Meena, none of them are comfortable in their own skin. Magid reinvents himself as Mark Smith to his English buddies and desperately wishes to be:

> . . . *in some other family*. He wanted to own cats and not cockroaches, he wanted his mother to make the music of the cello, not the sound of the sewing machine . . . he wanted to go on biking holidays to France, not day-trips to Blackpool to visit aunties; he wanted the floor of his room to be shiny wood, not the orange-and-green swirled carpet left over from the restaurant; he wanted his father to be a doctor, not a one-handed waiter. (Smith 126)

Millat, on the other hand, tired of his father's partiality to Magid and the constant racial tension experienced in school, turns to radical Islam to try to find an identity for himself because

> . . . he knew that he, Millat, was a Paki no matter where he came from; that he smelled of curry; had no sexual identity; took other people's jobs; or had no job and bummed off the state . . . that he could be a dentist or a shop-owner or a curry-shifter, but not a footballer or a filmmaker . . . that no one who looked like Millat, or spoke like Millat, or felt like Millat, was ever on the

> news unless they had recently been murdered. In short, he knew he had no face in this country, no voice in the country. (194)

Millat takes part in a riot to burn Salman Rushdie's controversial book *The Satanic Verses* along with other fellow radicals even though he admits that he hadn't read the book, or more importantly did not need to, because like Kureishi's protagonist in *My Son the Fanatic*, the event, however irrational it might be, gives him a sense of belonging in a hostile country which is otherwise intent on pushing anybody who is different to the peripheries of society. So when Millat decides to make an appearance at Marcus Chalfen's Futuremouse convention and shoot the genetically modified mouse poised to change the path of history, he does so with the desire of claiming a bit of that history and to show the world that he too has a voice. As he sits on the bench where his father had inscribed his name years ago in an attempt to leave a mark on this land, Millat is filled with contempt for his father – "a faulty, broke, stupid, one-handed waiter of a man who had spent eighteen years in a strange land and made no more mark than this" (419). But Millat promises himself that he will change all this by standing up against Marcus Chalfen and his brother Magid, who symbolise the onslaught of the West, and boldly declaring that he was there "... to finish it. To revenge it. To turn that history around. He liked to think he had a different attitude, a second generation attitude. If Marcus Chalfen was going to write his name all over the world, Millat was going to write his BIGGER" (419).

Smith, like Syal, comments on the visible/invisible binary here. Even with the considerable black and Asian presence in England, non-white faces were a rarity on national television. As Syal's protagonist Meena mentions in *Anita and Me*:

> According to the newspapers and television, we simply did not exist. If a brown or black face ever did appear on TV, it stopped us all in our tracks. 'Daljit! Quick!' papa would call,

> and we would crowd round and coo over the walk-on in some detective series, some long-suffering actor in a gaudy costume with a goodness-gracious-me accent . . . But these occasional minor celebrities never struck me as real; they were someone else's version of Indian, far too exaggerated and exotic to be believable. (Syal 165)

It was convenient to imagine immigrants did not exist; if they did, it was easy to depict them as grotesque caricatures good for eliciting a few laughs. In a remarkable passage placed somewhat centrally in *White Teeth,* from which the epigraph to the chapter is drawn, Smith contemplates this disturbing position that immigrants are forced to inhabit. She rightly points out "It makes an immigrant laugh to hear the fears of the nationalist, scared of infection, penetration, miscegenation, which is small fry, *peanuts*, compared to what the immigrant fears – *dissolution, disappearance*" (272). As the novel so eloquently demonstrates, it is this fear of utter invisibility, of disappearance, that makes immigrants develop this urgency to find a place for themselves. So while Magid Iqbal finds his identity by embodying the Western man of science, Millat does it through embracing fundamentalism and direct action, while fifteen-year-old Irie Jones, burdened with her mother Clara's West Indian lineage that she doesn't fully grasp, is enamoured with the English family, the Chalfens, in spite of their ridiculousness. Irie "just wanted to, well, kind of, *merge* with them. She wanted their Englishness . . . Their Chalfenishness. The *purity* of it . . . To Irie, the Chalfens were more English than the English" (273). In strikingly similar language to Meena's confusion in Syal's novel discussed previously, we are told that Irie felt an "illicit thrill" when she visited the Chalfens – "She was crossing borders, sneaking into England; it felt like some terribly mutinous act, wearing somebody else's uniform or somebody else's skin" (273). But Irie's attempts at pseudo-Englishness doesn't help in clarifying her identity; in an impulsive moment towards the end of the novel, she sleeps with both Millat and Magid and discovers she is pregnant, thus indicating her child's roots will remain as entangled as ever.

It is this same fear of invisibility, of disappearance, that makes Karim, in *The Buddha of Suburbia*, give in to cultural stereotypes. Karim is asked to perform the role of the boy-hero Mowgli in Kipling's Orientalist classic, *The Jungle Book*, even though the theatre director Shadwell is completely puzzled when he realises that Karim doesn't speak any Indian languages and has never been to the country – "Everyone looks at you, I'm sure, and thinks: an Indian boy, how exotic, how interesting, what stories of aunties and elephants we'll hear now from him. And you're from Orpington" (*The Buddha of Suburbia* 141). Still, Shadwell declares Karim perfect for the role – "You are Mowgli. You're dark-skinned, you're small and wiry, and you'll be sweet and wholesome in the costume . . . Certain critics will go for you" (143). Karim resists this imposition, particularly when he is forced to emulate an Indian accent to sound authentic in his role by declaring that "It's a political matter to me" (147). He doesn't see why, as an English subject, albeit the son of an Indian immigrant, he should be coerced into a specific ethnic identity. But when Shadwell insists that "You [Karim] have been cast for authenticity and not for experience" (147), he realises that for an aspiring actor like him, ideologies have to be shoved aside for the sake of artistic concession and the good of the production. He thus dons the requisite sing-song accent, the brown body make-up and loin cloth for the role, even though he can now see through Shadwell's purported veneer of racial tolerance. Karim's English identity is thus completely nullified as he is pigeonholed into the specific ethnic identity that exists in England. Shadwell's attitude towards Karim doesn't only reveal the blatant racial stereotyping of the 1960s but also punctures the myth about the openness of liberal London that Karim had constructed prior to his move. As Nick Bentley suggests,

"Karim's experiences at the hands of Shadwell is an example of what Paul Gilroy has identified as 'cultural racism': a form of prejudice that does not focus directly on biology but attempts to re-establish a power relationship based on the perceived cultural practices engaged in by a particular ethnic group (164). In fact, as a biracial immigrant, Karim is also branded a "half-caste in England . . . belonging nowhere, wanted nowhere" (*The Buddha of Suburbia* 141), clearly echoing the comments of National Labour Party leader John Steel following the Notting Hill riots of 1958 – "We will be a nation of half-castes. The result is that the nation will possess neither the rhythm of the coloured man, nor the scientific genius of the European. The only thing we will ever produce is riots, just as do the mixed races of the world" (Dawson 28). And even though he is still uncomfortable with the significance of his actions, Karim, like Haroon, eventually warms up to this forced self-exoticisation because it brings him the attention that he has always craved, especially in London's theatre circuit – "Despite the yellow scarf strangling my balls, the brown make-up, and even the accent, I relished being the pivot of the production" (*The Buddha of Suburbia* 150). John Clement Ball suggests, "Father and son both become faux-Indians, successfully marketing back to the English warmed-over versions of their own popular appropriations of Indian culture" (Ball 233).

Kureishi continues to show the cultural confusion and despair faced by immigrants in some of his later work. In his short story turned film, "My Son the Fanatic", Pervez works hard as a taxi driver and "dreams of doing well in England" (*My Son the Fanatic* 120) by giving his boy Ali a good education in the hopes that he will become a good accountant. He even relishes bacon and fried bread and instructs his wife to cook pork sausages because they were "not in the village now, this is England. We have to fit in" (*My Son the Fanatic* 126). But Ali, increasingly disenchanted by his father's liberal attitudes towards alcohol and women, and particularly because of his relationship with the prostitute Bettina, turns to radical Islam and accuses his father of "groveling to the whites" (128) and being "too implicated in Western civilization" (125). As Kureishi explains in "The Road Exactly", the introduction he wrote for *My Son the Fanatic*, "My father's generation came to Britain full of hope and expectation. It would be an adventure, it would be difficult, but it would be worth it . . . [but] the 'West' was a dream that didn't come true. But one cannot go home again. One is stuck" (*Dreaming and Scheming* 219–220).

ANXIETY ABOUT MISCEGENATION AND SEXUAL IDENTITY IN LATE TWENTIETH-CENTURY BRITAIN

In his essay, "Blacks and Crime in Post War Britain", Paul Gilroy states that, "Concern about criminal behavior of black settlers in the late 1940s and 1950s assumed a different form [to that of the 1970s], clustering around a distinct range of anxieties and images in which issues of sexuality and miscegenation were often uppermost" (Procter 71). Following the Notting Hill riots, anxiety surrounding miscegenation became one of the bulwarks of racial conflict in post-colonial Britain. Ashley Dawson points out:

> Anger over sexual relations between black men and white women was a crucial catalyst of the riots. Agitators such as John Steel played on fears that sex between Englishwomen and black male immigrants from the Caribbean would create a mongrel population in Britain. Notwithstanding their formal rights as British subjects, in other words, black migrants were viewed by the neofascists, by many members of the political establishment, and by much of the populace in general as a threat to racial purity and consequently, to national identity. (Dawson 29)

Rules regulating sexuality, especially female sexuality and marriage, were central to the imaginings of English national identity in the 1960s, and now that the black men had made their way into the metropole, the virtuous white women had to be protected at all costs. The erotic is inextricably linked with the exotic in *The Buddha of Suburbia*. Karim's easy masquerade where he enacts racial stereotypes doesn't serve him well when it comes to actual physical relations between immigrants and whites, and he quickly learns that the xenophobia he experiences everyday translates into ugly racism and open hatred when it comes to matters of sexuality. Karim's first lesson in this is when he goes to visit Helen, the girl he is beginning to like, as he weans himself away from his infatuation with Eva's son Charlie. Just as Karim calls out to Helen, Helen's dad appears in the yard and irately warns Karim to get off the premises because his daughter won't go out with " . . . boys. Or with wogs" (*The Buddha of Suburbia* 40). Helen's father then launches into a vitriolic attack on immigrants and warns Karim that "However many niggers there are, we don't like it. We're with Enoch. If you put one of your black 'ands near my daughter I'll smash it with a 'ammer! With a 'ammer!" (40), before setting the dog on him. Karim is disillusioned yet again through his experience with his fellow actor, Eleanor, in Shadwell's theatre group. He is initially intoxicated by his emotional and sexual encounters with her, but soon realises that she would never completely belong to him not simply because of her somewhat privileged class status and her easy accessibility to some of the most glamorous social circles, but because she is consumed by "white liberal guilt" (Buchanan 50) because of the suicide of her black lover, Sweet Gene, in the face of blatant racism within London's theatre community. Gene's sense of self-worth was tied up with his acting ambitions, and when he is repeatedly forced to enact stereotypes of black men, like criminals and taxi-drivers, on stage instead of being in "Chekhov or Ibsen or Shakespeare" (*The Buddha of Suburbia* 201), he internalises his frustrations, leading to his suicide. Further, when Karim is forced into a sexual orgy with Eleanor, Pyke and his wife Marlene because she fancied him, Karim realises that emotions have no place in this tableau of racial fetishism and that "the reduction of black men to sexual fetishes placed them in the passive position of the sex object" (Dawson 39). From his encounters with Helen and Eleanor, Karim realises that black men were either agents of contamination or sexual fetish objects.[6] In a telling statement, Karim acknowledges the futility of his actions.

> We pursued English roses as we pursued England; by possessing these prizes, this kindness and beauty, we stared defiantly into the eye of the Empire and all its self-regard – into the eye of Hairy Back, into the eye of the Great Fucking Dane. We became part of England and yet proudly stood outside it. But to be truly free we had to free ourselves of all bitterness and resentment, too. How was this possible when bitterness and resentment was generated afresh every day? (*The Buddha of Suburbia* 227)

Like Sweet Gene, Karim is finally disillusioned with his dream of England, this time as a land of sexual possibilities.

The Need for a Re-evaluation of British National Identity

If anything is apparent from these novels, it is the fact that Britain is nothing like what the Asian, African and West Indian immigrants had imagined and hoped it would be. Through the 1960s to almost the final decade of the twentieth century, Britain remained a xenophobic society, with traces of Powell's vitriolic rhetoric of contamination clouding the popular imagination. It is also worth noting that most of the novels discussed above make a reference to Powell's infamous speech, reflecting the widespread influence it had not only on public policy but also on the English imagination. In Kureishi's *The Buddha of Suburbia*, Helen's father lashes out at Karim for trying to date his daughter, declaring that "We're with Enoch" (*The Buddha of Suburbia* 40), and Meena in *Anita and Me* overhears her father and Uncles getting angry "over someone they referred to as 'That Powell Bastard with his bloody rivers' and had added, 'If he wants to send us back, let him come and damn well try!'" (*Anita and Me* 267). In *White Teeth*, Archie's company director, Kelvin Hero, fires him for marrying the West Indian Clara and bringing her to the company's social events. Kelvin tells Archie "I'd spit on that Enoch Powell . . . but then again he does have a point, doesn't he? There comes a point, a saturation point, and people begin to feel a bit uncomfortable . . . I mean, it's like Delhi in Euston every Monday morning" (61). Archie is too slow to get the full import of his words and is blissfully happy about his severance package instead, but Alsana is entirely dismissive of Powell's demagoguery. While she doesn't feel settled in the area of North London she moved to with Samad, she recognises it as a nice area: "Not like Whitechapel, where that madman E-knock someone-or another gave a speech that forced them into the basement while kids broke the windows with their steel-capped boots. Rivers of blood silly-billy nonsense" (Smith 52). Either way, the message in these novels is clear – Britain failed to fulfil the dreams of its immigrants and even with the implementation of so-called anti-racist, multicultural policies, the structures of colonial discrimination and representations persisted throughout most of the twentieth century. As Susie Thomas effectively sums up Kureishi's work, "It is not just the myth of tolerant England that is blown apart in the novel but the myth of a homogenous Englishness. Instead, the novel shows Englishness as changing and unstable, varying according to class and gender as well over time" (64). Much of the work of contemporary British writers, including Kureishi and Smith then, "is actually concerned with exploring the disjunction between London's 'hip' utopian potential and its sobering realities" (Mcleod 139). But interestingly, none of these writers are entirely able to relinquish their belief in England as the land of possibilities or give up their hope of a re-evaluation of British national identity.

Things seem to change a bit in the new millennium. In a much-celebrated speech in 2001, amidst the popularity of Indian cuisine and the mushrooming of Indian restaurants all over England, British foreign secretary Robin Cook tried to embrace Britain's racial and cultural diversity by declaring Chicken Tikka Masala as "the" British national dish (Cook). Then, in the summer of 2007, London hosted yet another Indian cultural festival, something that has also become fairly routine in the twenty-first century. Titled "India Now", this three-month-long event was meant to showcase India's art and culture in the sixtieth year of Indian independence. The festival, estimated to attract a million people, exhibited Indian cinema, theatre, music, fashion, food and business through over 1500 events spread across London. The main attraction was a giant replica of the Taj Mahal floating down the Thames. Inaugurating the festival, mayor of London Ken Livingstone described it as an opportunity to "experience the richness of Indian culture" while Indian celebrities like Shilpa Shetty waxed lyrical about how events like this would remind Londoners of the "amazing gifts" India had to offer the West (Saroor). On the surface of it, these events and the shift in tone seem to suggest that Britain was finally ready to re-examine issues of national identity and adopt a more inclusive approach. But as Stuart Hall has pointed out, in the 1970s "exoticism" had simply been reformulated into the discourse of "multi-culturalism" – "Nobody would talk about racism but they were perfectly prepared to have 'International Evenings,' when we would all come and cook our native dishes, sing our own native songs and appear in our own native costume" (Hall 56) and his words are still relevant in this context. Exoticism, as Hall suggests, becomes coded into the more sophisticated discourse of multiculturalism and through "cultural" festivals like "India Now", cultural difference becomes neatly packaged into events designed for metropolitan consumption. This becomes an effective way of still ensuring that cultures and ethnicities come into direct and actual contact and yet remain markedly distinct. Case in point is a series of twelve-inch dolls modelled on Bollywood celebrities launched by the department store Harrods in 2006. Created by London-based entrepreneur Shameen Jivraj in collaboration with toy manufacturer and distributor Spin Master Toys UK and promoted as India's answer to Barbie and Ken, these miniature dolls, priced at 24.99 pounds each, were part of the "Bollywood Legends" series and were replicas of popular stars like Shahrukh Khan, Hrithik Roshan, Kajol and Priyanka Chopra. Quite predictably, the doll versions of Kajol and Priyanka Chopra were resplendent in colourful ethnic outfits reminiscent of their roles in popular Bollywood films like *Dilwale Dulhaniya Le Jayenge*, while the male dolls were dressed in fashionable Western wear. Moreover, the official event launch happened at the world famous Harrods store in Knightsbridge, London, amidst an extravagant display of Bollywood glitz and glamour and the coveted presence of the Bollywood stars, much to the delight of the fans. Jivraj, a veteran of the toy industry in England, came up with the idea of these ethnic dolls in 2002 and brought it to the attention of the aforementioned Bollywood celebrities who were delighted with the concept and only too happy to collaborate with her on this project. As Jivraj explains, "I became intrigued by Bollywood a little while ago and was drawn into the movies with their mix of fun, fashion, music and dance. It's such a magical and emotive arena. . . . I wanted to create something that would allow the audiences to be able to take some of that magic home to treasure and enjoy in a unique and new way." ("Shah Rukh Khan, for Sale"). So the exotic world of Indian cinema is commodified into bite-sized dolls to be enjoyed in a more private setting. This in-your-face cultural commodification didn't seem to ruffle any feathers; in fact, Bollywood celebrities were only too happy to recreate a fairy-tale atmosphere, that is, an Oriental setting, by arriving at Harrods in a horse-drawn carriage and endorsing this commodification by autographing the dolls for their fans. But this racialised politics of marketing cultural and ethnic difference can have serious ramifications as Ann DuCille points out in her analysis of the increasing range of "ethnic" versions of Barbie dolls: "For me these dolls are at once the symbol and a symptom of what multiculturalism has become in the hands of contemporary commodity culture; an easy and immensely profitable way off the hook of Eurocentrism that gives us the face of cultural diversity without the particulars of racial difference"(3–4). So in spite of these superficial gestures towards inclusivity, the London subway bombings of 2005 and the rising tide of Islamophobia throughout Britain in the 2000s demonstrate the need to wipe out racism and work on the reconceptualisation of British national identity.

As we have seen in this chapter then, contemporary British writers, by demythologising England as a place of untold possibilities and revealing it to be plagued by racial and class tensions, have repeatedly tried to puncture the state-sponsored discourse of happy multiculturalism. At the same time, writers like Hanif Kureishi continue to argue for a new, more inclusive, definition of English-ness which is not based on an essentialised notion of Englishness: "If there is to be a serious attempt to understand Britain today, with its mix of races and colours, its hysteria and despair, then writing about it has to be complex. It can't apologise or idealize. It can't sentimentalize and it can't represent only one group as having a monopoly on virtue" (*Dirty Washing* 14–20). Perhaps Alsana in Smith's *White Teeth* has the last word on the issue of re-evaluation of Englishness when she declares: "You go back and back and back and it's still easier to find the correct Hoover bag than to find one pure person, one pure faith, on the globe. Do you think anybody is English? Really English? It's a fairy tale!" (196).

Works Cited

Ali, Monica. *Brick Lane*. New York: Scribner, 2003. Print.

Ball, John Clement. *Imagining London: Postcolonial Fiction and the Transnational Metropolis*. Toronto: U of Toronto P, 2004. Print.

Bentley, Nick. *Contemporary British Fiction*. Edinburgh: Edinburgh UP, 2008. Print.

Brah, Avtar. *Cartographies of Diaspora: Contesting Identities*. London: Routledge, 1996. Print.

Braithwaite, E. R. *To Sir, With Love*. New York: Jove Books, 1977. Print.

Chrisman, Laura. *Postcolonial Contraventions: Cultural Readings of Race, Imperialism and Transnationalism*. Manchester: Manchester UP, 2003. Print.

Constantine, Learie. "Colour Bar." *Writing Black Britain: 1948–1998: An Interdisciplinary Anthology*. Ed. James Procter. New York: St. Martin's P, 2000. 63–68. Print.

Cook, Robin. "Chicken Tikka Masala Speech." *The Guardian*. 19 April 2001. Web. 16 December 2015. <http://www.guardian.co.uk/world/2001/apr/19/race.britishidentity>

Dabydeen, David. "On Cultural Diversity." *Whose Cities*? Eds. M. Fisher and U. Owen. London: Penguin, 1991. 97–106. Print.

Dawson, Ashley. *Mongrel Nation: Diasporic Culture and the Making of Postcolonial Britain*. Ann Arbor: U of Michigan P, 2007. Print.

DuCille, Anne. "Dyes and Dolls: Multicultural Barbie and the Merchandising of Difference." *Differences* 6.1 (1994): 46–68. Print.

Ghosh, Amitav. *The Shadow Lines*. New York: Penguin, 1990. Print.

Gikandi, Simon. *Maps of Englishness: Writing Identity in the Culture of Colonialism*. New York: Columbia UP, 1996. Print.

Gilroy, Paul. "Blacks and Crime in Post War Britain." *Writing Black Britain: 1948–1998: An Interdisciplinary Anthology*. Ed. James Procter. New York: St. Martin's P, 2000. 71–78. Print.

Gooneratne, Yasmine. *A Change of Skies*. Sydney: Pan/Picador, 1991. Print.

Hall, Stuart. "The Local and the Global: Globalization and Ethnicity." *Culture, Globalization, and the World System: Contemporary Conditions for the Representation of Identity*. Ed. Anthony D. King. Minneapolis: U of Minnesota P, 1997. 19–39. Print.

James, C. L. R. "Africans and Afro-Caribbeans: A Personal View." *Writing Black Britain: 1948–1998: An Interdisciplinary Anthology*. Ed. James Procter. New York: St. Martin's P, 2000. 60–63. Print.

James, Louis. *Caribbean Literature in English*. New York: Longman, 1999. Print.

Joshi, Priya. *In Another Country: Colonialism, Culture, and the English Novel in India*. New York: Columbia UP, 2002. Print.

Kureishi, Hanif. *Dreaming and Scheming: Reflections on Writing and Politics*. London: Faber & Faber, 2002. Print.

———. *My Beautiful Laundrette and Other Writings*. London: Faber & Faber, 1996. Print.

———. *Sammy and Rosie Get Laid: The Script and the Diary*. London: Faber & Faber, 1988. Print.

———. *The Black Album*. London: Faber & Faber, 1995. Print.

———. *The Buddha of Suburbia*. New York: Penguin Books, 1991. Print.

———. "The Carnival of Culture." *The Guardian*. 4 August 2005. Web. 18 December 2015. <http://www.guardian.co.uk/world/2005/aug/04/religion.uk>

———. "The Rainbow Sign." *London Kills Me: Three Screenplays and Four Essays*. New York: Penguin Books, 1992. 3–37. Print.

Lamming, George. "Journey to an Expectation." *Writing Black Britain: 1948–1998: An Interdisciplinary Anthology*. Ed. James Procter, New York: St. Martin's P, 2000. 57–60. Print.

Lokuge, Chandrani. "'We Must Laugh at One Another, or Die' Yasmine Gooneratne's A Change of Skies and South Asian Migrant Identities." *Shifting Continents/Colliding Cultures: Diaspora Writing of the Indian Subcontinent.* Eds. Ralph J. Crane and Radhika Mohanram. Atlanta: Rodopi, 2000. 17–34. Print.

Macaulay, Thomas Babington. *Selected Writings*. Eds. John Clive and Thomas Pinney. Chicago: U of Chicago P, 1972. Print.

Maira, Sunaina. "Henna and Hip Hop: The Politics of Cultural Production and the Work of Cultural Studies." *Journal of Asian American Studies.* 3.3. New York: The John Hopkins UP, 2000. 329–369. Print.

McLeod, John. *Postcolonial London; Rewriting the Metropolis*. New York: Routledge, 2004. Print.

Moore-Gilbert, Bart. *Hanif Kureishi. Contemporary World Writers*. Manchester: Manchester UP, 2001. Print.

Naipaul. V. S. *An Area of Darkness*. London: A Deutsch, 1964. Print.

Phillips, Caryl. *A Distant Shore*. New York: Vintage, 2005. Print.

Powell, Enoch. *Freedom and Reality*. Ed. John Wood. Kingswood, Surrey: Paperfronts, 1969. Print.

Procter, James, ed. *Writing Black Britain: 1948–1998: An Interdisciplinary Anthology*. New York: St. Martin's P, 2000. Print.

Rhys, Jean. *The Complete Novels*. New York: Norton, 1985. Print.

Said, Edward. *Orientalism.* New York: Vintage, 1979. Print.

Sardar, Ziauddin. *The A to Z of Postmodern Life: Essays on Global Culture in the Noughties*. London: Vision, 2002. Print.

Sarkar, Parama. "England is [Not] the Place for Me: The Failure of the Immigrant Dream in Hanif Kureishi's The Buddha of Suburbia." *The Journal of Commonwealth and Postcolonial Studies*. 1.2 (2013): 39–60. Print.

Saroor, Hasan. "'Taj Mahal' afloat on the Thames." *The Hindu.* 18 July 2007. Web. 11 January 2016. [http://www.thehindu.com/todays-paper/taj-mahal-afloat-on-the-thames/article1875177.ece]

Selvon, Sam. *The Lonely Londoners.* Essex: Longman Group, 1956. Print.

"Shah Rukh Khan, for Sale!" *Rediff Movies.* 26 July 2006. Web. 11 January 2016. [http://www.rediff.com/movies/report/toys/20060726.htm]

Smith, Zadie. *White Teeth.* New York: Vintage, 2000. Print.

Soyinka, Wole. "Telephone Conversation." *Explorings: A Collection of Poems for the Young People of Southern Africa.* Compiled by Robin Malan. Cape Town: David Philip, 1988. Print.

Syal, Meera. *Anita and Me.* New York: The New P, 1996. Print.

Thomas, Susie, ed. *Hanif Kureishi: A Reader's Guide to Essential Criticism.* Basingstoke: Palgrave Macmillan, 2005. Print.

Varma, Balgopal. "Some Thoughts on English Fiction and the Reading Public." *Fiction and the Reading Public in India.* Ed. C. D. Narsimhaiah. Mysore: Wesley P, 1997. 1–7. Print.

Visram, Rozina. *Asians in Britain: 400 Years of History.* London: Pluto P, 2002. Print.

———. *Ayahs, Lascars and Princes: Indians in Britain 1700–1947.* London: Pluto P, 1986. Print.

Notes

1. See Rozina Visram's *Asians in Britain: 400 Years of History* and *Ayahs, Lascars and Princes: Indians in Britain 1700–1947* for a detailed history of Black British immigration to Britain.

2. See Page 1 of Ashley Dawson's *Mongrel Nation* for a full version of Lord Kitchener's song.

3. My discussion of Kureishi's *The Buddha of Suburbia* has been previously published in The Journal of Commonwealth and

Postcolonial Studies. For the entire article, read "England is [Not] the Place for Me".

4. As Procter points out, Stuart Hall's essay "New Ethnicities" "draws attention to the fact that the category 'black' actually houses a stressful, internally discrepant community that it can only claim to partially articulate" (5–6). The meaning of "black" as a category has been reconfigured, but it is essential to underscore its importance as a key organising category used to create solidarity among immigrant groups in a racially polarised Britain.
5. For the entire article on race and multiculturalism, read "The Carnival of Culture" by Kureishi.
6. As Dawson suggests, "Colonial and racist discourses, in other words, rendered black men as both hypermasculine and feminine at one and the same time" (40).

SIX

Postcolonialism and Beyond

Newer concerns in postcolonial writing

It's not war, it's not genocide, it's not ethnic cleansing, it's not a famine or an epidemic. On the face of it, it's just ordinary, day-to-day business. It lacks the drama, the large format, epic magnificence of war or genocide. It's dull in comparison. It makes bad TV. It has to do with boring things like water supply, electricity, irrigation. But it also has to do with a process of barbaric dispossession on a scale that has few parallels in history. You may have guessed by now that I'm talking about the modern version of corporate globalization.

—Arundhati Roy, *The Algebra of Infinite Justice*

As we have seen in preceding chapters, European colonialism was on its way out following the consistent decolonisation in Asia, Africa, the West Indies and South America in the second half of the twentieth century. The years following the Cold War witnessed the decline of the former Soviet Union. It also saw the unprecedented rise of the United States as a global superpower, with American corporations spearheading what many people termed neo-colonialism because of its uncomfortable similarities with the colonial process. For a few years before this, critics had started to point out that the market-driven processes of globalisation were the main impetus behind the rise of the new American

Empire. Writers like Ngũgĩ wa Thiong'o started worrying about this as far back as 1993. In his book, Thiong'o elaborates, "Today, US finance capital and the USA-based transnationals are equally on a mission of economic robbery and theft of the resources, the labour, and the produce of the entire Third World. The nations of Asia, Africa and South America are bleeding under the weight of unpayable debts" (50). Others like Hardt and Negri believe that the new empire has more in common with the Roman Empire rather than European colonialism. They argue that in contrast to the old imperial world, where different European powers were competing for the same prizes, the new empire:

> . . . establishes no territorial center of power and does not rely on fixed boundaries or barriers. It is a decentered and deterritorializing apparatus of rule that progressively incorporates the entire global realm within its open, expanding frontiers, and plural exchanges through modulating networks of command. The distinct national colors of the imperial map of the world have merged and blended in the imperial global rainbows. (Hardt and Negri xiii)

Even though Hardt and Negri do not identify the Unites States as the face of this new empire, it cannot be denied that the events of 11 September 2001 irrevocably altered the global landscape and the field of neo-colonial politics. The brazen attack on the World Trade Center was widely seen as an attempt to dislodge the US from its dominant seat in the global marketplace. Following 9/11, the so-called war on terror and the consequent US invasion of Iraq and Afghanistan have made writers and critics extremely uneasy about America's role in the current geopolitical landscape. On the one hand, there is a continued mistrust of what is termed the "McDonaldization" of the world and its impact on local communities; on the other, there is increased concern about the emerging culture of surveillance in modern nation-states that are obsessed with securing their borders against external threats and policing their boundaries through a proliferation of documentation (passports, visas, identity cards, birth certificates, etc.).

While writers like Jonathan Safran Foer and Lorrie Moore have tried to understand the effect of these momentous events on the American literary landscape, non-Western writers, especially those from the Middle East, have come under increasing scrutiny. Novels like Khaled Hosseini's *The Kite Runner* (2003) and Azar Nafisi's *Reading Lolita in Tehran* (2003) have been well received in the West, partly because they confirm some of the stereotypes about the East that exist in the Western imagination. Others have faced the same fate as Marjane Satrapi's autobiographical graphic novel *Persepolis* (2003), which was banned in Chicago public schools on the dubious grounds that the book contains graphic scenes of torture and is not appropriate for a seventh-grade curriculum. Thus questions of power dynamics, domination and resistance have acquired a new sense of urgency in postcolonial studies in the last two decades, albeit in a slightly different context than that of European colonialism. This final chapter will attempt to interrogate some of these issues and try to highlight some of the newest concerns in the field of postcolonial literary studies.

THE IMPACT OF GLOBALISATION

Although the term "globalisation" has come into prominence in the last two decades with the sustained impact of multinational capitalism all across the world and publication of books like Samuel Huntington's *The Clash of Civilizations* (1996), Benjamin Barber's *Jihad Versus McWorld* (1995) and Thomas Friedman's *The Lexus and the Olive Tree* (1999) and *The World is Flat* (2007), globalisation as a phenomenon has long been in existence and can even be said to predate the colonial enterprise. As Manfred Steger demonstrates in his book, the Chinese were invested in discovering trade routes in far-flung parts of the world way back in time – "By the fifteenth century CE, enormous Chinese fleets consisting of hundreds of 400-foot-long ocean-going ships were crossing the Indian Ocean and establishing short-lived trade outposts on the east coast of Africa" (Steger 25). Of course, the Silk Road was already in existence, connecting the Chinese and Roman Empires. The famous Moroccan merchant and traveller, Ibn Battuta, and his Venetian counterparts, extensively used this trade route to reach the court of the Mongol Khans in Beijing. But as Steger points out, a few decades later, the decision by the Chinese rulers to focus on their internal economy cut short Chinese industrial progress and "allowed much smaller European states to emerge as the primary historical agents behind the intensification of globalization" (25).

In his celebrated but controversial book *The World is Flat*, economist Thomas Friedman claims that globalisation occurred in three stages, starting with Columbus's discovery of the New World. The first phase, which he refers to as "Globalization 1.0", lasted from 1492 until around 1800, in which rapid industrialisation and events like the coming of the steam engine and the opening up of waterways aided the colonial project and paved the way for widespread international trade. During this period, according to Friedman, "the key agent of change, the dynamic force driving the process of global integration was brawn – how much muscle, how much horsepower, wind power, or later, steam power – your country had and how creatively you could deploy it" (9). The second phase of globalisation, that Friedman labels "Globalization 2.0", lasted from about 1800 to 2000. That era of globalisation, he argued, was spearheaded by multinational companies globalising in order to obtain cheaper labour and resources, aided significantly by the growth of technology and the early version of the internet. "It was during this era that we really saw the birth and maturation of a global economy, in the sense that there was enough movement of goods and information from continent to continent for there to be a global market, with global arbitrage in products and labor" (10). The activities related to this phase thus further broke down the barriers of international borders, trade, and cross-cultural connections. This period also saw the establishment of three new international economic organisations: The International Monetary Fund (IMF), The International Bank for Reconstruction and Development, popularly known as the World Bank, and the General Agreement of Tariffs and Trades (GATT), later succeeded in 1995 by the World Trade Organization (WTO).[1] The third and current ongoing phase of globalisation, "Globalization 3.0", began around the year 2000, aided by the development of the personal computer, the fibre-optic cable and work flow software. Friedman insists that what is really exciting about this era of globalisation is that it is built around the convergence of these three technological advancements which confers an inordinate amount of power to individuals. Thus individuals have a far more prominent role in this phase as opposed to countries or corporations in the earlier phases. "People all over the world started waking up and realizing that they had more power than ever to go global as individuals, . . . and they had more opportunities to work with those other individuals, not just compete with them" (Friedman 11).

Friedman's claims about the historical genealogy of globalising processes seem to be corroborated even in the literary arena. In his *In an Antique Land* (1992), Amitav Ghosh points out that there was a flourishing medieval trading network that extended from the Eastern Mediterranean to the Malabar Coast of India. As Ghosh illustrates, this centuries-old flourishing trade was destroyed by European greed and violence with the advent of Portuguese colonisation which took control of the trade "by aggression, pure and distilled" (*In an Antique Land* 287–8). However, contrary to Friedman's claims, most critics of globalisation agree that in the current phase of globalisation, the influence of giant transnational corporations headquartered in the West and other developed countries often outweigh the influence of the nations and local communities in which they operate. Since a lot of these corporations are American, like General Motors, McDonalds, Coca Cola and Walmart, critics claim that American neo-colonialism, under the veneer of globalising corporations, continue to exploit the labour markets in developing countries merely to increase their profit margins. Thiong'o is decidedly more critical of this globalising phenomenon, but also points out the increasing dominance of some Asian countries like Japan:

> A traveller in any one of the tri-continental countries will find the same familiar names: IMF; World Bank; General Motors, Firestone, Del Monte, Coca-Cola, Macdonalds, etc; Esso, Caltex, Mobil oil, etc; Hilton, Sheraton, etc; and of course other similarly familiar signs from Japan and Western Europe. In short the same tiny group of financial, industrial and commercial interests from the USA and the West generally still control the economies of the various 'Third' World countries. (50)

What Friedman describes as a flattening of the world brought on by the invention of the personal computer and rapid global network connectivity and aided by the dot com boom, is deeply suspect in developing countries; as is attempts by corporations to homogenise local cultures – a "McDonaldization" or "Coca-Colonisation" of the world. Coined by sociologist George Ritzer, the term "McDonaldization" was primarily used to describe the socio-cultural processes by which fast-food chains like McDonalds were increasingly permeating and dominating not only the American social fabric but spreading all across the world (Steger 73). The purported efficient service of making food available to consumers quickly is undermined by the bad nutritional value of the food served and the "sameness" of the restaurant, irrespective of its location. This has given rise to controversies about the erosion of local cultural values.[2] So even as the Western tourist is comforted by the familiar logo of Starbucks in a remote village in China, the infiltration of American brands and consumer goods in some of the most vulnerable places on the globe has raised some serious concerns. As Steger points out, "in the long run, the McDonaldization of the world amounts to the imposition of uniform standards that eclipse human creativity and dehumanize social relations" (73).

This onslaught of American cultural imperialism has re-invigorated postcolonial studies and has become an enduring concern in the field in recent years. As John Thieme points out, postcolonial studies "has itself variously been seen as a means of resisting the homogenizing practices of Western consumer capitalism and as a subject which colludes in such homogenization by aggregating the cultural productions of markedly different societies and groups together, thereby effectively operating as a kind of latter-day Orientalism that involves an essentialist exoticization of non-Western experience" (Thieme 108).

GLOBAL TOURISM AND NEO-IMPERIALISM IN POSTCOLONIAL WRITING

The impact of Western cultural imperialism brought on by globalising processes and leading to a homogenisation, and even erosion, of local cultures has become an object of analysis in the works of contemporary writers like Jamaica Kincaid, Pico Iyer, Aravind Adiga, Hari Kunzru, Arundhati Roy and others. One of the most important facets of neo-imperialism and cultural homogenisation is global tourism, and most postcolonial writers are scathingly critical of the tourism industry, especially in countries that depend on Western tourists for economic survival. In countries like Thailand, Indonesia and the West Indies, there has been a rapid development of the tourism industry centred around the rich Western tourist, while the native people have hardly seen any positive developments in their living conditions. In *Video Night in Kathmandu*, Pico Iyer compares tourism to colonial invasion:

> Tourists were the great foot soldiers of the new invasion; tourists, in a sense, were the terrorists of cultural expansionism, what Sartre once called 'the cool invaders.' Scarcely forty years ago, most of the world's secret places were known only to adventurers, soldiers, missionaries and a few enterprising traders; in recent years, however, the secrets were open, and so too was the world – anyone with a credit card could become a lay colonialist. (*Video Night in Kathmandu* 13)

Caribbean writers like V. S. Naipaul and Jamaica Kincaid are particularly critical of this new form of imperialism; however, both are also quick to hold the West Indies responsible for not resisting this new onslaught because of economic viability. In *The Middle Passage*, V. S. Naipaul asserts, "Every poor country accepts tourism as an unavoidable degradation. None has gone as far as these West Indian islands, which, in the name of tourism, are selling themselves into a new slavery" (210). But perhaps the most trenchant critique of mass tourism is Jamaica Kincaid's *A Small Place*. Kincaid, like Naipaul, unabashedly implicates Antigua in the development of the tourism industry that is the mainstay of the Antiguan economy, but is quick to illustrate that behind the veneer of the lush tropical paradise, the story of native experience is one of economic deprivation and injustice. Kincaid acerbically draws attention to Antigua's colonial legacy that resulted in Englishmen creating mini-versions of themselves wherever they went – "Everywhere they went they turned it into England; and everybody they met they turned English. But no place could ever really be England, and nobody who did not look exactly like them would ever be English" (Kincaid 24). This, like in other colonised countries, created a kind of slavish mentality in the natives that has persisted even after decolonisation.

Kincaid finds herself in a postcolonial Antigua where illiteracy is rampant; where the old library, the seat of learning, has been downgraded into a dilapidated building with books in old rotten boxes; where a country renowned for its beaches doesn't allow natives access to them and instead restricts it to hotel guests; where the government officials are corrupt and where there is a Minister of Culture, but no attempt to redefine themselves culturally. It is an Antigua where in 1985, because of Queen Elizabeth's visit, all roads she would travel on were paved anew so she would retain a favourable impression of the island, while ordinary people lived in poverty and squalor. Kincaid berates the Western tourist for his idyllic existence on the island, with little concern or understanding of native cultures and customs.

> An ugly thing, that is what you are when you become a tourist, an ugly, empty thing, a stupid thing, a piece of rubbish pausing here and there to gaze at this and taste that, and it will never occur to you that the people who inhabit the place in which you have just paused cannot stand you, that behind their closed doors they laugh at your strangeness. (17)

At the same time, she is quick to acknowledge the role of the Antiguans themselves in this difficult situation and hopes that Antiguans will one day be able to see the "relationship between their obsession with slavery and emancipation and their celebration of the Hotel training School" (55), and will be able to comprehend the real meaning of freedom.

Arundhati Roy's 1997 novel, *The God of Small Things,* also offers a blistering critique of Western tourism in the scene with the Kathakali man. We are told that the "Kathakali Man is the most beautiful of men. Because his body *is* his soul. His only instrument. From the age of three it has been planed and polished, pared down, harnessed wholly to the task of story-telling" (*The God of Small Things* 230).[3] The Kathakali man had been trained from his childhood to uphold the glorious mythic storytelling tradition of India. Even though he uses his body to earn a living, the implications are that as a performer of myths and epics narrating the story of gods, he has been traditionally imbued with a divine aura; "he has magic in him" (230). But economic unviability threatens the Kathakali man's very existence and he has become commodified and fetishised as a tourist attraction, completely vulnerable to the western gaze as he performs for Western tourists in the temple in Cochin – "In the *Heart of Darkness* they mock him with their lolling nakedness and their imported attention spans. He checks his rage and dances for them. He collects his fee." (231; emphasis added). The reference to Conrad's *Heart of Darkness* is unmistakable here – the implication is that globalisation, like colonisation, has ensured that cultural commodification remain a constant.[4] Roy's characters are aware of this cultural encashment as they argue over the use of the image of the Kathakali man alongside the "Paradise Pickles and Preserves" (46) sign on top of the Plymouth owned by the Ipe family. Though the very material task of making pickles is completely at odds with the aesthetic appeal of the Kathakali tradition, one of the main characters, Chacko, insists on it because "it gave the products a Regional Flavour and would stand them in good stead when they entered the Overseas Market" (47). By showing the Kathakali man as symbolising the regional flavour of Kerala and revealing his survival to be contingent upon his acting as a local cultural enticement to western tourists, Roy both laments the downfall of tradition and comments on the ill effects of incipient globalisation. In her book on Roy, Julie Mullaney aptly comments that, "The transatlantic networks and movements of goods, money, and labor that once were at the heart of the British colonial enterprise continue despite the ostensible dismantling of Empire with Independence" (*The God of Small Things: A Reader's Guide* 49). Roy is deeply suspect of both the domestic policies of the postcolonial government, primarily the privatisation of India's vast natural resources, and of the giant transnational corporations spearheading such efforts and bulldozing over local communities and cultures with dogged insistence on profits. Actively involved in the protest against the establishment of a dam across the Narmada River by the multinational corporation Enron at the cost of the displacement of millions of people, Roy is critical of this neo-colonialism which has assumed the face of corporate globalisation. She addresses this and a variety of other subjects including American imperialism after 9/11 and neoliberal capitalism in two provocative collections of essays, *The Algebra of Infinite Justice* and *An Ordinary Person's Guide to Empire*. In an essay entitled "The Ladies Have Feelings, so . . .", Roy asks: "Is corporate globalization about the 'eradication of world poverty' or is it a mutant variety of colonialism, remote controlled and digitally operated?" (*The Algebra of Infinite Justice* 200). Further along in the essay, she gives a graphic picture of this new threat.

> 'Trade not Aid' is the rallying cry of the headmen of the new Global Village, headquartered in the shining offices of the WTO . . . . This time around the colonizer doesn't even need a token white presence in the colonies. The CEOs and their men don't need to go to the trouble of tramping through the tropics risking malaria, diarrhoea, sunstroke and an early death . . . . They can have their colonies *and* an easy conscience. 'Creating a good investment climate' is the new euphemism for third world repression. (203)

Roy's mistrust of global organisations like the World Bank and the IMF and fear of techno-dominance is reflected through the disastrous effects they have, even on the quiet little town of Ayemenem in her novel – the Meenachal river, formerly the lifeblood of the people of the region now "smelled of shit, and pesticides bought with World Bank Loans" (*The God of Small Things* 13). Baby Kochamma's passion for gardening has been usurped by the appearance of satellite television and "in Ayemenem, where once the loudest sound had been a musical bus horn, now whole wars, famines, picturesque massacres and Bill Clinton could be summoned up like servants" (27). Baby Kochamma now exists in the make-believe world created by the western media. Roy's anxiety about individuals being engulfed by external forces like technology and losing touch with their inner selves permeates her book.

As is evident through Roy's writings, even though she is deeply suspicious of the disastrous effects of globalisation on the Indian landscape, she remains optimistic that the country will be able to rise above this new form of colonisation.

> Corporatizing India is like trying to impose an iron grid on a heaving ocean, forcing it to behave. My guess is that India will not behave. It cannot. It's too old and too clever to be made to jump through the hoops all over again . . . and . . . I hope – too democratic to be lobotomized into believing in one single idea, which is eventually, what corporate globalization really is: Life is Profit. (*Algebra* 214).

In spite of his scepticism of mass tourism, travel writer Pico Iyer, like Roy, remains optimistic that developing countries will be able to successfully resist the forces of globalisation in its myriad forms. In several of his books, including *Video Night in Kathmandu* and *The Global Soul: Jet Lag, Shopping Malls, and the Search for Home*, Iyer is constantly preoccupied with exploring, understanding and documenting how some non-Western cultures have struggled to adapt/resist Western cultural influences. As he points out in *Video Night in Kathmandu*:

> I was interested to find out how America's pop-culture imperialism spread through the world's most ancient civilizations. I wanted to see what kind of resistance had been put up against the Coca-Colonizing forces and what kind of counter-strategies were planned. And I hoped to discover which

> Americas got through to the other side of the world, and which got lost in translation. (5)

What emerges is an insightful account of Iyer's travels through India, China, Japan and South East Asia as he tries to explore the syncretic relationship between people and places through the prism of American cultural influence. In individual essays based on each country, Iyer rues the loss of the natural beauty of the island paradise of Bali by rampant commercialism spurred by Western tourism, is amused to see the inside of a McDonald's in a small city in the Philippines decorated like a Arizona coffee shop complete with pictures of John Wayne, the Lone Ranger and Chief Red Cloud (*Video Night in Kathmandu* 166–167), and is staggered by the dynamic frenzy of Hong Kong, "a city with none of the encumbrances of a state, the entrepôt provided a perfect movable feast for go-getters, over-achievers and rootless ex-patriots – driven, self-making men with no allegiances except to the self" (224–225). But what struck him the most is that while all the above-mentioned countries were more invested in simply imitating recent Western trends, be it food or fashion, India simply "naturalized" (280) them. Iyer points out that instead of importing McDonald's, India came up with fast food chains like Pizza King, Coca Cola was substituted with Campa Cola, and the most popular soaps of television happened to be a mix of the popular American *Dynasty* and the British *Pride and Prejudice* (280–281). In other words, India seemed "torn not just between tradition and modernity, but more specifically between the British and American Empires .... India was caught between two worlds, one dying, the other struggling to be born" (278). Iyer's travelogues seemingly end on an optimistic note with him claiming that in spite of the rampant Western cultural onslaught, none of the countries he visited, except perhaps the Philippines, had been transformed by it. In contrast, if anything, the West was now in the throes of Eastern cultural influence – "the Japanese provided Tokyo-made Plymouths; the Thais filled L.A. with Bangkok-style American bars; the Chinese served up sweet-and-sour pork (a dish created expressly for Western palates) . . . all suggested that the Asians had absorbed the West, and mastered it, more fully and more subtly than anything that could be imagined in reverse" (360).

POSTCOLONIAL "MIGRANT" WRITING AND QUESTIONS OF HOME AND BELONGING

As we have seen in earlier chapters, a lot of post-independent writers identified with nationalist causes and were invested in nation building, but geographic and cultural affiliations for a lot of postcolonial writers, like Pico Iyer, V. S. Naipaul and Jamaica Kincaid, have become increasingly fraught. In an important article, Revathi Krishnaswamy talks about a new kind of postcolonial "migrant writer".

> A new type of 'Third World' intellectual, cross-pollinated by postmodernism and postcolonialism, has arrived: a migrant who, having dispensed with territorial affiliations, travels unencumbered through the cultures of the world bearing only the burden of a unique yet representative sensibility that refracts the fragmented and contingent condition of both postmodernity and postcoloniality. Journeying from the 'peripheries' to the metropolitan 'centre,' this itinerant intellectual becomes an international figure who at once feels at home nowhere and everywhere. No longer disempowered by cultural schizophrenia or confined within collectivities such as race, class, or nation, the nomadic postcolonial intellectual is said to 'write back' to the empire in the name of all displaced and dispossessed peoples, denouncing both colonialism and nationalism as equally coercive constructs. (125)

Almost echoing Krishnaswamy's definition, writer Pico Iyer tells us that he spent eight months of the year in a boarding school in England and four months in California in an Indian household. So for him, "as a British subject, an American resident and an Indian citizen, I quickly became accustomed to cross-cultural anomalies and the mixed feelings of exile. Nowhere was home, and every where" (*Video Night* 24). For a variety of different reasons, writers like Iyer, with roots in one of the formerly colonised countries, have become the quintessential global soul by embracing this feeling of rootlessness, of carrying their "home" with them. Writer Salman Rushdie was born in Bombay, educated in England and continued to live there undercover following the issuing of the fatwa against him by Ayatollah Khomeini, before eventually making his home in New York. Jamaica Kincaid, born in Antigua, also calls New York her home. So does Nigerian writer Teju Cole and British writer Zadie Smith. V. S. Naipaul was born in Trindad but lives in London. So does British writer of Caribbean descent, Caryl Phillips, and Nigerian writer Ben Okri. Amitav Ghosh, born in India, educated in England, is a resident of San Francisco and divides his time between both India and the United States. And the list goes on. As Elleke Boehmer rightly points out, "Ex-colonial by birth, 'Third-World' in cultural interest, cosmopolitan in almost every other way, he or she works within the precincts of the Western metropolis while at the same time retaining thematic and/or political connections with a national background" (233). In her book, Barbara Korte suggests that "An internationalized view, which emphasizes transculturality, cultural hybridity, and syncretism, is certainly gaining ground" (169) in postcolonial writing.

Critics, like Arjun Appadurai in his book *Modernity at Large: Cultural Dimensions of Globalization,* have tried to examine the "migrant condition" by studying the relationship between globalisation and nation-states. Appadurai coined a set of neologisms, "ethnoscapes", "mediascapes", "technoscapes", "financescapes" and "ideoscapes" in order to explore the different dimensions of "global cultural flows" (Appadurai

33), and went on to explore how people, commodities, culture, increasingly travel in complex transnational circuits across the globe. Appadurai claimed "An important fact of the world today is that many persons on the globe live in such imagined worlds (and not just in imagined communities) and thus are able to contest and sometimes even subvert the imagined worlds of the official mind and of the entrepreneurial mentality that surround them (33). He further stated that this has often rendered nation-states obsolete and has created the necessity of establishing other forms of allegiance and identity. Contrary to this, Peter van der Veer established an indissoluble relation between migrant communities and the nation-state:

> Nationalism is a discourse that depends on notions of space, of territory. Outsiders do not belong, are not rooted in the soil, and indeed have immigrated from outside . . . . I would suggest that this opposition of nation and migrant has an ideological function. Nationalism needs this story of migration, the diaspora of others, to establish the rootedness of the nation. (6)

For writers like Pico Iyer, transculturalism becomes necessarily a two way process as he emphasises that "on a grand collective level, the encounters between East and West might well be interpreted as a battle; but on the human level, the meeting more closely resembled a mating dance"' (*Video Night* 21). So even as global cities like London, Tokyo and New York often serve as the bases of operation for postcolonial migrant writers and feature prominently in their works, so do formerly colonial cities like Bombay, Calcutta, Nairobi and Lagos, as they try to negotiate their de-territorialised identity in a postmodern world. At the same time, possibly because of this feeling of simultaneously being everywhere and nowhere, postcolonial migrant writing remains invested in questions of home and belonging, national identity, and the struggle to find one's roots. In *Back to Africa*, Ferdinand Dennis, a Jamaican writer living in

London, writes about how he is forced to question his rootless existence after a chance encounter with a young girl in Lagos. After the young girl insists that he looks like a Yoruba, Dennis mulls over his identity:

> That morning made me aware that I have in the past hungered for an identity more concrete than 'world citizen,' that I wear a mask which sometimes slips. Perhaps if I had arrived at this rootlessness, this lack of belonging, by a less violent route than the middle passage, the slave plantations of the Caribbean and migration as a child, I would never hunger for roots, which I know, in my composed moments, are irrevocably lost. (Dennis 170)

Vikram Seth, born in India but educated in England and the United States before returning to settle in India, writes of a similar feeling of rootlessness in *From Heaven Lake* – "I recall drinking sherry in California and dreaming of my earlier student days in England, where I ate *dalmoth* and dreamed of Delhi. What is the purpose, I wonder of all this restlessness? I sometimes seem to myself to wander around the world merely accumulating material for future nostalgia" (*From Heaven Lake* 35). The celebratory aspects of globalisation, cultural hybridity and multiculturalism thus often become mired in the schizophrenia and in-betweenness that plagues migrant writers.

Amitav Ghosh's 1987 novel, *The Shadow Lines*, captures the angst of migrant experience with astonishing finesse. Ghosh, himself a transnational migrant, knows the significance of crossing borders only too well. The book, written immediately after the 1984 religious riots in India following the assassination of Indian Prime Minister Indira Gandhi, captures a tumultuous phase of political turmoil. The novel also deals with the Partition of India, but much like the shadow lines erected between the two countries of India and Pakistan, the actual historical event is more of a spectral presence. Ghosh primarily attempts to emphasise the utter futility of constructing geopolitical borders prompted by petty nationalism as he reveals how traumatic historical/political events can leave indelible marks on ordinary citizens across three generations. Simultaneously, Ghosh tries to interrogate the meaning of freedom in a postcolonial world; national freedom had come at a heavy price, but in the modern transnational world, with its insistence on open borders and free flow of people and commodities, were postcolonial individuals truly free? Ghosh's unnamed narrator is a young Indian boy whose identity is shaped by the events of pre-Partition Dhaka, a war-weary London and 1960s Calcutta, but one of the focal points of the book is his relationship with his grandmother (Thamma). The narrator's family had relocated to Calcutta from Dhaka following the Hindu-Muslim riots after the partition of India, and as the book opens, Thamma constantly tries to inculcate nationalist feelings in her young grandson. The narrator reports that Thamma insists that "You can't build a strong country . . . without building a strong body" (*The Shadow Lines* 8) and encourages him to work out so he can serve his country better. Characteristically, Thamma is completely unsympathetic towards his cousin Ila when she is subjected to racial slurs in England by insisting that it is her own fault by choosing to stay in a place where she doesn't belong. Thamma's behaviour makes sense as it is revealed that she had been a revolutionary during the Indian freedom movement; on one occasion she even claims she wouldn't have had any qualms killing an English magistrate because "It was for our freedom: I would have done anything to be free" (39). Yet, as Ghosh reveals, freedom is an illusion and national borders, however intangible, can only constrain people into narrow definitions of home. Thamma realises this when she visits her original home in Dhaka for the first time since Partition. She is eager to see the actual border dividing India and Bangladesh but is told by her son that it doesn't exist. She asks, "What was it all for then – Partition and all the killing and everything – if there isn't something in between?" to which the narrator's father replies, "It's not as though you're flying over the Himalayas into China. This is the modern world. The border isn't on the frontier: it's right inside the airport. You'll see. You'll cross it when you have to fill in all those disembarkation cards and things" (149). Thamma is unable to comprehend the reality of the situation and falls silent. The narrator realises later on that her silence at that moment was because "she had not been able quite to understand how her place of birth had come to be so messily at odds with her nationality" (149), that freedom didn't necessarily guarantee peace and stability. Robi, the narrator's cousin, probably has the most poignant thoughts on this in the closing pages of the book. As he explains, postcolonial nation states are still plagued by the spectre of violence arising out of a desire to have separate states because "everyone's doing it to be free" (241). As Robi says, "Why don't they draw thousands of little lines through the whole subcontinent and give every little place a new name? What would it change? It's a mirage; the whole thing is a mirage. How can anybody divide a memory?" (241). Ghosh thus emphasises that migrants, like Thamma, are often victims of their own imagination – torn between a new home in which they find themselves and the idealised home they would like to believe in. Ila, Nick's cousin, has travelled widely because of her father's job in the Foreign Service, and on the surface, seems to have an easy time crossing borders between countries and cultures. She considers London her home because, as she tells the narrator after an episode at a Calcutta nightclub, in London she can be free, "free of your bloody culture and free of all of you" (87). But as the narrator slowly realises, Ila too, like Thamma, is handcuffed to history, torn between her Indian heritage and her idealised version of home in London, which for the most part remains just that, an ideal. So even as postcolonial novels like Vikram Seth's *A Suitable Boy* (1993), Salman Rushdie's *The Satanic Verses* (1989), Michelle Cliff's

No Telephone to Heaven (1987), Mohsin Hamid's *The Reluctant Fundamentalist* (2007), Hari Kunzru's *Transmission* (2004), Chimamanda Adichie's *Americanah* (2013) and others criss-cross the globe and link the new global cities to the former imperial centres, migrant writing often reflects a disillusionment and confusion with transnational globalisation and other neo-colonial processes. Issues surrounding home and belonging also remain fraught with complexities.

It is worth emphasising here that globalising processes are not always uniform in their reach and dissemination and postcolonial experiences are not always limited to one specific location or can be neatly packaged into easy stereotypes for Western consumption. As Pico Iyer perceptively points out in *The Global Soul*, "Perhaps the greatest danger of our global community is that the person in LA thinks he knows Cambodia because he's seen *The Killing Fields* on-screen, and the newcomer from Cambodia thinks he knows LA because he's seen *City of Angels* on video" (65).

POSTCOLONIAL WOMEN'S WRITING AND THE GLOBAL LITERARY MARKETPLACE

Just as a lot of contemporary postcolonial writers are resisting specific national affiliations, many postcolonial women writers are resisting labels and definitions forced on them by the Western publishing industry, and this recent trend in postcolonial studies is worth exploring in detail. Even the most vocal anti-globalisation critics will agree that the invention of the personal computer and the rapid advances in internet technology have revolutionised the way information flows across the globe. The rise of sites like Amazon, a global online literary marketplace, the proliferation of online reading groups and blogs, the popularity of social networking sites and the proliferation of e-readers have all contributed in various degree to reshaping the postcolonial literary canon. So as Julie Mullaney points out, questions like "who has access to these resources? . . . How are postcolonial literatures marketed? How are distinct audiences and genres of writing recognized or marginalized in the publishing of postcolonial literatures? What happens to indigenous language publishing with the ascent of English language publishing?" (*Postcolonial Literatures in Context* 37) have assumed a new sense of urgency. Interestingly, postcolonial women's writing has been a site of controversy in the past two decades and is well worth some consideration here.

In an article facetiously called "The God of Big Trends", clearly mirroring the title of Arundhati Roy's much celebrated novel, *The God of Small Things*, Noy Thrupkaew recalls an incident from 1998 when she was working on a newly launched imprint featuring "the writing of women of all colours" for a publishing company in the United States. In her conversations with booksellers from all over the country about authors they should publish, the following quote was the standard response: "'That Indian subcontinent is really hot. Oh, oops, do you say 'South Asia' now? . . . 'Nah, our customers don't really like stuff in translation. But have you read that Jhumpa?'" (Thrupkaew 299). In the late 1990s, "literary brown ladies were the new thing" (Thrupkaew 299) in the West with Roy winning the Booker Prize in 1997 and Jhumpa Lahiri winning the Pulitzer Prize for *Interpreter of Maladies*, her debut collection of short stories, in 2000. Indian women writers in the early twentieth century, like Attia Hossain, Santha Rama Rau, and Kamala Markandaya, always hovered on the peripheries of the literary marketplace, and even writers like Anita Desai, Bharati Mukherjee and Meena Alexander, who were quite prolific in the later decades, had limited appeal to Western readership. But Indian writing in English has become a hot commodity in the Western consumer market since the 1990s with Arundhati Roy's *The God of Small Things* (1997), Kiran Desai's *Hullabaloo in the Guava Orchard* (1998) and *The Inheritance of Loss* (2005), Chitra Banerjee Divakaruni's *Arranged Marriage* (1995), Indira Ganesan's *Inheritance* (1998) and Lahiri's short story collection as well as her novel, *The Namesake* (2003) among others, flooding bookshelves in Barnes & Noble and Waterstones, winning various awards and climbing the ladder in several national bestseller's lists on both sides of the Atlantic.

While this might seem like a welcome change given the Western publishing industry's former apathy to postcolonial writers, in a rather disturbing trend, instead of an emphasis on Roy's brilliant narrative act or Lahiri's succinct eye for detail, an inordinate amount of attention was suddenly devoted to the author's "exotic" beauty.[5] Roy was quickly named one of *People Magazine's* "50 Most Beautiful People in the World" and Lahiri was celebrated as a "Woman We Love" in *Esquire* magazine, and paparazzi stalked her 2001 Calcutta wedding to journalist Alberto Vourvoulias Bush as retailers and booksellers across Europe and America scrambled to find a place for the hot ethnic writer on their shelves.[6] Indian culture had become big business in the West in the 1990s with Madonna sporting henna tattoos in her 1997 "Frozen" video and Heidi Klum and Seal renewing their vows in a Bollywood-themed ceremony in Mexico. It was only a matter of time before the publishing industry claimed their stake. When writers like Roy and Lahiri entered the literary scene, the publishing and bookselling business went into a frenzy, as is evident from the glitzy magazine spreads that featured them and the numerous interviews with them that flooded the web.[7] As Marwan Hassan suggests, in the twenty-first century "Capital is concentrated, not in the creative process, but in the marketing, advertising, promoting and distributing sectors, where book production emulates the models of Coca-Cola, Pepsi, and McDonald's, striving for market share and saturation" (12). Moreover, publishing houses are not hesitant to readily deploy Orientalist stereotypes in book design and promotional materials if they are convinced that will translate into profits. Mustapha Marrouchi, when talking about the global consumption of exotic products, points out that "An exotic cast of features, myths, stereotypes and exercises in sensory seduction – scents of perfumes, spices, honeyed mint tea, jellaba, Casbah, Medina, babouche, sirocco, souk, story-tellers, snake-charmers, conjurors, water-sellers, even dentists with their own stalls, pliers ('teeth pulled on the spot'), seemingly deconstructed by writers, surface with a vengeance in the marketing designs of their literary productions" (17). This trend of mass marketing of ethnicity deliberately created and fostered by the Western publishing industry has also given rise to much critical debate within the field of postcolonial studies.

Roy Miki argues that unequal power dynamics continue to exist between writers, publishers and consumers "since publishers, reviewers, and critics (mostly white) control the conditions of receptivity and interpretation" (121). The scenario becomes even more complicated for writers from formerly colonised countries who are trying to find a niche in the global literary marketplace. Noted Indian critic Makarand Paranjape talks about the enormous influence the Western publishing industry has on postcolonial writing:

> Western media and publishing conglomerates exercise tremendous power over the production and dissemination of images about the Third World. These images not only determine how we are viewed by them, but also how we come to view ourselves. It is not that we are totally helpless or lack the agency to construct our own identities. But the fact is that the strength of these images is so overpowering that few of us can really resist the onslaught. (235)

Indian writers writing in English, especially diasporic writers, become the object of Paranjape's ire:

> . . . the positions of such diasporics is akin to that of African middlemen who sold slaves to the white traders. A Naipaul or Ved Mehta comes to India, invades our privacy, interviews us, makes us objects of analysis, captures our reality, then makes a marketable product out of it. When we don't like what he says about us or wish to speak up for ourselves, no one over there is prepared to listen. (Paranjape 239)

According to these critics, women writers are especially guilty of gross misrepresentations with their portrayal of promiscuous men and sexually repressed women as well as tongue-in-cheek presentations of specific Indian traditions like arranged marriage. Paranjape goes on to argue that such representations "may contribute to a continuing 'colonization' of the Indian psyche by pandering to Western market tastes which see India in a negative light" (238). Though Paranjape's accusations are not entirely invalid and writers like Nirad C. Chaudhuri, Kamala Markandaya, Santha Rama Rau and even V. S. Naipaul are all guilty of performing the role of cultural translators both consciously and unconsciously, it is more important to explore the socio-economic terrain of the postcolonial literary marketplace that often determines the nature of postcolonial narratives. Paranjape rightly indicts western publishing houses that completely disregard vernacular literature or native literature in translation, which are less popular in the West, and are instead actively involved in creating and preserving an orientalised image of South Asia. But at the same time, it is worth investigating the fraught position that postcolonial writers are often forced into because of the demands of the global literary marketplace.

It is true that when a "writer of colour" makes it big in the West, he or she is automatically cast into the role of a representative of the culture he or she comes from. In her book on South Asian writers in twentieth-century Britain, Ruvani Ranasinha points out that South Asian writers writing in the early decades of the twentieth century were "seen as exotic and oriental outsiders, were also often expected to embody 'foreignness', and provide 'alien' perspectives on Britain, usually in prescribed terms" (11). In an atmosphere inhospitable to South Asian writing except when it rehashed stereotypes about the East already dominant in the Western imagination, writers like Kamala Markandaya in Britain and Santha Rama Rau in America were often forced to embrace the role of cultural interpreters in their bid to assimilate into mainstream society. As such, they sometimes adopted certain prescribed modes of exoticism in their texts. Kamala Markandaya came to Britain with her English husband, Bertrand Taylor, in 1948, and as Ranasinha reveals in a detailed analysis of her novels, her British and North American publishers were significantly involved in underscoring the commercial appeal of her novels.[8] Ranasinha suggests the difficulty of publishing fiction about India in the West is the reason why Markandaya deliberately adopts exotic motifs and is willing to construct an image of India on orientalist terms for Western consumption (151). On the other side of the Atlantic, South Asian writer Santha Rama Rau also underscored her role as cultural translator and, as the titles of her two most popular books – *Home to India* (1945) and *This is India* (1954) demonstrate, she "entered the American scene as India expert" (Burton 4). But as Antoinette Burton points out, Rao also went beyond orientalist stereotypes of India and in fact often sought to refute it "by representing India as a site of multiple cultural influences, as the home of lively aesthetic and culinary practices both ancient and modern, and, above all, as an appealing tourist destination" (5).

This trend has continued well into the last decades of the twentieth century with the Western publishing industry determining the commercial process through which the work of an "ethnic writer" can be readied for metropolitan consumption. In her essay, Rita Wong rightly points out that even before we can pay attention to the writer's work, there is a large framework or machinery that determines what is "hot", that is, what gets published and what gets promoted. "Quality of writing is only one factor in this scenario; access to capital, profit margins, and preconceptions of what is 'marketable' also plays an important part in the process shaping the books to which we as readers have access" (Wong 40). In the genre of any kind of ethnic literature, this commercial process of publication and marketing assumes a whole new dimension. In a sarcastic answer to the question of what makes a certain ethnic genre hot, Thrupkaew notes:

> The mystical stuff and the food seem to reflect the way that some white people come to different cultures – through seeking religious or spiritual enlightenment, or by exhibiting their open-minded, adventuresome selves through eating our food. Our cultures are 'better' somehow – closer to the earth, purer, more attuned to sensory pleasure – but in nice, non-threatening ways, wrapped up neatly in fortune-cookie wisdom. (301)

But her statement is corroborated by British-born writer Bidisha Bandopadhyay in an interview with the *Guardian*. Bandopadhyay says of her first novel *Seahorses*, set in London's media world, "I stayed away from race because of the publishing industry's tunnel vision. English publishing is in love with India: writers are being outrageously successful confirming what English people think they already know about India – inter-caste relationships, jungle sensuality. They pander to colonial perceptions" (Jaggi "Where East is West"). She adds that critics scorned her first heroine Pale who was of an unspecified race:

> Loads of critics said I hadn't played the race card. I felt their terrible sense of offence that I hadn't tackled the traumas of being a young Asian girl – arranged marriage, irate father. They don't understand there are different kinds of Asian people. They can't handle Asians in the same position as them – only if they're phoning up for a takeaway. (Jaggi "Where East is West")

Even though writers like Bidisha Bandopadhyay and Arundhati Roy have repeatedly distanced themselves from orientalist stereotypes and from the forced role of cultural translators and have insisted on their subjectivity, few are willing to listen. When Roy won the Booker Prize for her debut novel in the 50th year of Indian independence, she was repeatedly asked what it meant to be an Indian novelist at that moment, clearly indicating that the Booker Prize, Britain's highest honour for any writing in English, had somehow given Indian writing in English yet another stamp of legitimacy after Salman Rushdie's 1980 win for *Midnight's Children*. At home in India, on the other hand, Roy drew significant criticism for her portrayal of strife-torn, caste-ridden Kerala.

In conclusion, it is important to draw attention to this dual critical trajectory to illustrate the tenuous position of female Indo-English fiction writers like Arundhati Roy who constantly have to "negotiate a double-bind, balancing an awareness of their work as a cultural commodity against the counter-hegemonic imperatives of their politics" (Tickell 75). The politics of the global literary marketplace at odds with their personal politics is what makes Roy enact a superb stylistic performance in *The God of Small Things*. In the novel, Roy uses the motif of performance to construct a critique of a society caught between a colonial legacy and the constant onslaught of trans-national rhetoric. But her overt critique of globalisation, which she believes to be a kind of neo-colonialism, effectively sidelines the representation of a strife-torn, class-ridden Kerala, something that could have otherwise drawn charges of misrepresentation and cultural fetishism. Further, she disrupts possible allegations of inauthenticity because of her writing in English by dovetailing the English language to a specific cultural context and by casting her narrative in the traditional Indian oral epic mode, thus signalling a metaphoric return to indigenous traditions. So it is not unusual that in his introduction to a volume of Indian

English writing, Amitava Kumar is cautiously optimistic that the new generation of writers like Roy and Jhumpa Lahiri, among others, will "rescue us from the stereotypical fare, which I have described elsewhere as 'the mistress of spices, the heat and dust, sweating men and women in lisping saris, brought together in arranged marriages, yes, the honking traffic, and the whole hullabaloo in the guava orchard'" (Kumar xviii).

And the last word undoubtedly rests with Arundhati Roy as she makes an impassioned plea for literary freedom for postcolonial, albeit, all artists in the twenty-first century:

> Painters, writers, singers, actors, dancers, filmmakers, musicians – they are meant to fly, to push at the frontiers, to worry the edges of human imagination, to conjure beauty from the most unexpected things, to find magic in places where others never thought to look. If you limit the trajectory of their flight, if you weight their wings with society's existing notions of morality and responsibility, if you truss them up with preconceived values, you subvert their endeavour. (*Algebra* 191).

Works Cited

Appadurai, Arjun. *Modernity at Large: Cultural Dimensions of Globalization.* Minneapolis: U of Minnesota P, 1996. Print.

Boehmer, Elleke. *Colonial & Postcolonial Literature.* Oxford: Oxford UP, 1995. Print.

Burton, Antoinette. *The Postcolonial Careers of Santha Rama Rau.* Durham: Duke UP, 2007. Print.

Dennis, Ferdinand. *Back to Africa: A Journey.* London: Sceptre, 1992. Print.

Friedman, Thomas. *The World is Flat: A Brief History of the Twenty-first Century.* New York: Farrar, Straus and Giroux, 2005. Print.

Ghosh, Amitav. *In An Antique Land.* New York: Granta, 1992. Print.

———. *The Shadow Lines.* New York: Mariner, 2005. Print.

Hardt, M. and Negri, A. *Empire*. Cambridge: Harvard UP, 2000. Print.

Hassan, Marwan. "Chain of Readers." *Paragraph* 16.3 (1994–1995): 10–4. Print.

Iyer, Pico. *The Global Soul: Jet Lag, Shopping Malls and the Search for Home*. New York: Vintage, 2000. Print.

———. *Video Night in Kathmandu, And Other Reports from the Not-So-Far East*. New York: Vintage, 1988. Print.

Jaggi, Maya. "Where East is West." *The Guardian*. 28 June 1999. Web. 28 December 2015. [http://www.theguardian.com/culture/1999/jun/29/artsfeatures.arundhatiroy]

Jana, Reena. "Arundhati Roy." *Salon*. 30 September 1997. Web. 28 December 2015. [http://www.salon.com/1997/09/30/00roy/]

Kincaid, Jamaica. *A Small Place*. New York: Farrar, Straus and Giroux, 1988. Print.

Krishnaswamy, Revathi. "Mythologies of Migrancy: Postcolonialism, Postmodernism and the Politics of (Dis)location." *Ariel: A Review of International English Literature*. 26.1(1995): 125–46. Print.

Korte, Barbara. *English Travel Writing from Pilgrimages to Postcolonial Explorations*. Trans. Catherine Matthias. London: Macmillan, 2000. Print.

Kumar, Amitava, ed. *Away: The Indian Writer as an Expatriate*. New York: Routledge, 2004. Print.

Marrouchi, Mustapha. "Fear of the Other, Loathing the Similar." College Literature. 26.3 (1999), 17–58. Print.

Miki, Roy. *Broken Entries: Race, Subjectivity, Writing*. Toronto: Mercury, 1998. Print.

Mullaney, Julie. *Postcolonial Literatures in Context*. London: Continuum, 2010.

———. *The God of Small Things: A Reader's Guide*. New York: Continuum, 2002. Print.

Naipaul. V. S. *The Middle Passage: Impressions of Five Societies – British, French, and Dutch – in the West Indies and South America*. New York: Vintage, 1962. Print.

Paranjape, Makarand. "What About Those Who Stayed Back Home? Interrogating the Privileging of Diasporic Writing." *Shifting Continents/Colliding Cultures: Diaspora Writing of the Indian Subcontinent.* Eds. Ralph J. Crane and Radhika Mohanram. Atlanta: Rodopi, 2000. 225–45. Print.

Ranasinha, Ruvani. *South Asian Writers in Twentieth-century Britain: Cultures in Translation.* New York: Oxford UP, 2007. Print.

Roy, Arundhati. *The Algebra of Infinite Justice.* New Delhi: Penguin Books, 2001. Print.

———. *The God of Small Things*. New Delhi: India Ink, 1997. Print.

Sarkar, Parama."Performing Narrative: The Motif of Performance in Arundhati Roy's The God of Small Things." *South Asian Review.* 28.2 (2007): 217–236. Print.

Seth, Vikram. *From Heaven Lake: Travels through Sinkiang and Tibet.* London: Chatto & Windus, 1983. Print.

Steger, Manfred. *Globalization: A Very Short Introduction*. Oxford: Oxford UP, 2009. Print.

Thieme, John. *Post-Colonial Studies: The Essential Glossary*. London: Arnold, 2003. Print.

Thiong'o, Ngũgĩ wa. *Moving the Centre: The Struggle for Cultural Freedoms*. London: James Currey, 1993. Print.

Thrupkaew, Noy. "The God of Big Trends: Book Publishing's Ethnic Cool Quotient." *Bitchfest: Ten Years of Cultural Criticism from the Pages of Bitch Magazine*. Eds. Lisa Jervis and Andi Zeisler. New York: Farrar, Straus and Giroux, 2006. Print.

Tickell, Alex. "The God of Small Things: Arundhati Roy's Postcolonial Cosmopolitanism." Journal of Commonwealth Literature 38 (2003): 73–89. Print.

Wiltz, Teresa. "The Writer Who Began with a Hyphen." *The Washington Post*. 8 October 2003. Web. 28 December 2015. [https://www.

washingtonpost.com/archive/lifestyle/2003/10/08/the-writer-who-began-with-a-hyphen/3714e7f7-542b-4fab-bea5-a256c9a3cd47/]

Van der Veer, Peter. "Introduction: The Diasporic Imagination." *Nation and Migration: The Politics of Space in the South Asian Diaspora*. Ed. Peter Van der Veer. Philadelphia: U of Pennsylvania P, 1995. 1–16. Print.

Wong, Rita. "Market Forces and Powerful Desires: Reading Evelyn Lau's Cultural Labor." *Culture, Identity, Commodity. Diasporic Chinese Literatures in English.* Eds. Tseen Khoo and Kam Louie. Montreal: McGill-Queen's UP, 2005. 39–58 Print.

Notes

1. For more on the objectives and functions of these organisations, see page 39 of Steger's *Globalization*.
2. For a more detailed exploration of this phenomenon, see page 73 of Steger's *Globalization*.
3. My discussion of Roy's *The God of Small Things* has been previously published in the South Asian Review. For the entire article, read "Performing Narrative."
4. In fact, the *Heart of Darkness* image is reiterated numerous times throughout the text, most often as an epithet for Ayemenem. When the police torture Velutha, and Rahel and Estha are forced to witness "History in live performance" (*The God of Small Things* 309) in the "Heart of Darkness", Roy clearly indicates that even though a hotel chain had recently bought the "Heart of Darkness", over three hundred years of colonial rule has left a disturbing legacy, for instance, "Man's subliminal urge to destroy what he could neither subdue or deify" (308). Ayemenem seems to be hopelessly caught between this legacy that the colonial rulers left and the onslaught of corporate globalisation and consumerism.
5. Lahiri, in an interview with *The Washington Post*, is described as "a slender, soft-spoken woman with a caramel complexion, large limpid eyes and a flair for fashion" (Wiltz "The Writer

Who Began with a Hyphen"). Similarly, a *Salon* interview with Arundhati Roy, after she won the Booker Prize, draws significant attention to her unusual good looks – "She's Arundhati Roy, and she's remarkably tiny – hovering around 5-foot-2 – despite the black platform shoes she's wearing and new literary lioness persona. An explosion of curly black hair frames her face, which showcases nearly childlike, saucer eyes and cheekbones that erupt the moment she talks or smiles" (Jana, "Arundhati Roy").

6. This was not the first time that Westerns readers, especially in America, had made a beeline for writers of a "hot" ethnicity. As Thrupkaew mentions, the early 1990s saw a proliferation of Latina narratives – Laura Esquivel's *Like Water for Chocolate* (1989), Sandra Cisneros's *The House on Mango Street* (1984) and Julia Alvarez's *How the Garcia Girls Lost Their Accents* (1991), among others (300).
7. After Roy's Booker Prize win, her novel was published in more than twenty nations, was listed at number one on the *Sunday Times* London's bestseller list and had earned her more than one million dollars.
8. For a detailed analysis of how Markandaya constructs an oriental India for Western consumption, see Ranasinha's *South Asian Writers in Twentieth-century Britain: Cultures in Translation.*

INDEX